organize
your
genealogy

organize
your
genealogy

STRATEGIES and SOLUTIONS
for EVERY RESEARCHER

Drew Smith

**FAMILY
TREE
BOOKS**

CINCINNATI, OHIO
shopfamilytree.com

CONTENTS

Introduction **6**

CHAPTER 1
Organizing Yourself **10**
Prep your mind and body for the rigors of research with this guide to optimizing you and your habits.

CHAPTER 2
Organizing Your Space **24**
Clean up your research space. This chapter describes the workspace arrangement and office supplies you'll need to build a productive genealogy headquarters.

CHAPTER 3
Organizing Your Goals **36**
Plan your way to genealogical success by using the techniques in this chapter to develop, manage, and evaluate realistic goals for your research.

CHAPTER 4
Organizing Your Notes and Ideas **58**
Never lose a train of thought again. This chapter provides suggestions for how to preserve and sort information, from your random musings to crucial, irreplaceable interviews with family members.

CHAPTER 5
Organizing Your Files **83**
Store your hard-earned research with this guide to organizing your physical documents and digital files.

CHAPTER 6
Organizing Your Research Process **105**
Plan your way to genealogical success. This chapter covers how to manage your research workflow and use tools such as genealogy software programs to document and manage your projects from start to finish.

CHAPTER 7

Organizing Your Communication 129

Sort all those pesky e-mails and letters by using the tips in this chapter to optimize your mail-sorting system, e-mail inbox preferences, and even social media accounts.

CHAPTER 8

Organizing Your Online Research 147

Surf the web with confidence. This chapter discusses how to keep track of your files, searches, and family trees on the ever-growing Internet.

CHAPTER 9

Organizing Your Research Trips 161

Travel far and wide for your research with this guide to having efficient research sessions abroad, whether at a stateside library or an archive in the old country.

CHAPTER 10

Organizing Your Learning 179

Expand your genealogical knowledge. This chapter details how to choose and manage important genealogy lectures, conferences, webinars, and more.

CHAPTER 11

Organizing Your Volunteering 204

Give back to the community with this guide to pitching in with (and even running) genealogical-society meetings and projects.

Conclusion 220

Appendix 222

Index 230

Introduction

Why Do We Organize Anything?

As I sat down with the intention of dictating the first words of this book, I realized I was missing a piece of electronic hardware that allows me to connect my wireless headset to my desktop computer. This device, a "dongle," is about the size of a USB flash drive. I had always kept this device in a special location in my desk drawer, but I couldn't find it when I looked for it there. I began looking in other drawers and on top of other furniture in the room, all to no avail. And the longer I looked, the more stressed I became. Without the dongle, I couldn't use the headset, and I would have to think of another way to dictate this book. The irony was not lost on me that my lack of organization was preventing me from beginning a book about organization!

Fortunately, it occurred to me to look behind my computer desk to see if the dongle had fallen. Sure enough, there it was on the floor, hidden between the wall and the woofer that provided the deep bass sounds for my computer's speakers. I was back in business, and so I began this book.

What lessons can we learn from this experience? First, when we're disorganized, we lose precious time. The time better spent searching for our ancestors, evaluating genealogical evidence, communicating with distant cousins, planning a research trip, learning new research techniques, or volunteering for a genealogy society is instead spent searching for misplaced equipment, notes, and documents. In some cases, we may even have to spend money to replace a missing item—money that could be better spent on new hardware, software, online subscriptions, books, magazines, webinars, conferences, and research trips.

Even setting aside the needless loss of time and money, the frustration we experience when we're disorganized increases our stress level, which can cause physical and mental harm. As a result, our ability to be careful and productive genealogists is diminished, and we get less pleasure from our genealogical activities. But when we're calm and organized, we can think more clearly and do better work.

Finally, when we're organized, other people find it easier to work with us. Many of us have contacted another genealogist and asked for information, only to discover the other person has misplaced our e-mail or misfiled the document we're asking about. When this happens, we question whether or not we want to work with this individual. An organized genealogist, however, can be a pleasure to work with.

What's more, the pitfalls of unorganized genealogical research aren't really that different from other activities. For example, misplacing a recipe or a kitchen utensil can make cooking difficult. Try gardening when you have lost the packet of seeds or the garden tool you need. Clearly, being organized has universal benefits.

Who Should Read This Book?

Most people can benefit from the organizational advice in this book, but let me discuss the most obvious groups. I hope this book will benefit new genealogists, as it's often easier to adopt good habits when you're starting a relatively new activity than to change the way you have been doing things for years. I especially enjoy writing books and articles for beginning genealogists, and I still remember what it was like when I started this hobby. This guide will hopefully be the kind of book I would like to have read as a beginner looking to establish good habits early on.

The next audiences for this book are intermediate or advanced genealogists. While they may already use some of the techniques discussed here, many genealogists who have been working for a few years still look for ways to examine their procedures and how to improve them. And more experienced genealogists may find it useful to learn about organizing techniques they can share with beginning genealogists.

Even professional genealogical researchers are motivated to be organized in the work they do. Being disorganized can result in dissatisfied customers and a loss of potential income. Genealogists must organize not only the research itself, but also correspondence and other business-related paperwork. Many professional genealogists, whether or not they take clients, may also engage in speaking and writing. These activities involve meeting deadlines, traveling to speaking venues, corresponding with editors and societies, and filing contracts and invoices. All those activities require the organization we'll be discussing in this book; editors appreciate organized writers, and societies appreciate organized speakers.

Many genealogists will also get involved with local, state, and national genealogical societies, work that involves a certain level of organization. Volunteering to serve as an officer or as a member of a committee will involve dealing with schedules, correspondence, documents, and possibly travel. When you're organized, you'll get more satisfaction out of serving a society, and the people working with you will appreciate how organized you are.

Finally, this book can benefit anyone who needs to work with large amounts of information. For instance, historians engage in many of the same activities as a genealogist, such as keeping track of documents needed to construct an historical narrative. Similarly, a journalist working on a story, like a genealogist, needs to organize (ideas, notes, and interview times and transcripts), communicate with sources and editors, and plan research trips. Although this book uses examples based upon genealogical research, the organizing principles laid out here apply to many types of activities.

How Can You Best Use This Book?

While this book can certainly be read from beginning to end, I expect that you'll find certain chapters more interesting than others, especially if you feel a strong need for improvement in a particular area. Review the table of contents and identify two or three chapters that you think will be most helpful to you immediately. Later, you can return to the remaining chapters to see if they contain ideas that will improve upon your existing procedures.

As you read this book, don't beat yourself up over the organizational problems you have. You may be well organized in some parts of your life, unaware that you could apply what you've learned in those areas to the areas needing better organization. This book doesn't point out a long list of things you're doing wrong. But rather, it highlights some useful techniques to stay organized. These may be techniques that you already use in the non-genealogical parts of your life and can apply to your genealogical work.

What Are the Basics of A Good Organizing System?

For an organizing system to be successful, it needs to adhere to a few general principles that we'll discuss throughout the book:

1. It needs to be simple. A simple system is easy to learn, easy to remember, and easy to use. Complex systems are frustrating and difficult to maintain.

2. It needs to work well with your existing way of doing things. This means that the system needs to be flexible enough that you can customize it to fit your workflow, making it that much easier to adopt. And because each of us is different in our personalities, preferred ways of doing things, and goals, the flexibility of the organizing system becomes essential.

3. It needs to be something you can implement in stages. Change is inherently stressful. By making small changes over time, you can keep your stress level low. Too many changes too quickly can cause you to revert to the way you used to do things. Even small improvements in organizing your genealogy should result in observable benefits, which will motivate you to continue.

And now with that in mind ... Let's get organized!

1

organizing
yourself

When picking up the typical book about organizing, you'd probably expect it to talk about organizing your physical space, your papers, your digital files, and your to-do lists—so you may not expect a book to begin by focusing on you. But genealogical research is primarily a mental activity (with the possible exception of traipsing through a cemetery). Your mind is without a doubt your most important genealogical research tool. If you don't make an effort to be at your most mentally alert, your research will suffer, and you'll find yourself missing important clues or making mistakes when evaluating evidence or entering data.

Genealogy is nothing if not a mental game, so you'll need to know about and take care of yourself to do your best work. This chapter discusses how to identify and implement ways of making yourself a more effective researcher, including improving your mental health, setting personal routines, simplifying your workspace, automating your workflow, and taking adequate breaks.

Maintaining Mental Wellness

Because genealogy is a mental activity, you'll need to make sure you focus on your brain's basic needs to be successful.

For example, psychologists don't agree on everything, but they've come to a consensus concerning the human need for at least one thing: sleep. You've probably heard the stereotype of the genealogist staying up all night in her bathrobe and bunny slippers, looking for just one more record before calling it a night. But fuzzy slippers aside, doing genealogical research when you are weary and bleary-eyed is not a good idea. Getting a full seven to eight hours of sleep each night—ideally starting and ending at the same time every day (on both weekdays and weekends)—will set your brain into a regular pattern and make it easier for you to figure out what time of day you're most productive.

I realize that what I'm suggesting here is stopping when you've reached a certain time of the night and going to bed, even if you're hot on the trail of an elusive ancestor. But don't worry: You can make notes about where you left off so you can eagerly resume the hunt at your next opportunity. After all, you don't really want to make a mistake late at night that sends you down the wrong family line, do you?

Your diet is another factor that affects your mental wellness. You want to stay well hydrated, but carefully use caffeinated drinks like soda and coffee if you're a fan of either. Avoid caffeine in the late afternoon and evening if it interferes with your ability to get a good night's sleep.

Monitor the foods you eat at different times of the day, and note how those foods affect your mental alertness. Keep healthy snacks handy so you don't find yourself distracted by thoughts of hunger between meals. In particular, avoid extreme highs and lows that might impact your blood sugar levels, as you'll have trouble focusing with high blood sugar and grow tired with low blood sugar, and either can cause your thoughts to be somewhat fuzzy.

Finally, don't neglect your emotional needs. For instance, as a pet owner, I enjoy having a cat or two snoozing near my computer desk so that I can observe them and thereby place myself in a calm, relaxed state. They put a big smile on my face and make my research that much more enjoyable. Having these reminders of things or people you love—like pictures of loved ones—can lower your stress level and give you motivation when the road gets rough.

Falling Into a Routine

How often have you driven to work or your favorite store but couldn't recall anything about the drive once you get there? Unless something unusual happened during that car ride, the details simply won't register with you.

That kind of lapse in memory is due to our tendency to establish routines, or sets of actions that we engage in automatically to minimize effort. Much of what we do is so automatic that we don't even have memories of our actions. We create routines because, if we had to think about everything we do during the day before we did it, we might never get anything done at all.

You probably have a morning routine that begins when your alarm clock goes off, when you wake up naturally, or when someone else nudges you awake, and ends with you showering, brushing your teeth, and getting dressed. You probably also have an evening routine that you perform every night before bed. You've likely done some of these routines for so long you no longer have to think about them.

One reason that we feel a bit scattered about our genealogical research is that we have not yet established good routines for it. Do you have a set of actions you always engage in when you sit down at your home computer to do research? Another set you do just before you get up from your research work to do other things? If not, establish routines that will make certain you're doing the things you should be doing. And once established, these routines will run without conscious thought.

Before we can establish a routine, however, we need to identify the specific activities that will be part of it, and how and when the routine will begin.

No two people are exactly alike, and we all have different times of the day when we are at our best. Perhaps you're a morning person who gets your best work done before lunch,

---

research tip

Be Patient

You may have heard or read that anything can be made into a habit if you do it every day for twenty-one days, but effective habits are more complicated than that. That particular myth is a misinterpreted version of a study that found twenty-one days to be the *minimum* length of time for habit establishment. Later studies have shown that habits may take as long as two months or even eight months to establish. You'll need to judge for yourself when the habit has become second nature—when you aren't even giving it a conscious thought when doing it.

or maybe you're a night owl who is most productive after dinner (or even later). Depending on your work and household obligations, you may find that certain days of the week are best for your research.

Allow yourself the opportunity to experiment doing different kinds of research on different days of the week or at different times of the day, and begin building your routine around that optimal research time. Certainly, work or family obligations may limit your flexibility, but you may find that you can get up earlier than usual and get a great deal accomplished before you need to head off to work or take care of the household. Understanding when you work best and what time you have available to you is crucial when setting and sticking with a routine.

Later in this book, we'll look at a lot of instances in which a routine would be helpful. But at this point, let's talk about the general process of creating a routine.

If we look carefully at a routine, we see that it is composed of a sequence of activities, linked together like a chain. Each activity is a habit, and the first habit in the routine is started as the result of some sort of trigger. Once you have linked together these habits into a routine, each habit becomes a trigger for the next one.

In the sections that follow, I'll discuss triggers and habits and why they're important for creating a genealogical research routine.

Identify and Use Triggers

What are triggers? A trigger is a change in your environment, either natural or artificial, that causes you to respond in a particular way—here, to focus on an activity you need to perform.

Living things are designed to respond to triggers. Plants react to changes in light, temperature, and water. Animals respond to their internal feelings of hunger, thirst, and tiredness. Humans have long responded to sunrise and sunset and to the change of seasons, but we've created artificial, technological triggers as well: clocks to measure the hours of the day, calendars to measure the months of the year, and push notifications on our desktop/laptop computers and mobile devices.

As genealogists, we have external triggers (e.g., an e-mail from a relative in our inbox, a document we ordered in our mailbox, or a conference registration deadline), and triggers we create for ourselves (e.g., doing genealogy at a certain time of day on a certain day of the week). Your job is to figure out what behavior to engage in when you encounter a trigger.

Fortunately, genealogy (unlike activities like gardening) doesn't depend much upon the time of day or the season of the year. With the exception of visiting a cemetery, genealogical activities are generally conducted inside. Some of our activities will depend

CASE STUDY: Paper Workflow Habit

Say you have a physical tray that will serve as your inbox. Where will the incoming paper come from? It could be from the mail (perhaps a genealogical document that you ordered), something from your computer's printer, or a sheet of notes you collected while on a trip to the local library or an archive. Your old, bad habit may be putting this paper in all kinds of places, such as on top of your computer desk, on your regular work desk, on the dining room table, on top of a stack of books, or even directly into a drawer. So let's establish a new habit: Every piece of paper that comes into your household and concerns genealogy will go into the inbox on your desk and nowhere else. (For now, you can do whatever you like once it's in that inbox. We'll eventually get to what you should next, but again: one step at a time.)

We've defined the habit, so what is the trigger that will precede it? The trigger is genealogy-related paper coming into your house, and the habit to develop is placing the paper (no matter how it got there) in the inbox. It's a small habit that takes almost no time to do, but it's important to prevent paper from ending up in multiple places and even lost somewhere on your desk.

Don't beat yourself up if you slip up in adopting a new habit. Thinking "well, nothing bad will happen if I set this new piece of paper down over here on this table," rather than putting the paper directly into the inbox, is perfectly human. Start again, and each time you find that papers are not lying about and are all in the inbox, congratulate yourself on a job well done. If you think it will motivate you, give yourself a small reward. Perhaps each week you go without breaking the habit, you get to read a genealogy magazine or post a favorite family photo online. Pick a reward that is something you enjoy.

upon the day of the week and the time of day when a repository is open for business. But beyond that, we have a great deal of flexibility to engage in research whenever (and, for the most part, wherever) we choose, limited only by our other obligations. This means that we are free to create triggers for ourselves based upon our availability, research goals, and personal preferences.

Create Habits

So now that we've seen the importance of routines and triggers, let's talk more about the habits that make up routines and how to establish them. Bad habits are hard to break, and good habits are hard to create. In many cases, we may be trying to replace a bad habit with a good one. To establish *any* habit, we need to associate it with a trigger, either the trigger that begins the routine or a habit already in the routine that will in turn serve as a trigger for the next habit.

You'll experience many benefits by establishing habitual ways of dealing with each trigger, including:

- less decision fatigue, as you won't have to make a conscious choice of what to do
- an easier and more consistent workflow, with each step in the process (such as scanning a paper document or backing up your changes to your digital files) becoming automated
- fewer mistakes and missed steps in your research

The mistake that many people make when establishing a new habit is trying to make too many changes at once. Remember that in order to implement an organizing system, we want to do it in stages, a little bit at a time. This allows us to keep our stress levels low, fit the change into our existing practices, and refine the new step before we move on to the next change. We should focus on one new habit at a time, working on that one step until it becomes second nature. And once we're comfortable with that, we can see which habit we want to work on next. See the Case Study: Paper Workflow Habit sidebar for an example of how to form (and encourage yourself to keep) a habit.

As you continue to read this book, think about routines, habits, and triggers. These concepts will come up again and again, moving you in the direction of being more organized and productive.

research tip

Find an App For That

If you like high-tech solutions, look for an app for your computer, tablet, or smartphone that will help you track your habits and give you reminders each day. Then you'll be able to look back at your successes and see that you're making progress toward becoming a more organized genealogist.

Simplifying Your Workspace

One of the reasons we're disorganized is that we're surrounded by too much complexity. For example, the office or desk you've set aside to do genealogical work may be messy or too cluttered for you to focus. Or maybe you have too many genealogical to-dos and can't decide which one to work on first. I mentioned at the beginning of this chapter that decision fatigue is a problem that can cause stress and lead to making errors when we are engaged in genealogical research. One way to minimize this fatigue is to simplify our environment and the work we're doing, allowing us to focus on what needs to be done with just the right tools and resources immediately at hand.

In the past, the idea of simplifying may have conjured an image of throwing away your personal belongings and moving to the woods or a deserted island. Don't worry: Simplifying isn't about that. Rather, in the context of genealogical research, simplifying means only that, at any given moment, you're able to focus on the important things you want to accomplish, aided by just those resources and tools needed to accomplish them.

In chapter 2, I'll discuss your research space in greater detail, but let me offer an example how to simplify that space. I used to keep a holder on my desk for pens and pencils (image Ⓐ). When I needed a pen, I would need to make a choice as to which pen to use (and hope the one I chose still had ink). It did not occur to me that even this trivial act of selecting a pen might diminish my later ability to make choices, not to mention briefly distract me from what I was trying to accomplish. Today, I no longer have a penholder on my desk. I keep a single pen in a convenient desk drawer for those times when I need one.

You're probably thinking that the time and effort it takes to select a pen is so trivial that it's silly to even think about. But what happens when you have dozens of these little decisions in your environment? These instances add up and can distract us from what we are trying to accomplish. The more distractions we can eliminate from our workspace, the easier it will be for us to focus on our genealogical research.

In a later chapter, I'll discuss how to organize your files, both paper and electronic, but for a moment let's talk about how simplifying them can be beneficial. When you sit down to do research, what papers are in front of you? Can you see files and folders that are unrelated to your current work? This visual clutter may cause you to think about other things that will distract you from your work. Ideally, the only paper that should be visible is what you need right now. In the same way, when you turn on your computer, what files and applications are showing on your desktop? To avoid distraction, all you should see are files you need immediate access to and the applications you will be using to work with

While it may seem trivial, simplifying your workspace by removing superfluous items (like extra pens and pencils) can improve your productivity.

them. If at all possible, everything else should be invisible. You want to see only what you want to focus on that day or in the very near future: a short, manageable list of to-dos for each time you begin your genealogical work.

Automating Your Workflow

After you've simplified your physical research workspace, physical and digital files, and to-do list, what's the next major way you can set the stage for organizing your genealogy? Simple: time management and the importance of automating whatever processes you can.

The term "time management" is something of a misnomer. You can't really "manage" time; we all have the same amount, and it passes at the same rate for all of us no matter what we do. But what we can manage is us: the choices we make and how we use our time. So this aspect of organizing refers to those choices. Are we choosing to spend our limited time in activities that could be done without our direct involvement? By using some form of automation, we can free ourselves from wasting our time in activities that we shouldn't have to think about doing.

Ways to automate your specific genealogical activities will be covered later in the book, but let's look at a list of some of them to see what they all have in common:

- scheduling an automatic daily backup of your digital files
- setting up auto-renewal for your genealogical subscription services

Microsoft Office Suite

Because my full-time job requires Microsoft Outlook <**www.microsoft.com/en-us/outlook-com**>, I use it for many of my calendaring activities, such as monthly meetings of my genealogical society and its associated board meetings. I also add dates for when I'll attend genealogical conferences. If you don't have a job that pays for your access to Outlook, consider a monthly subscription to Office 365 Home <**products.office.com/en-us/office-365-home**>, which for about ten dollars per month provides Word, Excel, PowerPoint, OneNote, and Outlook, as well as Publisher and Access for PC users. This subscription allows you to install these applications on five different PCs or Macs, plus five tablets or smartphones. It also comes with 1TB (terabyte) of online storage, and sixty minutes per month of Skype calling to mobile phones and landlines. Almost all genealogists (especially professionals) will want access to Word and Excel, and those who make presentations will also want PowerPoint.

Having said that, you may find that Outlook doesn't best fill your e-mail needs. Be sure to look for calendar tools that work best for you.

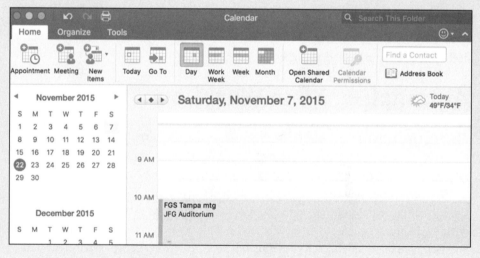

- creating filters for certain kinds of incoming e-mail messages (such as those from mailing lists) so they go into assigned folders

- developing a checklist of online websites to check when researching a genealogical question

- using a travel app to automatically notify you of any changes to your flight itinerary when flying on a research trip or to a genealogical conference

Most of these automation methods use technology, although printed checklists and schedules also qualify as tools for automation. When you use a printed or online checklist/schedule, you can immediately see the next thing you should be doing without having to think much about it. You already put in the work up front when creating the checklist or schedule. By investing that time only once at the time of creation, you save time you would have spent thinking about it later every time you use it.

Every day, developers release new apps that can automate some aspect of life. By seeking out and using these apps, we can reduce the time we spend making choices about what needs to be done and use the saved time to engage in the fun and rewarding parts of genealogy. Two popular online services, IFTTT **<www.ifttt.com>** and Zapier **<www. zapier.com>**, can automate connections between different apps and services you use. For instance, you can set up one of these automation services so that every time you receive an e-mail in Gmail **<mail.google.com>** with an attachment, a copy of the attachment is automatically saved in Dropbox or Google Drive. Or you can set them up so that every time you read Twitter and like a tweet, a copy of that tweet is saved to Evernote **<www. evernote.com>**.

As you read through this book, think about more ways to automate your genealogical activities.

Using Calendars

Our distant ancestors developed calendars to track where they were in the course of a year. In this way, they could predict the overall change of seasons, even though individual years might have variations in temperature and rainfall that threw off their predictions. Eventually, calendars became important not only in hunting and agriculture, but also in religion and commerce. Today, we still use calendars to define months, weeks, and days for religious observances, holidays, memorial activities, and academic schedules, as well as to synchronize our work-related events, medical and business appointments, and shared time with family and friends.

Certainly, we'll need to use calendars for genealogy as well: when repositories are open for business, when societies meet and conferences are being held, when webinars are being offered, and when we're traveling for research or to visit family. Many of these dates are beyond our personal control, but we *can* control how and when we spend our free time, especially at home. Online genealogical websites are effectively open 24/7, so we can use them whenever it best fits our own schedules (apart, perhaps, from times when they're down for maintenance or overwhelmed during a few days of free access).

If you prefer a hard copy of your calendar, you may want to invest in a daily planner notebook of some type. Your nearest office supply store will have these in a variety of colors and styles, and you can decide for yourself (and your budget) what kind you'll need. You may also want a standard wall calendar that you can hang in your genealogical workspace—I used to buy a large erasable wall planner each year. The advantage of wall calendars and planners is they don't take up any space on your desk and are always visible for a quick glance to see what is coming up in the near future and when.

However, you don't have easy access to wall calendars and planners when you're away from your workspace, and they (especially planner notebooks) can be lost or destroyed. You can overcome these shortcomings by using online calendars and planners instead. In a later chapter, we'll discuss applications designed to track projects and to-dos and assign due dates to them. But for now, let's focus on online calendar tools for recording important dates and regular schedules.

While many software applications can provide calendar features you're going to want, two are your best bet to fill the role of your primary calendar app: Google Calendar **<www.google.com/calendar>** (image **B**) and Apple's iCloud Calendar application (previously known as iCal). By choosing one of these popular options, you'll find many ways to synchronize your calendar across multiple devices and link your calendar to other apps (as described in the previous section on automating). You may like a particular calendar app for its attractiveness or ease of use on your desktop computer, laptop, tablet, smartphone, or smartwatch, but ideally that app will get its calendar data from Microsoft Outlook, Google Calendar, or Apple's iCloud Calendar.

Once you've decided which calendar app to use, you should install it on every device you use, spend some time learning its features, and (in particular) focus on its ability to synchronize its data across all of your devices. Certainly, you'll use it to schedule one-off events, such as a society meeting, conference, or webinar. But the strength of the calendar will come from its ability to schedule recurring events. Some genealogy-related events you will want to appear on your schedule once a year (such as reviewing your big-picture goals) while others should appear monthly (such as reviewing your projects or checking for new records that have been uploaded to an online database) or even weekly (such as

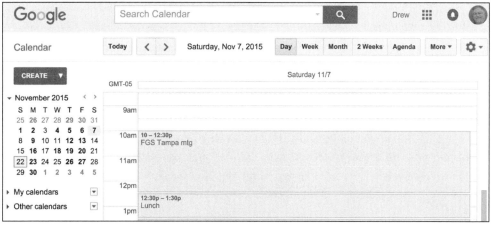

Google Calendar offers one of the most popular digital calendar platforms.

reviewing your to-do list for the upcoming week). We'll come back to the calendar in a bit more detail when we talk about goals, projects, and to-do lists.

Taking Breaks

In the first section of this chapter, I talked about how good mental and physical health are important to being an organized, productive genealogist. Beyond getting enough sleep each night and engaging in a regular schedule of healthy nutrition, you should incorporate one more thing in your workflow to minimize your stress levels and maximize your mental and physical effectiveness: regular breaks.

You've probably lost track of time while searching for information. Whether sitting in front of your computer at home or poring over documents at a repository, you may have sat for hours, blissfully unaware of anyone around you or the passage of time and being "in the zone" (or, in modern popular psychology terminology, "experiencing flow") and being highly productive and effective.

Unfortunately, long stretches without breaks are bad for your physical and mental well-being. Recent medical research has found that sitting for long periods can increase your risk for heart disease, high blood pressure, diabetes, obesity, anxiety, and other health problems. I have a few coworkers who have switched to using a stand-up desk for this reason. Even if a stand-up desk were to solve your inactivity problem at home, you may not be in a position to work that way at a repository. My personal solution is to use an automated system that reminds me to stand each hour. This could be something you set on your desktop or laptop computer or something that runs as a health app on your smartphone or smartwatch.

When I take a regular break from my seated genealogical activities, get up, and walk around (sometimes engaging in random household chores), I gain a clearer head and more energy. When I return to my work, I'm more interested in what I'm doing and reduce any nagging worries that I have neglected something going on outside my workspace.

This isn't to say that you have to ban doing anything related to genealogy during your stand-up break. You could take a smartphone or digital voice recorder with you and record your thoughts on how you've spent the last hour or ideas you've generated for future research. Or you could listen to fifteen minutes of a genealogical podcast while doing a household chore or stand at a kitchen counter and flip through a genealogical magazine, maybe flagging articles for later, closer study.

You may be worried that you'll lose track of where you were right before you took the break. But you can remedy this in one of two ways: You can leave the windows open on your computer screen so you can see what you were doing last, or you can use your research log (discussed later in this book) to make a note that describes what you were doing and what needs to be done next.

Being a genealogist may not require the physical level of an Olympic athlete, but that doesn't mean we should neglect our mental and physical health. Take good care of yourself and use tools to establish good habits, and you'll find that your most important genealogical research asset—you—will be at its best for the work to be done.

Drew's **To-Dos**

☛ Start organizing by paying attention to yourself: When in the day/week are you most productive? What bad habits do you have that you need to break?

☛ Get plenty of rest, eat properly, and keep an eye on your daily energy levels before engaging in research.

☛ Establish good research habits and link them together to form routines.

☛ Eliminate the unnecessary and automate as many repetitive activities as possible.

☛ Use a synchronized calendar on all of your devices to schedule your research activities for the best available dates and times.

☛ Take regular breaks to refresh your body and mind.

RESEARCH HABIT TRACKER

Organizing your genealogy really starts with organizing yourself and developing good personal habits that will help fulfill your research goals and keep your life in order. Use this worksheet to jot down the habits you want to develop, each habit's trigger, and what time of day/day of the week you anticipate the habit will occur. You can also download a Word-document version of this form at **<ftu.familytreemagazine.com/organize-your-genealogy>**.

Habit 1: _____   Day/Time: _____

Trigger: _____

_____

Habit 2: _____   Day/Time: _____

Trigger: _____

_____

Habit 3: _____   Day/Time: _____

Trigger: _____

_____

Habit 4: _____   Day/Time: _____

Trigger:_____

_____

2

organizing
your space

Apart from traveling to record repositories, homes of relatives, or genealogical conferences, most genealogy work is done at home. My spouse (also a genealogist) often jokes about adding a genealogical wing to the house. Our work takes up quite a bit of room in our home, and we're quite fortunate in being able to repurpose the two smallest bedrooms of our house into home offices, with each bedroom closet serving as an office supply closet. Of course, our home offices aren't strictly for genealogy, since they're also used for storing the home computer and its accessories, reviewing general mail, and handling personal finances. Nevertheless, genealogical research and related activities represent the most significant use of our home office space.

In this chapter, we'll discuss what equipment you'll want to have in an ideal research space.

Identifying the Perfect Workspace

Choosing an ideal workspace largely depends on your needs as a researcher, but most productive work environments have certain things in common. The space needs to be hospitable for old documents and sometimes delicate electronic equipment, so avoid a space that may get too warm or too humid. In addition, good workspaces are normally quiet, but not *so* quiet that any minute noise distracts you; having some quiet instrumental music play in the background can help you strike an appropriate balance of noise and silence. Good workspaces are also free of distracting sights or devices, such as windows overlooking busy streets or television screens.

In addition, you should keep utility in mind when organizing your supplies. The more frequently you use something, the closer it should be to where you sit, while the items you use less often should be stored farther away. Over time, this means that you may be relocating items as your need for them changes.

Overall, your genealogy workspace should be a place you enjoy spending a great deal of time, meaning that it should be both functional and attractive.

Genealogy Rooms

In a perfect world, you'd have a dedicated room for your genealogical work (image Ⓐ). You need space for computers, files, books, and magazines, plus large flat surfaces on which you can spread out documents for study and review. A separate room to house computer furniture, file cabinets, bookcases, and desk furniture is ideal for this. Having a separate room also allows you to close the door, which is desirable if you don't live alone and want to minimize distractions as you work. You also want a room with good lighting and a temperature conducive to long periods of sitting and working.

If you haven't yet set up your ideal genealogical workspace (or if you're in the market for a new home and such a space is on your desired feature list), you have a handful of options for a room dedicated to genealogy. If your house doesn't have a room that is already identified as a study, you can use an extra bedroom, attic/loft, basement, or converted garage for this purpose. The suitability of some of these options may depend on your local climate and whether or not the space is insulated and properly heated/cooled.

Alternative Spaces

Sometimes it's simply not possible to have an entire room or equivalent space dedicated to our genealogy passion. However, genealogists can be inventive when it comes to making do with space that also serves other purposes. For instance, you can create a usable

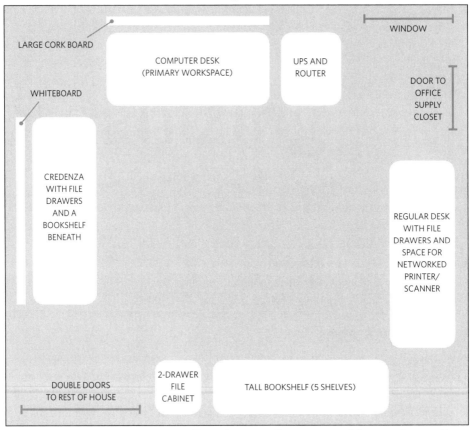

Everyone's workspace will look somewhat different, but most will contain some of the same elements. My workspace, for example, has a computer desk and another large flat space to lay out documents and hold my printer/scanner. I also have a credenza with file drawers, a two-drawer filing cabinet, and a tall bookshelf.

genealogical workspace as part of a bedroom, dining room, family room, living room, or kitchen. The most common option is likely a guest bedroom that's only used for special occasions. In that case, the room can serve both purposes; for example, you could have a bed that folds up into a couch but still provides plenty of space for a portable table that you can set up as needed. Ideally, you'll still have enough room for a lockable cabinet for your computer equipment, as well as for lockable file cabinets and a bookcase. If you have more than one bedroom closet, one of them can still serve as a guest closet while the other is used for office supplies and storage.

A master bedroom, if large enough, may also be able to house a genealogy corner even while serving its daily bedroom purpose. However, if you share this room with a significant other who doesn't share your passion for genealogy, this may turn out to be a less-than-ideal situation.

In a similar way, a corner of a family room, living room, or dining room may be large enough for a piece of furniture that opens up and folds down to become a computer desk with drawers and shelves. In the case of the dining room, the table may serve double-duty as the place to lay out working documents. When using a family room or living room, you may need to bring in a portable table for that purpose.

Kitchens are probably the most difficult spaces to cordon off portions of for genealogical work (not to mention that food and documents don't mix). Nevertheless, if there is space near the breakfast nook table, it may be serviceable.

What You'll Need

Whether you have the perfect genealogy office or are making do with a limited space that serves multiple functions, you've got a long list of tools to fill that space so you have what you need at hand (image **B**). If you're setting up a new space, this list should help you get started. And if you have an existing space, use this list to review what you already have and what can be improved.

Furniture

The first and foremost need for a research space is two pieces of furniture to serve as working surfaces: one for the computer display, keyboard, mouse, and related equipment, and one to spread out documents for reading and analysis. A computer desk can usually fulfill the first purpose, while the second may be a regular office desk.

This leads us to the ideal layout for your working surfaces. Because you want to be able to use your computer as well as review documents, the best furniture configuration is an L shape, with the edges of the furniture coming together to form a right angle. The L-configuration lets you reach everything you need without getting out of your chair. Not surprisingly, unless you're able to create your space in a large room, you'll probably place this L-configuration into the corner of the room.

When selecting a computer desk, look for one that allows you to adjust its height. The industry-standard 29-inch-high desks may fit well for a male of average height but may not be at an ergonomic height for others. If you're purchasing a new desk and can afford it, you may want to investigate desks that can be converted between a sitting desk and a standing desk.

What will you need room for on your computer desk or office desk? Certainly the computer desk will need to have room for at least one display, but I would highly recommend enough room for at least two displays. (While I wouldn't rule out the benefit of having three displays, this is probably beyond either budget or available workspace.) We'll come back to displays later when we talk about computers.

When I look around my own desk setup, I also see space for a holder for my smartphone and, perhaps most useful of all, a tray for my glasses. By having a set place to lay my glasses, I never lose them! I also have enough room on either side of my computer display for my pair of computer speakers, handy for listening to genealogical webinars. I also recommend space on the office desk for an inbox tray that collects incoming mail, documents, and magazines. And let's not forget that you'll need enough room for a drink coaster!

PAPER FILING SYSTEMS

One decision to make about genealogy workspace furniture is whether your paper-based filing system uses three-ring binders or manila folders (with or without hanging folders). While the plusses and minuses of these two popular systems will be the subject of chapter 5, you'll need more bookcases if you choose binders and more filing cabinets if you choose folders.

If you end up with fewer files, you may be able to make do with the two filing drawers found in a typical office desk or side credenza. With more files, you'll need at least a separate two-drawer filing cabinet, which provides additional flat surface space for other workspace-related things like a multi-function printer. At the moment, I'm getting by fine with two drawers in a credenza, two drawers in an office desk, and a two-drawer filing cabinet. Personally, I'd like to avoid the need for a four-drawer filing cabinet. But I won't be able to make that final decision until I have gone through all of my untouched material, discarded what is obviously discardable, scanned the more important documents, and archived the remaining paper to a more distant location.

DRAWER AND SHELF SPACE

Computer desks, office desks, and side credenzas may also offer you some important drawer space. This is what you're going to need to store both the things you need often and the things you use only occasionally. As with items on your desk, the drawers that are within easy reach should be reserved for the items you use most regularly, such as pens, batteries, magnifying glasses, charging cables, scissors, USB flash drives, and sticky notes. Drawers that are a bit farther away can be used for lesser used gadgets and office supplies. By keeping all of these items in drawers, you avoid distractions and preserve your desktop space for those things absolutely essential for your work.

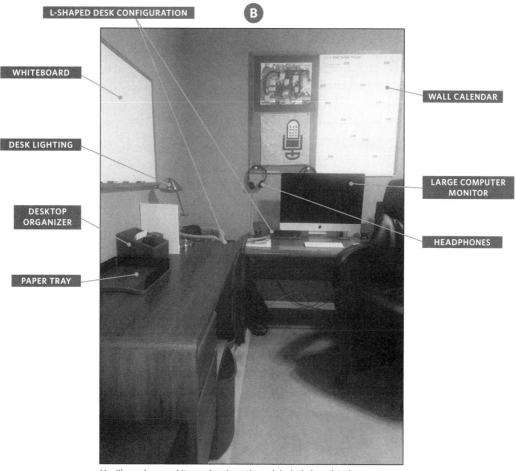

L-SHAPED DESK CONFIGURATION

B

WHITEBOARD

WALL CALENDAR

DESK LIGHTING

LARGE COMPUTER MONITOR

DESKTOP ORGANIZER

HEADPHONES

PAPER TRAY

You'll need several items (such as those labeled above) to have an efficient, organized workspace for genealogy.

In addition to the shelves used for books, magazine boxes, and three-ring binders, you may have a nearby shelf or two for other useful research items. I have a shelf at the bottom of my credenza that is occupied primarily by large map books, but I'm finding that I use those less and less frequently as I use more online maps instead. As a result, I'm thinking of relocating these to a more distant location.

ADDITIONAL STORAGE SPACE

In addition to your furniture and shelf and drawer space, you'll also need some sort of storage area for office supplies. Ideally, the room you're using will have a closet of some kind that can handle all those ink cartridges, file folders, envelopes, special printer paper, and reams of regular printer paper. This may also be a place to put lesser-used reference material, such as boxes for magazine archives or manuals for your electronic devices. If a closet isn't at hand, you may be able to use a drawer in a file cabinet instead or purchase plastic bins for storage.

Electricity

The next area of concern for the modern genealogical workspace is electricity. In this day and age, you can't have a research space in part of your house with no nearby power outlets. If you have set up your L-shaped space in the corner of a typical home office, you should have an outlet on each of those two walls. For one of my outlets (the one nearest the side desk), I have a power strip with surge protection plugged in. This provides power to items that won't be affected if the power is interrupted or surges, such as desk lamps, paper shredders, staplers, and rechargeable batteries. As a side note, I like power strips that have slides to cover the outlets that aren't in use; this keeps dust from settling in unused outlets.

My other outlet, nearer to the computer equipment, provides power to my uninterruptible power supply (UPS). Because I live near Tampa, Florida, I have to be concerned not only about brief power outages but also lightning strikes that might damage my electronic equipment. (There's a reason they call the local professional ice hockey team the Tampa Bay Lightning.) To minimize risk to my equipment and to keep things running long enough that I can safely shut off my computer, I use a heavy-duty UPS that can not only power my computer and its display, but also my modem/router and printer/scanner. As a result of my UPS, I cannot recall the last time I lost any significant amount of genealogical work to an unexpected loss of power. While a number of companies sell UPS devices for home use, I have long depended upon those made by APC **<www.apc.com/home/us/en>** and am currently using their APC Back-UPS XS 1500. Another company that makes comparable products is CyberPowerPC **<www.cyberpowerpc.com>**.

When you shop for these online or at an electronics or office supply store, look primarily at the number of outlets that the UPS provides (typically ranging from six to ten). As a general rule, the more outlets the UPS provides, the more power the unit can supply (measured in volt-amperes, abbreviated as VA). Unless you're buying a UPS for a home-based business with large numbers of electronic devices to support, you'll pay between $50 and $150 for an appropriate unit. Because lightning strikes can also cause power surges and damage over other pathways (such as phone landlines and copper-based cable Internet systems), make sure you can run those landlines and Ethernet cables through the UPS to serve as a surge protector.

After you have set up a safe and secure system for providing uninterrupted power to your critical stationary electronic devices, make sure you still have enough outlets available to plug in chargers for your portable devices, such as laptops, tablets, smartphones, and smartwatches. Like laptops, these devices may be able to charge using your computer's USB ports (though printers and headsets may occupy those ports and you may not have enough available to do the job). If the mobile device does not need to sync to your computer at that moment, you may simply want to plug it into a convenient nearby surge-protected power strip. You may want to purchase extra chargers so you have one near your computer desk, one wherever your mobile device sits overnight (such as by a bed), and one as part of your research travel kit.

Internet Connection

Your lifeline to the world of online genealogical information is going to be your home's Internet connection, whether your access is broadband or dial-up. While dial-up access may be sufficient for display of text-based information, much genealogical information consists of record images, which will display very slowly at dial-up speeds. And if you want to watch genealogical video tutorials or real-time genealogy webinars, broadband Internet access is especially important.

The typical broadband setup will include a modem (the device that translates between your service provider's data network and your home devices) that doubles as a router to provide Internet access to a combination of your wired and wireless devices. Obtain a router that is strong enough to provide a Wi-Fi signal to anywhere in your home so you won't have to worry about using your mobile devices in range. After all, your home Wi-Fi network may include not only desktop computers, laptop computers, tablets, and smartphones, but also networked printers, scanners, and external hard drives. Don't forget to set up your network's security features so people outside your home can't gain unauthorized access.

Lighting

Genealogical work requires reading books and magazines, as well as studying documents (some of which require close work to decipher). This means your research workspace must be set up to allow for plenty of good lighting, as this will help you make out faint or otherwise difficult-to-read printed documents. Although a window can help with this, sunlight may cause glare problems with your computer screen depending on where it's positioned. Good overhead lighting should work well as long as it isn't so far behind you that your own body will cast shadows on what you are trying to read. If there's a place for it near your work surfaces, a floor lamp may provide additional lighting, or you may find that a desk lamp is the right tool when you need extra light. You may need to experiment with this as you set up your workspace.

Computer Displays

Regardless of whether you use a desktop computer or a laptop as your primary home computer, you'll need a display large enough that you can clearly see genealogical records and ancestral photos. In the case of a laptop, you may need to hook it up to an external computer display so the display is large enough for your research purposes. Ideally, however, you'll want both a desktop computer with a large display for home use and a light laptop computer to take on research trips and to conferences.

Furthermore, see if your budget and desk space will allow for a second computer display. Multiple displays make it easier to simultaneously compare two documents or to review a document while using your genealogical software, browser, or word processing program. While one large display may allow for displaying two windows side-by-side, having two displays makes it possible to have three or even four windows up at the same time. You can dramatically increase your productivity when you don't have to constantly click around to switch between windows, trying to remember what was on each one.

Scanners and Printers

The next most important electronic device among your genealogical tools will likely be your scanner. While small portable scanners may work for scanning small photos, you'll probably need to scan documents or book and magazine pages that are letter-size or larger. Although I'm finding my tablet or smartphone's camera can substitute as a scanner when I'm traveling or the quality of the scan doesn't have to be high, neither substitutes for a high-quality flatbed scanner when one's available. The flatbed scanner is the only type that works well for documents or photos that either can't physically go through some sort of sheet feeder or that are at risk of being damaged.

And what specifications should this scanner have? Nearly all scanners scan at a resolution of at least 600 dpi, which is sufficient for typical genealogical preservation. You won't need higher resolutions unless working with slides or negatives, but you may find that taking them to a commercial service will be easier and cheaper than buying a device just for that purpose. Another feature to consider when purchasing a scanner is whether it can scan documents larger than letter-size paper (such as legal-size paper). If your desk space is limited, you may want to consider purchasing a multifunction printer, a single device that will handle all your printing, copying, and scanning needs.

Speaking of multifunction printers, the next device on our list of essential genealogical devices is a printer. To be honest, I use my own less and less every year in my efforts to be as paperless as possible. But I still find the occasional need to print. (This is where, if you share your household with other computer users, you may be able to share access to a single household printer via your home computer network.) I also find my printer handy for printing name badges for our genealogical society events. Of course, if you run a home-based genealogy business, you may find yourself printing a lot of things for your clients or for financial purposes. While I'm not quite ready to dispose of my printer entirely, I do see that it could easily be relocated farther away from my primary research workspace, perhaps freeing up space for my more frequently used items.

Other Equipment

As a librarian, I cannot imagine a home without books, and I've yet to meet a genealogist who doesn't own quite a few. Despite the trend toward having an e-book library, I still own reference books that I like to have nearby. I have a shelf under my nearby credenza that holds my most frequently used reference books, such as guides for writing and citation. But most of my genealogy reference books find space on a nearby bookcase. Magazine boxes are also on some of my bookshelves. (We'll discuss organizing books and magazines in a later chapter.)

A home office, no matter what it is used for, would not be complete without those tools to dispose of documents. In addition to a trash can, you may also want a separate bin for recyclable paper. Because the typical genealogy home office can double as a space for handling home finances (and may be the place for a home-based business, such as genealogical research services), you'll also want a paper shredder to dispose of more sensitive documents. When you shop for shredders, avoid the cheapest variety, as these will be insufficient for properly disposing financial documents and old credit cards. However, unless you're in a home-based business that deals with large amounts of sensitive paper, you probably also don't want the highest-end shredder either. Aim for the middle in this category. Fellowes **<www.fellowes.com>** is a respected brand, and you should be able to buy a good model for between $150 and $250.

Another important aspect of your workspace (especially if it's located in an otherwise unused corner of a room) is wall space for corkboards and whiteboards. For some, the corkboard is the place to stick a wall calendar. For me, it's a place to hang decorative art provided as gifts by friends, as well as two very large push pins at the two bottom corners that hold my computer headsets when I'm not using them. Because my corkboard is immediately behind my computer display, I can even leave my wired headset plugged into the back of my computer. To my left and above my credenza is a large whiteboard, with a tray at its bottom for the dry erase pens and the eraser. I find this most useful for important reminders to myself, and I make sure it's visible every time I enter my research space.

Finally, I also have my favorite tool: a Brother P-Touch label printer. Because I don't use it every day, I keep it almost hidden behind another item. But when I'm in the middle of a big labeling job (whether file folders or binders), the device is easy to pull out and put to work.

Drew's **To-Dos**

☞ Identify the best location in your home for your genealogical workspace.

☞ Acquire the right furniture and equipment needed for research, considering your research goals and habits.

☞ Store your materials according to their relevance to your research, with more useful items closer to your primary workspace and less useful items farther away.

YOUR GENEALOGY WORKSPACE CHECKLIST

Most genealogy work can be done at home, so having a productive and efficient workspace is crucial to your genealogical research. Make sure the items below find their way into your genealogical workspace, and add your own to the list.

Furniture

☐ large computer desk
    ☐ with large flat space?
    ☐ with drawers?
☐ small desk
    ☐ with drawers?
☐ bookshelf
☐ file cabinets
☐ closet space
☐ extra bins
☐ _____
☐ _____
☐ _____

Technology

☐ desktop/primary computer
    ☐ small enough to carry to conferences?
☐ charger/power adapter
☐ uninterruptible power supply (UPS)
☐ modem/router
☐ power strips
    ☐ with surge protection
☐ extra display monitor
☐ phone charger
☐ hi-res scanner
☐ printer
☐ _____
☐ _____
☐ _____

3

organizing
your goals

n the last half of the nineteenth century, Lewis Carroll and L. Frank Baum created two of the most popular characters in all of fiction: Alice, a seven-year-old English girl, and Dorothy Gale, a Kansas farm girl. Dorothy's character was influenced by Carroll's Alice, but another similarity between the two characters interests us here.

In *Alice's Adventures in Wonderland*, we have the following exchange:

> One day Alice came to a fork in the road and saw a Cheshire cat in a tree. "Which road do I take?" she asked. "Where do you want to go?" was his response. "I don't know," Alice answered. "Then," said the cat, "it doesn't matter."

In Baum's book *The Wonderful Wizard of Oz*, Dorothy's first encounter with the Scarecrow doesn't involve a choice of paths. However, in the well-known 1939 film version, Dorothy comes to a crossroads and doesn't know the best way to proceed. The Scarecrow, somewhat unhelpfully, indicates that people use all of the routes: "That way is a very nice way...it's pleasant down that way, too. Of course, people do go both ways."

Select the Right Surname

Because you'll normally have many surnames to choose from in your ancestry, you'll need to begin your research with a surname that will yield the greatest results. Avoid researching a very common surname, as it can be difficult to distinguish between your own relatives and individuals you're not related to. Save these more difficult surnames for later. You'll also want to avoid working on a line that someone else has already documented, as you'll likely be less motivated to re-research this branch of the family tree knowing the documentation already exists.

Unfortunately, some genealogists are more like Alice than they are like Dorothy. They lack a clear goal, and as a result, they have no rational basis for choosing the best course of action. At least Dorothy, unlike Alice, has a specific goal in mind: reaching the Emerald City. Dorothy settles on the path she chooses, and she (with some help) arrives at her destination.

Certainly, you might think you're engaging in genealogical research "just for the fun of it," with no particular goal in mind. But if that were really the case, why would you care whether or not you were organized? If you give it some additional thought, you'll likely realize you really do want to get somewhere and have at least a vague idea of where that is. Meaningful research is purposeful research, so you'll need to know where you want to go in order to get there. In this chapter, I'll help you find out what it is you want to accomplish and suggest how you can begin pursuing that goal.

Identifying Your Genealogical Goal

Your goals for genealogy research largely depend on your experience level and relationship with genealogy as a field of study. For example, because genealogy is a hobby for most people, many genealogists choose research goals based on what they think they would enjoy most. And beginning genealogists will probably enjoy an initial goal that is reasonably easy to attain; as you gain education and experience, your preferences may turn increasingly toward more challenging goals.

One of the most common goals amongst genealogical hobbyists (and even professional researchers) is identifying, through documented research, a set of related individuals. In terms of realistic steps toward this goal, you might first try to identify the names and vital details of all eight of your great-grandparents. As a general rule, recent ancestry (like the most recent three generations) is going to be easier to research than more distant ancestry, making this an achievable first step for most genealogists.

Of course, your case could be an exception. One or more of your more recent ancestors may be from a geographical area where the records are sparse, difficult to obtain, or in a language you don't currently speak. (I say "currently" because genealogical

research sometimes sparks an interest in learning a foreign language.) Again, your first genealogical goal should be something that won't frustrate you too much, but still gives you initial experience doing research.

Nothing says you need to restrict yourself to only one goal at a time, but you'll want to be selective. If you're working toward too many goals at one time, you'll likely find yourself jumping from one to another so often that you aren't making real progress on any of them. An ideal balance might be to have two or three genealogical goals at a time, letting you move between projects either when you hit a brick wall or have temporarily lost interest in one of them. There's nothing wrong with putting a research goal on hold, then returning to it later with fresh eyes and more experience. Sometimes the records you need to make progress on your goal haven't yet been made easily available, or you may be planning a future research trip and your goal will have to be on hold until that trip happens.

If you've achieved the eight-great-grandparents' goal (or if that's not the goal that interests you), you might choose another project:

- **Take a particular surname line as back as far as you can.** This goal is a bit trickier because it doesn't have a built-in way to know when you've achieved it, but you could break down that goal into phases. For example, a first-phase goal might be identifying the line back to the immigrant ancestor, followed by a second phase of researching the records from the country of origin. With any luck, you may even connect with a distant cousin, making it possible for the two of you to work together.

- **Identify all of a documented ancestor's descendants.** Often investigating an immigrant ancestor can lead to finding previously unknown cousins, some of whom may even be other genealogists.

- **Create a full family tree for a family reunion or event.** Your goal might have origins in sharing your history with family members at a reunion, wedding, anniversary, or birthday. For example, I began seriously working on my own family's

---

research tip

Make a Gift Out of It

Decorative family charts and binders can also make great wedding, anniversary, or birthday gifts. Making these projects doubles as an excellent research goal because you can visualize the end product, quickly determine how close you are to reaching that goal, and establish a concrete deadline.

---

ancestry in 1992, and I wanted to prepare a fairly complete family tree back a number of generations for my parents' fiftieth wedding anniversary in early 1993. Like me, your goal might be to complete a certain number of generations back from the common ancestral couple, and/or identify all of the known descendants of that couple. (In case you're wondering: I was successful.) The interesting thing about planned family events is that they not only provide you with a justification for your goal, but also an actual deadline to keep you motivated!

- **Research and produce a family history publication.** Here, your goal has a tangible finished product. While, of course, no genealogical research is ever technically "finished," you can always publish updated editions or post your work entirely online where it can be revised. In a similar way, professional genealogists might produce a client report, presentation, article, book, video, or podcast episode. In each of these cases, the tangible product that you can visualize can serve as a goal.

- **Complete work for a genealogical society or library.** If you're volunteering for a project at your local genealogy society, your society or one of its committees may have set your goal for you, such as completing a cemetery survey or preservation project, scanning a set of records, or indexing scanned images. Or perhaps you have been put in charge of an event for your society, which means that having a successful event is your goal.

In summary, when it comes to the research goals of the typical genealogist hobbyist, choose a goal that has a realistic and concrete result and allows you to track your progress and remain motivated over time.

Breaking Down Your Project

Goals and the projects that achieve them can be intimidating, especially when they require a lot of work and won't produce a final result for months or even years. In the case of a genealogical project, genealogists may be especially intimidated if they're new to the field or know they can devote only a limited amount of time each week to achieving it.

The best way to attack an ambitious project is to break it down into smaller sub-projects. When I first envisioned this book, for example, I knew that I would first need to create an outline so I could define the content of each of its chapters. My publisher asked to see an even more detailed outline so each chapter could be even further subdivided. Once I had that detailed outline, I realized I could complete the book one chapter at a time, and each chapter one section at a time. Each section required about one thousand words, a figure I could easily write each evening with additional work on weekends.

Dividing your goals into smaller sub-projects, such as finding a great-grandfather's SS-5, can keep your goals from seeming too large to achieve.

Setting Deadlines

As mentioned earlier, projects and sub-projects can be assigned deadlines. In some cases, someone else may impose a deadline on you. Clients, for example, expect work to be done in a timely fashion as outlined in a contract; publishers and editors give deadlines to their writers; and conferences and societies give deadlines to their presenters. Volunteer project managers may specify deadlines to their volunteers. But if you're working on a personal research project, you may feel that no deadline is necessary (unless it needs to be finished in time for a family event). However, a deadline, even if essentially artificial, will better motivate you to make ongoing progress with your work. You'll have a sense of accomplishment in saying to yourself, "This year I want to accomplish genealogical Goal X!" and at the end of the year finding that you were successful.

Being able to estimate how long it will take you to complete a genealogical project can be difficult, especially if you're relatively new to genealogical research. Certainly, any number of factors can influence the duration of your project, such as your amount of available free time, health status, or encounter with an unexpected brick wall, so when you're first giving yourself a deadline, be generous in your estimate. Then create a timeline between now and the deadline, assigning intermediate checkpoint dates on your timeline for each of your sub-projects. Post your timeline in a highly visible location in your genealogy workspace, such as on your whiteboard, corkboard, or computer's desktop. Even better, put each date on your calendar (whether a wall calendar, daily planning notebook, or online calendar). This will make it easier to monitor your progress and, if necessary, adjust your timeline.

B

DEATH OF ROBERT B. KING.

Following a long period of illness, Mr. Robert B. King died Friday night at one o'clock at the home of his son-in-law, Mr. Fred Rickman, Mills street. On Sunday morning at 10 o'clock funeral services were held at the home of Mr. Rickman, the Rev. John C. Davis, pastor of the Second Methodist church, officiating. At the conclusion of these services interment was made in the city cemetery.

Mr. King was in the 77th year of his age and is survived by his widow and had proceeded to Charleston several weeks before actual hostilities broke out. On the Morning of April 12 he was on the floating battery in the harbor of Charleston when the historic first gun was fired on Fort Sumter. While he laid no claim to the honor of having fired the first round, he did maintain that he pulled the lanyard that caused his piece of artillery to send the second charge into the camp of the enemy. He went through the entire four years' struggle and was engaged in many of the

Break your projects down into easier-to-achieve tasks to make steady progress on your genealogical goals. Doing so will lead you to small successes, such as this obituary for another of my great-grandfathers.

In the same way, almost any genealogical project can be broken down into smaller sub-projects. Instead of trying to tackle learning about all eight of your great-grandparents at once, instead focus on smaller, more immediate tasks, such as finding an application for Social Security (SS-5) form for one ancestor (image **A**) and an obituary for another (image **B**). If the entire project has a deadline, each sub-project, too, can be given its own deadline. This will not only maintain momentum on accomplishing the project, but also provides a way to monitor the project to see if it's going according to plan.

Depending on the type of genealogical project, you can subdivide it by generation, geography, genealogy, or some combination of the three:

- **Generational sub-projects** encourage you to focus on one generation at a time. As you work backwards in time, this may seem rather obvious, but consciously doing so prevents you from overlooking your ancestors' siblings before you move on to the next generation.
- **Geographical sub-projects** focus your research on a particular geographical area, which is useful because documents are usually filed and preserved together in repositories at a national, state, or local level. This can save time when you're using a set of online record collections based on the same geography or scheduling a research trip.
- **Genealogical sub-projects** are based on particular family lines, such as a sub-project for each child of an ancestor. This ensures that each descendant gets the proper research and isn't overlooked.

Pedigree Chart - Andrew Martin Smith

Chart no. _____
No. 1 on this chart is the same as no. _____ on chart no. _____

8 Charles Henry SMITH
b: 30 May 1859
p: Newark, Essex, New Jersey, United States
m: 4 Jan 1880
p: Newark, Essex, New Jersey, United States
d: 22 Apr 1906
p:

4 William Henry SMITH
b: 21 Sep 1889
p: Newark, Essex, New Jersey, United States
m:
p:
d: 9 Feb 1961
p: Irvington, Essex, New Jersey, United States

9 Mary Ann BANNON
b: 13 Jan 1863
p: Oldbury, Birmingham, England
d: 10 Oct 1940
p:

2 George Thomas SMITH
b: 8 Nov 1917
p: Newark, Essex, New Jersey, United States
m: 31 Jan 1943
p: Newberry, South Carolina, United States
d: 3 Nov 1999
p: Richland, South Carolina, United States

10 Louis WEINGLASS
b: 13 Feb 1865
p: Markowa, Przeworsk, Rzeszów, Poland
m: 24 May 1887
p: New York City, New York, United States
d: 2 Feb 1903
p: New York County, New York, United States

5 Rachel WEINGLASS
b: 20 Nov 1890
p: Manhattan, New York, New York, USA
d: 1 Jun 1976
p: Broward, Florida, United States

11 Sarah GRODOWITZ
b: Mar 1871
p: Poland
d: 11 Aug 1944
p:

1 Andrew Martin SMITH
b:
p:
m:

Since my mother and father came from significantly different geographic places, I can organize this project by geography, grouping my paternal ancestors into one project that researches New York/New Jersey, England, and Poland.

CASE STUDY: Subdividing Projects

Let's apply these ideas to the types of genealogical goals/projects already discussed. In the section that follows, "Project 1" will be to document all eight of my great-grandparents, "Project 2" will be to take my Smith ancestry as far back as I can manage, and "Project 3" will be to identify all of the living descendants of my immigrant seventeenth- and early eighteenth-century English ancestor William Boddie, who died in Isle of Wight County, Virginia. As you can see, Project 1 is a good beginner's project, Project 2 will probably start off easy and get more difficult as I work backwards, and Project 3 will be complex and time-consuming with varying amounts of difficulty from the very beginning.

For me, Project 1 (image C) can be subdivided first by geography. I know that my father was from New Jersey and that my mother was from South Carolina. This means that I'll be doing research in two different geographic areas, so I'll subdivide Project 1 into Project 1a (Dad's side) and Project 1b (Mom's side). This means that I'm dealing with only seven people in each sub-project (Dad, his two parents, and his four grand-parents in 1a; Mom, her two parents, and her four grandparents in 1b). I can then make even smaller sub-projects by focusing on each individual, one generation at a time.

Smith Ancestors of Andrew Martin Smith

First Generation

1. **Andrew Martin Smith**

Second Generation

2. **George Thomas Smith** was born on 8 Nov 1917 in Newark, Essex, New Jersey, United States. He died on 3 Nov 1999 at the age of 81 in Columbia, Richland, South Carolina, United States. George Thomas Smith was married on 31 Jan 1943 in Newberry, Newberry, South Carolina, United States.

Third Generation

4. **William Henry Smith** was born on 21 Sep 1889 in Newark, Essex, New Jersey, United States. He died on 9 Feb 1961 at the age of 71 in Irvington, Essex, New Jersey, United States.

Fourth Generation

8. **Charles Henry Smith** was born on 30 May 1859 in Newark, Essex, New Jersey, United States. He died on 22 Apr 1906 at the age of 46. Charles Henry Smith was married on 4 Jan 1880 in Newark, Essex, New Jersey, United States.

Taking a family's line back as far as possible (as I do in Project 2, a portion of which is represented here) will best be organized by generation.

Once I have identified and documented all eight great-grandparents, I'll know that we have completed this project.

Project 2 (image D) lends itself immediately to the generational approach, starting with myself, then my father, grandfather, and so forth. If I already have an idea as to approximately when and from where my ancestor in this direct surname line immigrated, I might want to create a Project 2a for research on the immigrant in the United States and Project 2b for research on the immigrant from records in his country of origin. The idea here is to define at least one doable sub-project that has a beginning and an end.

Project 3 (image E) is relatively complex. First, it might require a sub-project to establish the documented relationship of myself back to my supposed immigrant ancestor. After all, I wouldn't want to do a great deal of work on someone in the past only to learn that I wasn't really descended from him after all! So Project 3a might be exactly that: a genealogical sub-project that links me to the immigrant. Once I've completed

---

Descendants of William Boddie of Virginia

First Generation

1. **William BODDIE** was born between 1633 and 1635 in Ingatestone, Essex County, England. He died about 25 Feb 1717 at the age of 84 In Isle of Wight County, Virginia.

William BODDIE and Elizabeth were married in 1683. **Elizabeth** died after 1699 in Isle of Wight County, Virginia.

William BODDIE and Elizabeth had the following children:

> 2 i. **Elizabeth BODDIE**, married Alexander MATTHEWS.
> 3 ii. **John BODDIE**, born 1664, Isle of Wight County, Virginia; married Elizabeth THOMAS, 1694, Isle of Wight County, Virginia; died Mar 1720, Isle of Wight County, Virginia.

William BODDIE and Anna were married before 1683 in England. **Anna** died about 1683 in Isle of Wight County, Virginia.

William BODDIE and Anna had the following child:

> 4 i. **Mary BODDIE**, born 1653, Ingatestone, Essex County, England.

William BODDIE and Mary HUNT were married after 1699. **Mary HUNT**, daughter of William HUNT and Judith BURTON, was born between 1648 and 1650 in Isle of Wight County, Virginia.

Second Generation

2. **Elizabeth BODDIE** was born (date unknown).

Elizabeth BODDIE and Alexander MATTHEWS were married. **Alexander MATTHEWS** was born (date unknown).

More complex projects such as researching all living descendants of an immigrant ancestor (Project 3) will require a more complex organizational structure.

that sub-project, I can move forward in time with the immigrant's descendants, one generation at a time. This could be subdivided into sub-projects in a number of ways. For instance, if one branch of the family relocates to another state, it may make sense to set this up as its own sub-project.

However, this method isn't without its own complications. I have reason to believe that two different descendant lines of William Boddie left South Carolina at different times but ended up in the same place in Louisiana, even intermarrying there. Due to the complexity of this project, I'll likely have to define sub-projects as I go and decide how to define them based on what I learn.

Creating To-Do Lists

Once you have your goal, the project(s) to achieve it, and the sub-projects to make it more manageable, you still need to get down to the level of specific actions you can take on a given day. Even a sub-project will take some time and consist of many individual tasks, and each task may take a few minutes or a few hours to complete (anything longer should probably be split into multiple tasks). Whether you call it an activity, a task, or a to-do, you'll need to figure out what they are in order to accomplish your goal.

Like triggers, your to-do system can also be used as a way to track the formation of habits. If there's some genealogy-related habit you want to track, put it into your to-do system as a recurring task outside of your regular projects (unless you want to make a project just for your habit development). You will likely be able to set up your habit as a recurring task that needs to be done every day (or on some other regular basis).

The to-do system reminder you can set up will serve as the temporary trigger you may need for the habit. For instance, if the habit you want to acquire is putting any incoming documents into the inbox tray, you can add that recurring task to your to-do system, where it will remind you to perform the action. When the action becomes habitual and part of your routine, you can safely remove it from your to-do system. And don't worry about not knowing some of the needed tasks when you start your project; you can always add new tasks to your to-do system as you become aware of the need for them.

Perhaps you've been tracking your to-dos for years using a notepad of some kind. Some people even use their daily planner notebook (the same one used for calendaring events) to record their to-do list. Paper-based to-do systems can be difficult to review and search, move from one date to another without some effort, and hide completed tasks so they don't distract you from what remains to be done. Also, a paper-based system requires you to have a physical to-do list with you, not only when you're at home, but also when you're on a research trip or attending a conference. With that comes the risk of losing it.

> **research tip**
>
> **Track Your Collaboration**
>
> In some cases, your projects will be shared projects with other people. Perhaps you and a cousin are working on a family line together. You can use the to-do system to assign specific tasks to each individual, then track what they have done in the past week or month.

You gain a lot of benefits by using a paperless system. You can store your to-do list on your desktop computer, laptop, tablet, smartphone, and even smartwatch (if you have one). You can use the same software to track your to-dos for both genealogical and non-genealogical purposes and organize your to-dos to focus on just one at a time without being distracted by anything else. The best to-do list apps allow you to set due dates (if the

Picking Your To-Do App

Mobile apps are hot right now, and (like for many aspects of daily life) many apps can keep track of your to-do lists. But which application is the right one for you? Help select the app that best fulfills your research needs by asking yourself these questions:

- Does it run on my current computer's operating system (and on the operating system of a computer I am likely to get in the near future)? Does it provide an app for my tablet or smart-phone's operating system?

- Does it synchronize between multiple devices so that updating it on one device makes that change visible on all devices?

- Does it let me define projects or sub-projects so I can categorize my to-dos by them?

- Does it let me associate my to-do with a context, such as being at a certain location (say, a repository), having access to a particular device (such as a computer), or having a certain energy level (since some tasks require more mental energy, some less)?

- Does it let me set a due date and/or a defer date? Is it easy to change the date quickly so I can move it forward a day, a week, a month, etc.?

- Does it let me flag certain projects or to-dos as being especially important so I can focus on them first?

- Does it let me assign a to-do to a different person, such as when I'm waiting on a response from a repository or from another researcher?

- Does it allow me to add to my to-do list by forwarding an e-mail to the tracking system? Does it let me add notes to a to-do, including links to relevant documents?

- Does it let me create a to-do that repeats on a regular basis, such as weekly, monthly, or annually?

- Does it make it easy to do a regular review (for example, weekly) of what remains to be done in each project or sub-project?

- Does it provide a notification system to my computer desktop or to my mobile device to remind me of to-dos that are important or nearly due?

- Is the software free? If not, does it offer a free trial version?

project or task has a due date) and, even better, a defer date so you won't even see a to-do on your list until the day you want to do it or are able to do it (though different software applications refer to this function differently).

There are countless to-do applications, ranging from free to expensive. Some have free versions that can be upgraded to premium versions for more features. You may need to play with several different ones until you settle on one that best fits your needs and research practices. See the Picking Your To-Do App sidebar for some questions to consider as you look at the available tools.

CASE STUDY: Using OmniFocus to Track Research Progress

Let's see how this works in practice. Which system do I use? I previously used Toodledo **<www.toodledo.com>** and tried out Wunderlist **<www.wunderlist.com>**, and I've heard good things about Remember The Milk **<www.rememberthemilk.com>**, Todoist **<www.todoist.com>**, and Asana **<www.asana.com>**. But I'm currently using OmniFocus **<www.omnigroup.com/omnifocus>**, which doesn't have a free option (not necessarily something I would recommend if you don't already have experience using a to-do system). OmniFocus is available only for Mac OS X and iOS devices, but you should be able to replicate most of what I do with OmniFocus on whatever system you choose since many of these applications have the same (or similar) functions.

STEP 1: DOWNLOAD THE APP

Once you've settled on an app (such as OmniFocus), make an account and download the app on all the devices you use and that the app supports. The main advantage of using wireless apps is that you can edit and access them from anywhere, and making your to-do lists available on all your devices will help you do this.

To obtain a copy of OmniFocus for your Mac, go to the store on the OmniGroup website **<store.omnigroup.com>**. The Basic license for Mac is $39.99, and apps for the iPhone (image **F**) and iPad are sold separately in the Apple Store. All devices share the same data, and changes made on one device will automatically sync on other devices.

I should note that, although OmniFocus synchronizes across all of my devices, I don't use it in the same way on each device. On my mobile devices, I am more likely to view my to-do list, check off completed items, and quickly add a to-do that occurs to me while I'm away from home. However, when I need to set up a new project or sub-project and define a long list of to-dos or do a weekly review of my past accomplishments and what I plan to achieve in the coming week, I normally go to my desktop computer with its large screen.

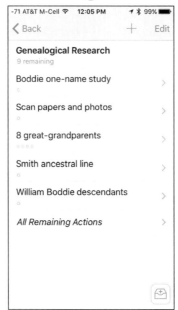

Look for apps that you can download on all of your devices, including mobile phones.

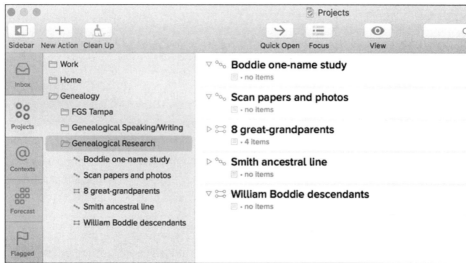

OmniFocus allows you to organize your tasks into projects and sub-projects.

STEP 2: SET UP PROJECTS AND FOLDERS

Now that you've made your to-do list accessible on all your devices, you'll need to organize your data. Many of these apps sort your tasks by project, organized into a folder. Because I use my to-do list system during my full-time job and for my non-genealogical home activities, I went to the Projects area of OmniFocus and created three folders: Work, Home, and Genealogy. Each of my projects, sub-projects, and tasks will appear in only one of those folders so I can focus on that particular area when I need to.

Within my Genealogy folder (image **G**) are some sub-folders: one for my genealogical society, one for my genealogy speaking and writing, and one for my personal genealogy research. When I highlight the Genealogical Research folder, I can see all of my research projects. At the moment, I already have a project for a one-name study I'm doing for the Boddie family name and another project for scanning papers and photos (we'll come back to that one in the chapter regarding organizing your files). So now I'll add the three projects discussed in the previous section (eight great-grandparents, the Smith ancestry, and the William Boddie descendancy).

OmniFocus allows you to define different kinds of projects. For instance, you can have a project in which each task has to be completed before the next one can be started. Or you can have a project in which more than one task can be worked on at the same time. The software also provides a "single action" type of project, but that's really just a way to hold a bunch of stuff in the same place without a particular final goal in mind, such as "books to read" or "movies to see." You might want to choose a sequential project when dealing with some genealogical research, making sure you have completed work on a particular generation before you move to the next one. I'll make my Smith project a sequential project, which will keep me from jumping around, while I'll make my great-grandparents and the Boddie project parallel projects so I can work on different parts of them as I choose.

STEP 3: DEFINE SUB-PROJECTS AND TASKS

Now that I have set up the projects, it's time to define sub-projects and tasks. (OmniFocus refers to sub-projects as "action groups.") For my great-grandparents project (image **H**), I start by creating a sub-project called *Research paternal line* and another called *Research maternal line*.

research tip

Track Your Tasks

Create a text file on your computer with a generic list of research tasks, allowing you to copy and paste the appropriate ones into your to-do system and modify them as needed for the particular individual research case.

H

▽ **8 great-grandparents**
   · 4 items

   ▽ Research paternal line
      · Genealogy

         Locate, scan, and archive father's SS-5
            · Genealogy

   ▽ Research maternal line
      · Genealogy

         Locate, scan, and archive mother's SS-5
            · Genealogy

   ▷ **Smith ancestral line**
      · no items

   ▷ **William Boddie descendants**
      · no items

With OmniFocus, you can designate sub-projects and create tasks within them.

Once I have my two sub-projects, I can think about all of the tasks I will need to accomplish to complete it. For now, I'll skip over the detail of documenting my own relationship with my two parents, and focus instead on each of them. For my *Research paternal line* sub-project, I'll add a task of *Locate and scan father's SS-5* because I know that document will name his two parents. I'll do the same thing for my maternal line research. I'll also add *Look for father in 1940 census and save a copy* and create similar tasks for 1930 and 1920. Again, I'll do the same thing for my maternal research project, omitting the 1920 census because my mother was born after it was taken.

I would also want to add tasks for finding other kinds of records, such as birth certificates, marriage certificates, death certificates, and obituaries, plus any other records that could document an individual's relationship to their parents.

Remember that my overall project (the eight great-grandparents) is a parallel project, so it doesn't matter if I work on my father's side or my mother's side first. I can also switch back and forth whenever the mood strikes me. (Remember I can also make each sub-project sequential, forcing me to step through the tasks for each generation one task at a time, reducing the possibility of overlooking an important document.)

OmniFocus also lets me set a defer date and/or a due date (image **I**). Knowing I can use this feature, I'll decide that I want to work on my father's side starting today and my mother's side next Saturday. So I use the defer date field to set those up. That way, those tasks won't bother me until the appropriate day arrives. For now, I'll leave the due date blank, as I have no external pressure to get this done by any particular date.

Finally, I'll input some information, such as where I think I've got these documents filed, into the Note field. When I'm ready to work on that task, I can review the Note area for any helpful information or links.

STEP 4: COMPLETE AND RECORD YOUR TASK

Now that we've set up our app, all that's left to do is the actual research! When I pull up the eight great-grandparents project, I can see which tasks have been completed, which I can work on now, and which ones are deferred to a later date (image **J**). If the only task for this project I can work on now is the one involving locating and scanning my father's SS-5, I should do so, then mark it complete in my to-do system when I'm done.

Again, while performing this task, additional tasks may arise, so I should be ready to add new tasks if needed. For instance, if I were to realize that I don't have a copy of my father's SS-5 but think my brother did, I would create and add to my list a new task of *Contact Jeff for Dad's SS-5*.

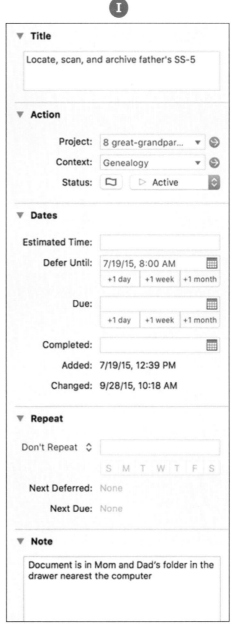

The defer date feature allows you to schedule certain tasks for certain days, keeping you on schedule and allowing you to focus your efforts.

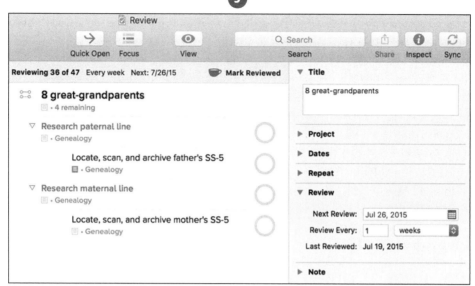

Monitor your progress and plan future sessions with OmniFocus' Review feature.

Plotting Out Your Tasks on a Calendar

Once you've defined your projects, sub-projects, and tasks, and have put them into some kind of system, spend some time thinking about when you want to accomplish them. In the previous section, I talked about using defer date and due date options to help schedule your tasks. Again, unless your work is tied to an upcoming event or you've promised something to someone else, you won't have any need for due dates for your personal genealogical research. So let's look again at defer dates, this time as they apply to your calendar.

If you're working on several projects at the same time, your to-do system might quickly become overwhelming with the number of possible tasks you can do. If you have the entire day to work on genealogy tasks, you can probably accomplish (on average) five major tasks. These tasks might take one to two hours each to complete. Some people find it more manageable to use a "3+2" system, in which you work on three major tasks and two smaller ones.

However, I wouldn't necessarily categorize "major" and "minor" strictly on how much time the task takes. You could also categorize them based on how much mental energy it will take to focus on the task. A task requiring you to review several documents and come to a conclusion about the genealogical facts will likely take a lot more effort than one that just involves filing some papers in your folders or binders. If you don't have the luxury of spending the entire day doing genealogy and can only squeeze in an hour or two at the end of your day after your other obligations, you'll want to consider whether you can do more than one major task (or a handful of minor ones).

At this point, pull out your calendar, view it with your to-do system, and start scheduling your tasks on the calendar (image 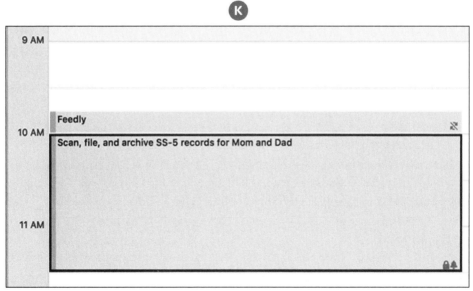). I often use the "all-day" field at the top of my calendar's daily view to list the two or three things I want to accomplish or focus on that day. The text can even be the name of a sub-project, which allows me to see which task in that sub-project I should probably work on next just by looking at my to-do list).

In some cases, you'll want to schedule a task for a particular time. For instance, you might know the best time to reach your cousin on the phone is during the noon lunch hour, so you can schedule a call for that exact time. Another option is to simply block out large chunks of time (one to two hours) for a particular sub-project, which will motivate you to work on that and not be distracted by other, equally fun genealogical work.

As mentioned in chapter 1, don't forget to schedule breaks in between work periods. Block out time for meals, and add shorter breaks between your other work sessions so you can stand at least once every hour. If your genealogical work is heavily computer-based, use your break time away from the computer.

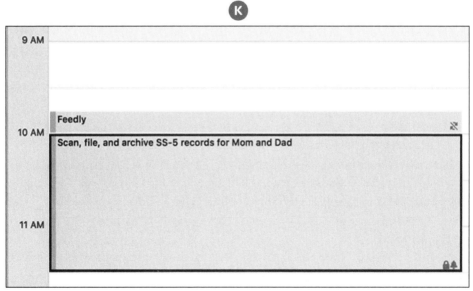

Ensuring your tasks appear on your calendar app will help you meet your goals.

If you're the type of person who benefits from reminders and won't find them too annoying, set up alerts on your calendar so you'll be notified of what to work on at any given time. You may need to turn off notifications from other systems (such as Facebook) so you won't be tempted to leave your research and spend that time on social networking. Don't worry: There'll be plenty of time for that once you're done!

Monitoring Your Progress

In any good project management/to-do system, you want a way to easily monitor how you're doing. You want to be motivated by what you've already accomplished and see at a glance what you need to do in the coming days, weeks, and months.

At least once a year, look at your system to review each of your projects. Your annual review does not need to take place during the last week of December or the first week of January (when you might be busy with holiday-related activities or making great progress in your research because you have more free time than usual). Rather, if you're starting your system while reading this book, consider setting your annual review for whatever today's date is. You can always adjust that date forward or backward by a week or two if you need to avoid some important personal date or holiday.

As you conduct your annual review, try to answer the following questions for each project:

- Has the project been completed? If so, you may want to archive it so you can refer to it later while keeping it from showing up in your list of active projects.

- If the project isn't yet completed, is it because it's a complex project that still requires more time? Or is it because you've lost interest in it? If you think there's a chance you'll return to a project at a later date, mark it as "on hold" in some way and remove it from your view until your next annual review. Otherwise, mark the project as "dropped" and archive it in case you want to refer back to it later. (OmniFocus lets you mark the status of a project as Active, Completed, On Hold, or Dropped.)

- Do you have ideas for new projects? Add them at this time. Although nothing prevents you from adding new projects at any time during the year, you may want to make sure you've completed a project or two before adding new ones.

Being able to review your genealogical research work on an annual basis not only will ensure that the projects you're engaged in are the ones you still find interesting, but also will document your growth as a genealogist as you move from simpler projects to more complex ones. It will also assist you in determining how long projects take to do, which is especially helpful if you think you'll be doing genealogical work for others, either professionally or pro bono.

You should also plan to do a monthly review of your projects. As with scheduling the annual review, you're not obligated to do your monthly review on the first of every month. Pick whatever date works best for your own schedule. The monthly review is a good time to see if a particular project is making progress or is stalled due to some unforeseen issue. Perhaps a repository has failed to respond to a document request, and you need to follow up. Or maybe you realize you've been focusing on other projects and neglecting one of them, resolving to devote more time to that project in the coming month. The monthly review is a good time to see whether you or others are the stumbling block in making progress.

Finally, you'll want to do a weekly review. In this review, you see specifically what you have done in the past week as well as start scheduling the things you want to work on in the coming week on your calendar.

Schedule your annual, monthly, and weekly reviews on your calendar, preferably on the same day of the week and at the same time so it becomes habitual and a part of your routine. Your to-do system may allow you to indicate the date of each project's next review and how often you want to review it (such as monthly).

After you've performed your reviews, consider sharing them with the appropriate people. A good way to maintain progress on any project is to have someone else you can discuss it with. Perhaps you have a genealogy friend whom you can arrange to have a weekly or monthly visit, phone call, or online chat. Knowing that your friend will be asking how your projects are going will give you additional motivation to honestly review your work and identify where any problems are.

Drew's **To-Dos**

➤ Create concrete, realistic, long-term genealogical research goals that interest you and answer questions about your family history.

➤ Break big projects into smaller pieces and give each piece a due date.

➤ Track tasks using a paper-based or online management to-do system and schedule time-dependent activities on your calendar.

➤ Monitor your progress on a regular basis (annually, monthly, or weekly) to keep yourself on track.

GOAL PLANNING WORKSHEET

Good genealogical research is purposeful. To accomplish your goals, you'll first need to articulate them and draft some ways to accomplish them. Use the table below to record some goals that you have, why you want to pursue them, and what resources you can use to fulfill them. You can also download a Word-document version of this form at <ftu. familytreemagazine.com/organize-your-genealogy>.

Goal	Estimated time of completion	Why do you want to accomplish this?	What do you need to accomplish this? What resources should you consult?

PROGRESS REVIEW WORKSHEET

Once you've established your goals (and, as discussed later in this book, have come up with a plan of action for accomplishing them), you'll need a way to evaluate your progress. Fill in the table below with questions to ask yourself during weekly, monthly, and annual reviews for each of your genealogical goals. You can also download a Word-document version of this form at <ftu.familytreemagazine.com/organize-your-genealogy>.

Goal	Weekly	Monthly	Annual

4

organizing
your notes
and ideas

The human brain is a funny thing. We can be anywhere when we have an idea. It can be triggered by something we read, hear, or see. Genealogical ideas come to us both in the middle of our research time and when we're doing nothing related to our research. It happens to all of us.

Unfortunately, we also usually forget to record these ideas. Later, we may recall that we had an idea but can't remember what it was. With any luck, it'll resurface at a later date, but it would certainly be less frustrating if we had recorded the idea when we first had it. You want to take the necessary steps to have something around you at nearly all times that can be used to record your thoughts, so a brilliant idea for your further research won't disappear in the fog of memory. And when you no longer have to worry about remembering those great ideas (because they have been safely recorded), your mind will be more relaxed and better able to generate even more ideas! In this chapter, I'll discuss how to record your ideas and notes with notebooks, digital recorders, and software like Evernote **<www.evernote.com>** so you'll never be disconnected from a sudden stroke of genius.

Recording Your Notes and Ideas

So how do we record our ideas so we don't lose them? One way is to make sure we have tools constantly available for this purpose. While it may be impractical to have a recording device in your shower (for example), you can usually arrange to have something record ideas in most other scenarios. In this section, I'll discuss some tools you can carry with you to deposit your ideas as they come to you.

Paper Notebooks

Let's start with the lowest tech solution: some sort of paper notebook or journal. For reasons I'll explain later, I use a Moleskine notebook marketed by Evernote <**www.evernote. com/partner/moleskine**> (image Ⓐ; see Research Tip: Use Moleskine to Convert Photos to Text), but any kind of notebook/journal will do. I especially like notebooks that have a ribbon to act as a bookmark (letting me quickly get to the first blank page) and an elastic band to hold it shut when carrying it around.

If you're going to use a paper journal, your biggest deciding factor will be the size, and which size you select will depend a great deal on what you wear and what you tend to carry with you. Most of the notebooks I've seen come in three sizes (the exact dimensions will vary according to the company that produces them): 3.5x5.5 inches (let's call this "pocket"), 5x8.25 inches ("large"), and 7.5x10 inches ("extra large"). Obviously, the pocket-sized notebook will work well in a shirt pocket or purse. The large size will work well in a purse or computer bag, while the extra large will fit in most computer bags or briefcases (does anyone still use a briefcase?) but otherwise will be cumbersome to travel with. My personal preference is the 5x8.25-inch large size, and I carry one in my computer bag together with a few pens—you don't want to run out of ink in the middle of writing down an idea.

research tip

Use Moleskine to Convert Photos to Text

Take advantage of apps that can scan and convert handwritten notes into searchable text such as the Moleskine notebooks marketed by Evernote. I can take a photo of the handwritten text on a Moleskine page with my Evernote app, and (in addition to the image being added to my Evernote database) the text in that image will become searchable in Evernote. Evernote also provides some special stickers with the Moleskine notebook that can be applied to specific pages so the digitized image can automatically be filed in a particular notebook in Evernote.

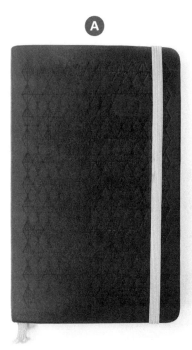

The Moleskine notebook is a useful tool for recording your thoughts, as Evernote will automatically transcribe your handwritten notes.

Idea-capturing notebooks don't need to be organized in any particular way, although I usually start a new page when I'm capturing a new set of ideas. I may write something at the top of the page if it's relevant, such as a title to describe what the ideas or notes are about so I can quickly scan through my various pages to find what I want. I also make notations at the beginning of some lines, such as an asterisk, to highlight something that should become a to-do.

I also use my paper notebook to record notes from meetings and presentations I'm attending. Oddly enough, I've found my brain is wired in such a way that I don't necessarily refer to these notes later (especially the ones from presentations). Rather, the act of writing them down and reading what I have just written helps me to remember more of the presentation itself.

Voice Recorders

What about situations in which writing isn't a good option? In particular, what if an idea occurs to you while you're driving or while your hands are busy cooking or cleaning? In this case, your best option may be to have a digital voice recorder. You can find voice recorders from many manufacturers that are priced from inexpensive to expensive. The two well-known companies that have different models at affordable prices are Olympus <www.getolympus.com/us/en/audio/digital-recorders.html> and Sony <www.sony.com/electronics/voice-recorder-products/t/voice-recorders>. I've long used Olympus voice recorders, and prices range anywhere from forty to three hundred dollars. Many models double as USB flash drives, which is handy if you want one less thing to worry about carrying when you travel. These are also useful to have when you're traveling to relatives' homes for recording family history interviews.

For capturing spoken ideas and notes, you won't need any fancy features or huge amounts of data storage, so purchase well within your budget. Just remember to check your recorder's battery level on a regular basis (especially before going on a trip) so you don't run out of power in the middle of an important capturing session!

Mobile and Computer Apps

If you have your smartphone or tablet with you, you may find that you don't need a separate digital voice recorder. Instead, you can use an app on your mobile device to record spoken notes. Many apps serve this purpose (including Evernote, but more on that later), and they range in price from free to only a few dollars. Although your smartphone or tablet might have a built-in voice recorder app, the free or inexpensive apps are generally going to be better and offer far more features.

Whether you use a paper-based system, a digital voice recorder, or a voice recorder app on your mobile device, you'll need to create a routine for yourself in which you transfer these into a more appropriate location. Ideally, you'll want to turn your handwriting and your voice recordings into searchable, digital text. In this way, you can copy and paste the information into applications (such as for word processing, project management, or recording genealogical information) on your computer.

---

research tip

Privatize Your Data

Because many people use Evernote in their personal lives as well as for genealogy, you may not want to store certain kinds of data in the cloud, such as financial data or passwords. To account for this, Evernote allows you to create local notebooks that are stored only on your desktop or laptop computer, and which are not synchronized to any other location. Take advantage of this feature to lock down your sensitive material. (As for passwords, an entire category of software safely stores those in an encrypted format, so you probably don't want to store important passwords in Evernote.)

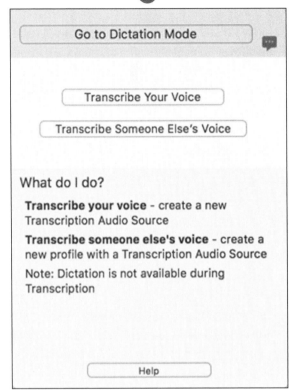

Having voice recording apps or devices (like my Olympus WS-821) ensure you never lose a spoken thought.

Some apps, like this Nuance Dragon app, transcribe spoken words into text for you.

Some tech will do all this for you. When transforming spoken words into digital text, I use one of the Dragon applications sold by Nuance Communications **<www.nuance. com/dragon/index.htm>** (image **B**). Nuance lets you know which digital voice recorders work best with their software, and that guided my most recent purchase decision. For about sixty dollars, I was able to purchase an Olympus WS-821 **<www.getolympus. com/us/en/ws-821.html>** (image **C**), which can store up to nearly five hundred hours of recording (even more if I were to use a microSD card with it) and has a battery life of thirty-seven hours.

However, although the quality of voice recognition technology has improved dramatically in the past few decades, interpreting recorded speech is not as accurate as interpreting speech delivered live through a microphone. Have realistic expectations regarding how much will be accurately transcribed from your digital voice recorder, and expect to spend a bit of time making corrections.

Brainstorming and Preserving Ideas with Mind Maps

In the previous section, we focused primarily on capturing the random ideas that occur to us, usually while we're busy doing something else. In this section, I'll talk about how to handle ideas that come from dedicated brainstorming sessions. You might decide to brainstorm when you've hit a roadblock while researching, and you want to consider all of your available options going forward. Some other examples could include

- planning a research trip and wanting to visualize everything you need to do to make it successful

- creating new topics for your work as a professional genealogy writer or presenter

- developing ways to attract new members or getting more people to attend monthly meetings of your genealogy society

Certainly you could brainstorm using a paper notebook, a whiteboard, or a word processing document on your computer. If text works best for you, then a word processing document may be your best option. Or even better, you could use a tool like Evernote (discussed later in this chapter) that is designed specifically to capture ideas and make them easy to organize and find. But if you benefit from expressing your ideas more visually, then a paper notebook or whiteboard could work better, as you could draw connections between your ideas and/or position them in different places on the page or whiteboard. This helps you see which of your ideas relates best to your other ideas, and which ideas are more isolated. And if you use a paper document or whiteboard when brainstorming, you can always scan the document or take a photo of the whiteboard and store the image electronically with your other digital files, though you wouldn't be able to easily manipulate these to make further changes.

But what if you could visualize your ideas and automatically save those visualizations and edit them in the future? "Mind mapping" allows you to do exactly that. Although mind maps have been created on paper for centuries, the computer age has resulted in software specifically designed for mind mapping on desktop computers and mobile devices. Because of its value to the business world, some high-end mind-mapping software can be expensive, but free or inexpensive mind-mapping applications exist. My favorite apps for mind mapping are web-based, which allow me to access my mind maps from any Internet-connected device.

At the moment, my mind-mapping app of choice is Coggle <coggle.it> (image **D**), a free British creation that is web-based and provides an unlimited number of mind maps. My maps can be organized, stored in Google Drive (you will need a Google account in

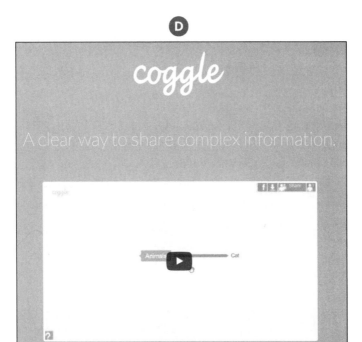

Apps like Coggle let you digitize your mind maps, allowing you to edit, share, and quickly organize them.

Sharing Mind Maps with Coggle

As you use tools such as Coggle and Evernote to capture your ideas and notes, you'll likely want to share the results of your work privately or publicly or even collaborate with others in creating the information in the first place.

You have several options for how to share your work through Coggle, including:

- e-mailing your mind map as a file to others or incorporating it as part of a Word document or web page
- exporting an MM-format copy of your mind map to a different mind-mapping application at a later date
- sharing your mind map on Facebook or Twitter
- embedding an HTML code in a web page
- giving another individual a URL to your map
- making your map discoverable via search engine, potentially attracting an unknown cousin
- collaborating with other Coggle users and giving them permission to view, download/copy, or edit your mind map

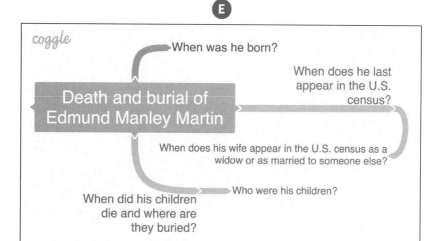

By making a mind map, you can visually represent the relationships between ideas.

order to use Coggle), and even shared with others (more about that in the Sharing Mind Maps with Coggle sidebar). The Coggle software lets you download a copy of your mind map in a number of different formats: PDF, PNG (a popular graphics format), TXT (basically a colorful text-based version of your map), and MM (a format that can be imported into several other mind-mapping applications).

Although I'll be using Coggle in my example, you'll find that nearly every popular mind-mapping application will have similar features.

Just as typical genealogy charts link individuals by lines of relationships (parent-child, spouse-spouse), a mind map has nodes (sometimes ellipses, rectangles, or similar shapes with rounded corners) that are connected by lines. The central node is the mind map's central subject.

For instance, let's imagine that I have a brick wall: the death and burial of my great-grandfather, Edmund Manley Martin (image **E**). I'm uncertain of the exact date and location, so I'll brainstorm how to get past this brick wall. I would start by creating a new mind map with the central node saying something like "Death and burial of Edmund Manley Martin." Now that I have my central node, which also serves as the title of my mind map, I can start to add additional nodes to either end. I might brainstorm a list of relevant questions, such as "When was he born?," "When does he last appear in the U.S. Census?," and "When did his children die and where are they buried?"

The nice thing about brainstorming using a mind map is that you can make the map as simple or as complex as you need. For instance, I might take the questions I already have

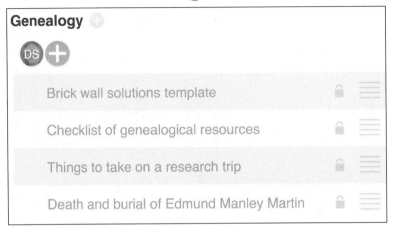

Mind-mapping apps like Coggle allow you to organize mind maps into folders, such as this one for creating genealogy mind maps.

and create related questions linked to them ("Who were his children?"; "When does his wife appear in the US census as a widow or as married to someone else?"). Or if I have an answer, I can link that answer and its associated question to sourced evidence. In this way, I can immediately see which questions have been already answered and which still need research.

Like most mind-mapping tools, Coggle lets me play around with the layout and appearance of the map. I can move branches from one side to the other, make the text bigger/smaller or bold/italic, have the branches appear in different colors, and more. I can link nodes to URLs (perhaps to pages that have more information), add images to the map (such as thumbnail-size pictures of people or documents), and even create a list of checkboxes so I can identify which of my ideas to turn into to-dos in my task management system.

Even if some of your ideas aren't very good (and though you'll be tempted to edit as you go), don't throw out too many ideas during a brainstorming session. Consider your mind map to be an informal tool; unless you plan to share it with others or to publish it online or as part of a document, don't worry too much about the details.

As you produce a larger and larger number of mind maps, take advantage of your mind-mapping tool's organizational features. For example, Coggle lets me create folders (image **F**), so I could have a different folder for each of my genealogical projects. Once I've created a folder, I can quickly create new mind maps in the same folder just by clicking the plus icon next to the name of the folder. And while you'll only use some of your mind maps once before discarding, others may serve a more permanent purpose. You could create templates to copy onto new maps whenever you need to work with that kind of question or problem, customizing it for the problem at hand. For example, you might have templates called *Brick wall solutions*, *Check list of genealogical resources*, and *Things to take on a research trip*.

Another way to use the mind maps is for inspiration/motiva-tion. You might print a mind map and stick it to your cork board so that you can look at it whenever you need to be reminded of what comes next in your research. Or you can turn a mind map into an image file and make it your computer's or mobile device's background image, helping you to focus on the particular problem you're dealing with. These visualizations can help you avoid unwanted distractions.

If anything, playing with mind maps helps unlock parts of your brain that you may not use otherwise. As genealogists, we deal with a lot of factual information, read a lot of text (typed or handwritten), and often work through our problems in a very linear fashion, from start to end. Mind maps can be a colorful way to reach our more creative thoughts, letting us not only see the big picture but also to zoom in as needed to look at the details. By experimenting with mind maps, you may see new connections between different ideas and facts.

research tip

Take a Quick Break
If you run out of ideas, consider taking a break, working on something different for a while, or even setting the mind map aside for a day or two. When you come back to your mind map, you may find that your brain has been working in the background, providing you with new things to add to the map.

Using Evernote to Create and Preserve Notes

As we've mentioned earlier, most of our ideas don't take place during brainstorming, but at random times of the day and night. As a result, an awful lot of information we acquire doesn't neatly fit into a typical filing system. Prior to the availability of mobile devices and better computer applications, we turned to scraps of paper and sticky notes to record our bits of information. Needless to say, this led to a lot of lost information.

Today, a category of software application can handle the acquisition, preservation, and organization of relatively small pieces of information, regardless of format. Two products dominating this field are Evernote **<www.evernote.com>** and Microsoft OneNote **<www.one-note.com>**. Both products are available for the Windows, OS X, Android, and iOS operating systems (as well as a few others), and they also provide access to the content via the web. I'll be using Evernote for the examples in this section and in other parts of the book, but the two

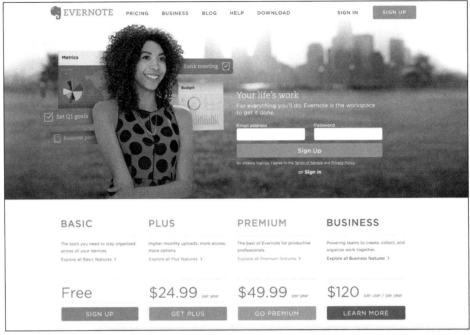

Evernote can hold vast amounts of data and sync them across multiple devices, and its paid subscription plans offer additional features.

products have similar features. As a result, you should be able to reproduce most of what I demonstrate even if you're using Microsoft OneNote instead of Evernote.

Evernote (image) can work wonders for your genealogical (and even non-genealogical) life. Indeed, blogger and Evernote user Kerry Scott wrote a whole book about it: *How to Use Evernote for Genealogy* (Family Tree Books, 2015), available on ShopFamilyTree.com **<www.shopfamilytree.com/how-to-use-evernote-for-genealogy>**. Now, we'll discuss how to use Evernote as it's relevant to organizing your ideas.

The Basics

Evernote is primarily a note-taking software, but one of Evernote's most important features is that it runs on multiple operating system platforms, all able to access the same underlying set of data. This means you can create notes on your desktop computer (in my case, my desktop computer at home and my desktop computer at work), your laptop computer, your tablet, and your smartphone. Evernote even runs on the Apple Watch!

When you create notes on one of your devices, those notes are synchronized in (copied to) Evernote's own servers, or "the cloud." Then, the data is synchronized on your other devices. As a result, you'll want to download and install the free Evernote software for each device you'll be using to access your Evernote note collection.

DATA STORAGE AND LIMITS

Your content is stored both in the cloud and on the hard drives of your desktop or laptop computers. However, as you can imagine, all that data would quickly overwhelm the storage capacity of your tablet or smartphone if they were stored internally. As a result, your tablet or smartphone only has a copy of the *index* to your notes (not the notes themselves). Because your tablet or smartphone is generally connected to the Internet, the program pulls a copy of a specific note from the cloud for display and editing only when you try to open it.

The amount of information you can store in Evernote is not unlimited, but it might as well be. You can store up to one hundred thousand notes in Evernote, and each note can be as large as 25MB in the free version, 50MB in the Plus version, and 200MB in the Premium version. That translates to 2.5TB (terabytes) for the free version, 5TB for the Plus version, and 20TB for the Premium version. If you become a regular Evernote user, you'll likely bump up against the monthly upload quota: Users of the free version can upload only 60MB of new content each month, while Plus users have a 10GB monthly upload limit, and Premium users have no limit at all.

TYPES OF CONTENT

So what kinds of genealogical information would fit well into Evernote? The answer is surprisingly broad, as Evernote can handle many types of files: text, images, PDFs, and even e-mails.

Your typical Evernote note (image Ⓗ) will be text that you type in yourself on whatever device you have. That content could be a single word or sentence or several paragraphs (for instance, I store my public library card number in Evernote so I don't have to carry around my library card in my wallet) or many, many paragraphs of information (such as a draft of an article you're writing).

Of course, the content of a note doesn't have to be something you typed yourself. It could be something you copy-and-pasted from a document, e-mail, or web page. For example, you could save an e-mail with instructions that you'll need to revisit later. You can copy and paste the content from the e-mail into an Evernote note, then safely delete the e-mail if there was nothing else that needed to be saved from it.

In addition, if the device you're using supports handwriting (such as a tablet or smartphone using a stylus), you can add handwritten notes to Evernote. This may be especially useful if you need to include a drawing. Evernote is also capable of interpreting handwriting, making the note's words searchable (though this feature can be hit-or-miss).

Notes are Evernote's basic building blocks. Notes can be made up of text, images, PDFs, audio files, or some combination.

Your note may consist of one or more images that can be accompanied by text. The Evernote app for tablets and smartphones lets you take a photo with your mobile device and import it directly into Evernote. This is especially useful if you're recording pages from a source (together with the cover or title page) so you can properly cite them later. This could be a photo of an instructional sign at a repository, a menu at a favorite restaurant during a research trip, a map leading you to a family cemetery, or any other helpful image for a genealogical researcher. As with handwriting, Evernote is capable of automatically transcribing text that it finds in an image. I've even had it transcribe names and dates that were in a tombstone photo! Not only can you put images into Evernote using the camera on your mobile device or the webcam on your computer, but you can also upload photos that were already stored on your device.

You can also use Evernote and your device's built-in microphone to record a note. This is especially useful if you're on a trip or visiting a cemetery and your smartphone is the most convenient device you have. For Plus and Premium users, Evernote can also store e-mails (more on this in chapter 7).

THE EVERNOTE WEB CLIPPER

As a genealogist, I type a number of notes into Evernote and often add images, but my most common practice for getting content into Evernote is saving online things directly from my web browser. Whether a blog post, news article, genealogical how-to document, or something else related to my research, lots of web content catches my eye and makes me want to keep it. In the days before the web, genealogists might have dealt primarily with paper, making a clipping file from the most useful articles in genealogy magazines. Evernote has done something similar, and clipping useful content from the web is as easy as installing the free Evernote Web Clipper <www.evernote.com/webclipper>.

Evernote's Web Clipper is available directly on your browser, making it easy for you to clip content from the web and save it to your account.

The Web Clipper offers a variety of ways to clip content, allowing you to save just the content you need.

The Web Clipper, a browser add-on, works with Microsoft Internet Explorer (versions 7 and later), Chrome, Firefox, Safari, and Opera. (At the time of this writing, the new Microsoft Edge browser for Windows 10 does not support add-ons, but it may soon do so.)

The Evernote Web Clipper (image) sits at the top of your browser as an icon, allowing you to click on it when you're on any web page that contains useful content you want to preserve. For instance, suppose you're reading Lisa Alzo's blog, *The Accidental Genealogist* <www.theaccidentalgenealogist.com>, and want to capture a post about her mother's autograph book (as a reminder to look for things like that in your own home). While viewing the blog post, click the Evernote Web Clipper icon. You'll be given a number of capture options (image):

- **Bookmark** captures just the URL, which is handy if that is all you want. But keep in mind that web pages sometimes change or are removed, so it's not the best option for anything other than the home page of major websites.

- **Full page** captures everything on a web page, which is certainly useful if the entire web page has value to you. In most cases, though, you'll be capturing content you don't want, such as headers, footers, sidebars, and advertising.

- **Article** and **Simplified article** are normally good choices for blog posts because they automatically detect the part of the page that is the article and will capture just

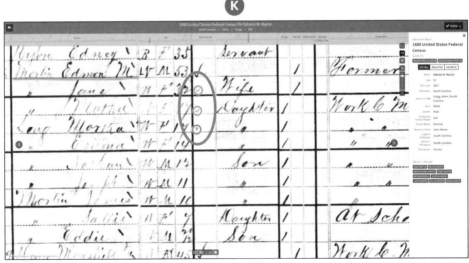

Using the Screenshot feature of Evernote's Web Clipper allows you to highlight or annotate your captured image with checkmarks, arrows, lines, and more.

that content. Unless the layout and font of the article are critical to your capture, you may prefer the Simplified article format.

- **Screenshot** lets you clip any rectangular portion of a web page, most useful when you want to capture all or part of an image of a genealogical document. Even better, the Web Clipper (image Ⓚ) lets you annotate a screenshot in a number of ways: a virtual highlighter (in eight different colors) to emphasize areas of the screenshot; arrows, lines, and several different shapes to draw attention to an area; the ability to draw or type on it; "stamps" such as a circled checkmark, X, exclamation mark, question mark (e.g., to mark something to follow up on), or heart; and pixilation to make part of the image unreadable (e.g., to protect sensitive information).

As you can see, nearly any method you can think of for creating digital content can work with Evernote: text, handwriting, images, audio, e-mail, and web pages. When used in conjunction with your computer's filing system and your genealogy software applications, Evernote becomes a powerful tool for tracking all that miscellaneous information that doesn't otherwise have a good place to reside.

Organization in Evernote

Yes, Evernote can hold lots of data. But how can you make sense of it? You're unlikely to have as many as one hundred thousand notes anytime in the near future, but you may find that with regular use of Evernote, you already have hundreds if not thousands of notes. The search system within Evernote is quite powerful, so organizing your notes or locating a specific piece of data can be done fairly easily.

But depending solely on Evernote's all-text search to find what you need may lead to some frustration. For instance, you may want to find all of your notes that are specifically about marriage certificates, but you don't want to pull up every note that has the word *marriage* somewhere in it. You may want to share one particular collection of notes with another researcher. Or you may want to see all of the notes that pertain to a particular research project together in a list, making it easier to work with them in relation to each other.

Fortunately, Evernote provides two different ways to organize your notes, and you can use either one or both together. In this section, we'll discuss these two options: notebooks and tags.

NOTEBOOKS

Think of notebooks like three-ring binders or file folders that hold other documents. Notebooks are a collection of similar notes that have been organized by subject (image Ⓛ). The benefit of notebooks is you can share them with other individuals (more on that

Genealogy	🔖	17
!Genealogy Inbox		26
DNA		5
FGS FORUM		2
FGS Tampa		18
FHISO		26
Genealogy - Bannon/Hyland		5
Genealogy - Bodie		11
Genealogy - general		35
Genealogy - volunteer lookups		37
Genealogy Guys Podcast		1
Genealogy presentation/ writing ideas		5
Lynn's genealogy 👥 Andrew M. Smith		45
Newspaper presentation		1
Organizing Your Genealogy		8

Evernote's three-tiered system (notes, notebooks, and stacks) allows you to organize data by subject, such as by record type or event.

in the next section). They can also act as a table of contents for your entire Evernote filing system, with each note like a chapter or section that has a proper place.

Notebooks are not without their downsides. For starters, a note can reside in only one notebook at a time. This means that if you have a notebook for your Smith research and another notebook for your Martin research, and you've created a note that talks about both your Smiths and your Martins, you're going to have a dilemma regarding which notebook to put it in.

The other big problem with notebooks is that you can't have more than 250 personal notebooks. (Yes, Evernote does provide a business version of its software that allows for a larger number of notebooks for an entire organization or company, but that isn't going to fit the typical usage of a genealogist. We'll ignore that here, where notebook refers to that level of organization in an individual's private account.) This means you're likely not going to be able to create a separate notebook for every surname you are researching, even if you wanted to. Instead, you'll probably only have notebooks for your main lines of interest.

Personally, I like to use notebooks for specific purposes, such as for organizations I work with, ongoing research/ writing/presentation projects, and upcoming events. The decision of how to use notebooks is a personal one, based on how you like to think about the things you work with. I recommend you start with a small number of notebooks and add to them slowly as you work. If you find they don't fit into your personal workflow, skip to the next section on tags.

If you're researching backwards in time, you could at least have a notebook for every surname back to your 128th great-grandparents. If you're researching from an ancestor forward in time, you could easily run out of notebooks fairly quickly in a few generations. And you're going to want a lot of notebooks for things other than just ancestral surnames, since many genealogists who use Evernote use it not only for genealogy but also for work-related and home-related functions. What to do?

TAGS

Notebooks have their drawbacks, but don't worry: Evernote provides tags (image **M**), a whole separate system of organization that solves both the "one notebook per note problem" and the 250-notebook limit. A tag is typically a unique word or term that can be applied to any note as a kind of label. For a genealogist, a tag could be a name (such as a surname or a last name-first name combo), place (such as a city, county, state, or country), date (such as a year), type of record (such as a census record or marriage record), or status (such as *To be researched* or *Completed research*). A single note can have up to one hundred different tags (shattering the "one notebook per note" problem), and you can have up to one hundred thousand tags per account.

Evernote offers users an alternative way of grouping notes: tags, which organize notes by words or short phrases.

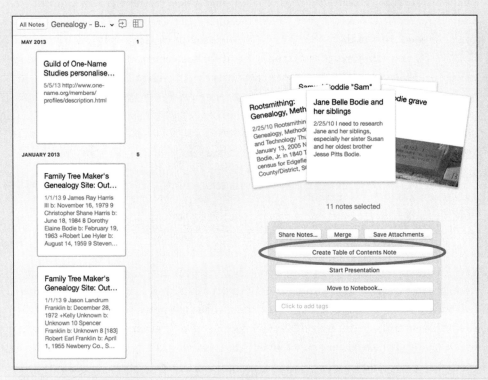

Creating an Evernote Table of Contents

If you have a notebook that contains a fairly large number of notes, browsing in alphabetical order may not make the most sense when searching for a note. Perhaps the various notes in the notebooks are related to each other in some other way, such as chronologically or by topic.

Fortunately, you can create a table of contents (TOC) note for your notebook. You can also edit the contents of the TOC note to rearrange the notes' order or add links to notes in other notebooks, which can be helpful.

Here's how to create a table of contents note in Evernote:

1. Select a group of notes. You can select all your notes by hitting Control-A (Windows) or Command-A (Mac).

2. Choose the option to Create Table of Contents Note. Note that you won't see this option if you're in the Expanded Card View.

3. Edit the title and individual entries. You also have the ability to rearrange the notes' order. You might start the title of your note with an exclamation point, such as !TOC or !Table of Contents, so it appears first in the list of notes for that notebook when you sort your notes alphabetically.

Some Evernote users are such fans of the tagging system that they don't use notebooks at all. But again, notebooks can give you some features that tags can't, and I recommend that you make good use of both notebooks and tags. For instance, you can specify that a notebook be local so its contents are not synchronized to the cloud version of Evernote (perhaps in cases where the data it contains is somewhat sensitive). If you're using a paid version of Evernote, you can even specify that a particular notebook be available offline so you can get to all the notebook's contents when you don't have an Internet connection. If you're depending on access to a map to a family cemetery in an area where phone connectivity is spotty, for example, this might be an important feature for you! And as already mentioned, notebooks facilitate sharing of sets of notes with others, a feature tags can't offer.

Evernote Tips

Now that we've identified the basics of how to use Evernote and the software's features, let's dive into some best practices for using Evernote.

TITLE YOUR NOTES AND NOTEBOOKS CAREFULLY

When you open up a notebook to see the notes it contains, you can choose to sort them by the date they were last updated or by note title. While seeing recent notes can be handy, you may want to sort by title if, for example, you're looking for an older note. Because of this, having a good title is important. When you create the note yourself, you can give it whatever title you think best. (But don't worry about making titles final: You can change a note's title, even if you're importing it using a Web Clipper capture or via e-mail import.)

The quickest way to find something in a list of titles is listing the most important word first. This means that you want to avoid starting a note title with *The*, *A*, or another article. Instead, think about which word you are most likely going to be thinking about when trying to find the note. A note about my Smith ancestors in the 1900 census should be titled *Smith - 1900 census*, not *The Smiths in 1900*. I can't say enough about this concept, and it applies to all forms of organizing information. (You'll see it again in chapter 5.)

Another issue when titling notes is consistency. Not only do you want to be consistent within the system you're using (such as Evernote), but you want to be consistent *across* your filing systems. This means that whatever system you adopt for titling notes in Evernote should resemble whatever system you use for giving file names to the files on your computer. This may mean using a consistent spelling for a surname in the title of a note (even though the surname might be spelled differently within the note itself).

Another thing to consider when titling notes for alphabetization is which word will appear first. You'll usually want to lead with a word that will help you group information together. This means that the title of a note might be *Smith, James* (not *James, Smith*) so

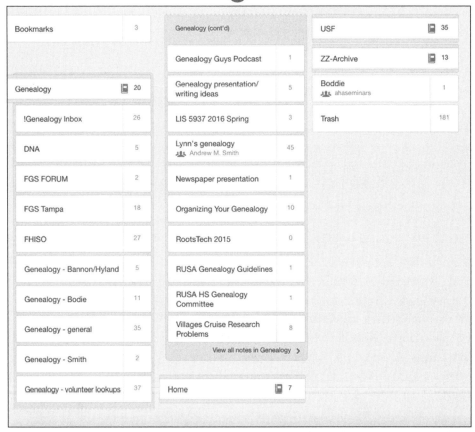

Stacks (groups of notebooks) can help you separate your personal, professional, and genealogical uses for Evernote. For example, my account has separate stacks for Genealogy and Home.

all of the Smith-related notes will be sorted together. (You're not likely going to want to group all the notes starting with "James" together.) Consider the same for geographical names. Instead of *Newberry, SC*, use *SC, Newberry* so all of the South Carolina notes will be together—and remember to abbreviate South Carolina as *SC*!

GROUP NOTEBOOKS INTO STACKS

Most genealogists who use Evernote use it for more than genealogy, so it can be confusing if your alphabetical list of notebooks is a mixture of genealogical and non-genealogical notebooks. To solve this problem, Evernote lets you group notebooks into stacks (image).

You can quickly create a stack by dragging one notebook on top of another. When you've done so, the program will ask you to name the stack. You may want at least one stack just for genealogy, one for home-related notebooks, another for work-related notebooks, and so

forth. If you find you're creating a lot of genealogy-related notebooks, you may want to create
different stacks for different aspects of your
genealogical work: one for society work, one
for personal research, one for research you're
doing for friends and family, and so forth.

CREATE A NOTEBOOK ARCHIVE

Since you don't want to run out of available
notebooks (exceeding your 250-notebook
limit), you may want to create one special notebook as an archive. I call mine *ZZ-Archive* so it
alphabetically sorts to the end of the list of all
notebooks and stacks (just above Trash). When
I am done using a notebook for active purposes
and want to archive its contents, I create a tag
with the original notebook's name and affix it
to all of the notes in that notebook, then move
all those notes into the ZZ-Archive notebook.

COLLECT TAGS INTO HIERARCHIES

While organizing a few dozen notebooks
doesn't seem like an overwhelming problem,
consider that you could have hundreds, if not
thousands, of different tags. Because these will
appear in alphabetical order in a list, you can
imagine the confusion when you've got a mix
of names, places, and record types (plus other
miscellaneous tags). At the very least, it would
be a good idea to be able to group all name-
related tags together, all place-related tags
together, and all record-related tags together.

Just as notebooks can be organized into
stacks, tags can be organized into hierarchies
(image ). However, creating a tag hierarchy
is a bit different from creating a notebook
stack. To create a tag hierarchy, start by creating a tag with the name you want to use for the

Like notes can be grouped into notebooks,
and tags can be sorted into tag hierarchies,
giving users another tool to organize their
data in Evernote.

hierarchy. This tag won't actually be used as a tag (i.e., you won't be tagging any notes with it). Instead, it's just a placeholder tag to drag other tags into so they'll appear together. For example, you could have one hierarchy called *Surnames* or *Names*, one called *Places* or *Locations*, and another called *Records* or *Events*. You may also want a fourth hierarchy for miscellaneous tags, which you could call *Z-Misc* to force it to sort to the bottom. And, if you're also using Evernote for non-genealogical purposes, you can create additional hierarchies if you think they would be helpful.

MAKE SMART SEARCHES

Evernote has a powerful search feature that lets you search across all your notes, including note title, note content, and any associated tags. If you have attached PDF files or Microsoft Office documents to a note and are an Evernote Premium user, Evernote will even search the content of the attached file. But what if you want to be more precise in your search? If you want to limit your search to a phrase in a particular notebook, such as for *Martin* in a notebook called *Smith Research Project*, start your search with the name of the item you want to search in: notebook:*"Smith Research Project" martin*. In the same way, you can use *tag:* or *stack:* to restrict a search to finding notes with a particular tag or notes within a particular stack.

In addition, if you find yourself repeatedly doing the same search, you can save and name your search. Then you will see that named search as an option when you go to do a search.

ADD SHORTCUTS

One more feature helps organize your notes, notebooks, tags, and searches: the Shortcuts area. You can add an item to this handy list by dragging it over the word. This does not remove it from its normal location, but basically makes a copy that is now visible at the top left of your screen (image **P**). If you have a note, notebook, or tag that you are using frequently (e.g., for a project you're currently working on), you'll find that it speeds your work to have this immediately available to you in a prominent screen location. If you have multiple shortcuts, you can arrange them in whatever manner you like. Once you're no longer using that particular item on a frequent basis, remove its shortcut status so it doesn't clutter your Shortcuts area.

SHARE YOUR WORK AND COLLABORATE WITH OTHERS

Evernote (like Coggle; see Sharing Mind Maps With Coggle sidebar) also gives you a variety of ways to share your work and invite collaborators. You can post a note or a link to a notebook on Facebook <www.facebook.com>, Twitter <www.twitter.com>, or LinkedIn <www.linkedin.com>. You can e-mail a copy to someone or generate a link to the note. Keep in mind that when you e-mail a note to someone, she's seeing the note as it was when you

Shortcuts

- Smith, George Thomas - questions to be researched
- Smith, George Thomas - when and where was he born?
- Genealogy Table of Contents

Recent Notes

- The Genealogy Guys Podcast #277
- FGS Tampa notes
- Smith, George Thomas - when and where was he born?
- Additional images and text
- Notes on edited work

Evernote allows you to create one-click shortcuts, allowing easy access to your most frequently used notes. A Recent Notes classification also floats your most recent projects to the top for quick reference.

sent it. However, if you e-mail a *link* to the note instead, the person who receives it can follow the link to see the most current version of the note. At any point, you can choose to stop sharing the note, which will deactivate the link.

If you're working on a project with others and you have an Evernote notebook for that project, you may want to share your notebook with the other people working on the project. For each individual, you can allow them to view the notebook, view and edit the notebook's contents, or view and edit the notebook and invite others to join. If you want to publish the entire contents of your notebook so others can view it, you can generate a URL for the notebook that you can then publicize in whatever way you choose.

Drew's **To-Dos**

- Carry a notebook or recording device with you at all times to capture your ideas.

- Preserve your notes using a system such as Evernote.

- Name and organize your files carefully, using notebooks and tags to make your research easy to find.

- Visualize your ideas and questions using a mind-mapping tool and share your mind maps and notes with other genealogists.

EVERNOTE ORGANIZATION WORKSHEET

Think about how you want to organize your notes within Evernote. Use this worksheet to sketch out ideas for your organization scheme. For items that don't fit into obvious categories, you may find it helpful to jot down potential notes first, then look for common themes to group them into notebooks or stacks. You can download a Word version of this worksheet at **<ftu.familytreemagazine.com/organize-your-genealogy>**.

Stacks	Notebooks	Sample Notes

5

organizing your files

n my opinion, the most common question when it comes to organizing research is "How do I organize my genealogical files?" Whenever the topic comes up on mailing lists, in message boards, or on Facebook groups, people offer their own solutions, including color-coding folders (both paper and electronic), naming schemes for files, paper versus electronic or hanging folders versus three-ring binders, and so on.

Perhaps the most important consideration as we tackle the subject of organizing files is that there is no perfect answer and certainly no "one size fits all" solution. Different people have different likes and dislikes. What works well for one may turn out to be a non-starter for someone else, whether due to varying comfort levels with technology, differences in familiarity with a particular system, or just sheer personal preference. Read this chapter (more than once if helpful) and see what resonates with you and your workflow (and what doesn't), then adopt the ideas that make the most sense to you.

As I've mentioned before, I like to start with big principles to see what they tell us, then apply them to the problems in front of us. So what are the big principles in terms of organizing information? First, we organize information so we can quickly access it later.

After all, if we never planned to use the information again, we could simply discard it or use any random system to file it away. So whatever organizational scheme we adopt, that system should make the process of finding what we want as quick as possible. Another general principle, discussed in chapter 1, is that organizing should be simple. This makes the organizing system easy to remember and quick to implement. A complex system for organizing will take too much time and effort, and you'll likely throw your hands up in frustration and abandon it.

In this chapter, we'll discuss practical organization schemes and formats that will help you develop a simple plan for organizing files and quickly retrieve your stored information.

Organizational Schemes

Before there was such a thing as genealogical database software (such as RootsMagic <www.rootsmagic.com>, Legacy Family Tree <www.legacyfamilytree.com>, Family Tree Builder <www.myheritage.com/family-tree-builder>, and Family Tree Maker <www.familytreemaker.com>), genealogists depended almost entirely on well-organized paper-based systems. And because these were paper-based systems, they had to be browsable (i.e., optimized to manually page through).

Keeping track of thousands of related individuals means you need a system to give each individual a unique identifier and, if possible, indicate how one individual might be related to another. Some systems just assign new, unique numbers to relatives as they're entered into the system (though without any way for the number to indicate how each individual is related to any other individual).

Let's review some of these schemes that will help us create modern paper-based systems, as well as give us some ideas of how to create good, browsable electronic systems.

Ahnentafel

The easiest numbering system for genealogical purposes is the *Ahnentafel* system (*Ahnentafel* is German for "ancestor table"; image Ⓐ). In that system, the person whose ancestors you're researching (often yourself, though you could certainly start with a child, grandchild, parent, or spouse) is assigned the number 1, then each generation back is numbered by doubling the individual's number for father and adding one to the father's number for his mother. This means that if you're number 1, your father is 2, your mother is 3, your paternal grandfather is 4, your paternal grandmother is 5, your maternal grandfather is 6, your maternal grandmother is 7, and so forth.

In such a system, all direct ancestors are assigned a number, and no two individuals have the same number. If none of your ancestors are related to each other, every number

Ahnentafel of Andrew Martin Smith

20 December 2015

Generation 1

1. **Andrew Martin SMITH**.

Generation 2

2. **George Thomas SMITH**: born 8 Nov 1917 in Newark, Essex, New Jersey, United States; married 31 Jan 1943 in Newberry, Newberry, South Carolina, United States; died 3 Nov 1999 in Columbia, Richland, South Carolina, United States.

3. **Altha Corinne MARTIN**: born 19 Dec 1920 in Newberry, South Carolina, United States; died 16 Jun 2007 in Newberry, Newberry, South Carolina, United States.

Generation 3

4. **William Henry SMITH**: born 21 Sep 1889 in Newark, Essex, New Jersey, United States; died 9 Feb 1961 in Irvington, Essex, New Jersey, United States.

5. **Rachel WEINGLASS**: born 20 Nov 1890 in Manhattan, New York, New York, United States; died 1 Jun 1976 in Fort Lauderdale, Broward, Florida, United States.

6. **George Washington MARTIN**: born 12 Jan 1882 in Edgefield, South Carolina, United States; married 3 Nov 1901 in Laurens, Laurens, South Carolina, United States; died 12 Nov 1964 in Newberry, Newberry, South Carolina, United States.

7. **Elizabeth Estelle KING**: born 7 Oct 1884 in Laurens, South Carolina, United States; died 1 Apr 1973.

Generation 4

8. **Charles Henry SMITH**: born 30 May 1859 in Newark, Essex, New Jersey, United States; married 4 Jan 1880 in Newark, Essex, New Jersey, United States; died 22 Apr 1906.

9. **Mary Ann BANNON**: born 13 Jan 1863 in Oldbury, Birmingham, England; died 10 Oct 1940.

10. **Louis WEINGLASS**: born 13 Feb 1865 in Markowa, Przeworsk, Rzeszów, Poland; married 24 May 1887 in New York, New York, United States; died 2 Feb 1903 in Manhattan, New York, New York, United States.

11. **Sarah GRODOWITZ**: born Mar 1871 in Poland; died 11 Aug 1944.

12. **Edmon Manley MARTIN**: born abt 1827 in Edgefield, South Carolina, United States; married abt 1872 in Edgefield, South Carolina, United States; died from 1894 to 1900.

13. **Jane Belle BODIE**: born 12 Feb 1845 in Edgefield, South Carolina, United States; died 22 May 1907 in South Carolina, United States.

14. **Robert Benjamin KING**: born 15 Apr 1834 in Sc; married 27 Jan 1869 in Cross Hill, Laurens, South Carolina, United States; died 8 Apr 1911 in Laurens, Laurens, South Carolina, United States.

15. **Elizabeth FOSHEE**: born 6 Aug 1844 in South Carolina, United States; died 30 Nov 1928 in Spartanburg, Spartanburg, South Carolina, United States.

Organizing your files by *Ahnentafel* number can be an effective and consistent way to keep track of your research.

will refer to a different person. But if there is "pedigree collapse" (in which you discover that the same ancestor appears in different parts of your direct ancestry), multiple ancestors will end up having multiple numbers in the *Ahnentafel* system. This isn't really a serious problem, but it does mean that you may have to cross-reference one set of numbers in the scheme to a different set of numbers. (Of course, if we could document our ancestry in each family line without limit, we would all eventually discover a pedigree collapse situation. In reality, you may hit brick walls on all of your lines well before that hypothetical point.)

An *Ahnentafel* system can be used to organize your paper files, so long as you focus only on your direct ancestors and don't spend much time with any of their other offspring. For instance, you could create a folder for files about yourself and label it 1, a folder for information about your parents and label it 2/3, a folder for your paternal grandparents labeled 4/5, a folder for your maternal grandparents labeled 6/7, and so forth. Then you could easily sort these folders numerically in whatever filing system you're using.

You may already see some issues with these labels. The numbers alone make for poor folder labels, since they don't tell you who they refer to, and it's not likely that you're going to remember the *Ahnentafel* number for more than a handful of your most recent relatives. So you'll want folder labels that provide not only the pair of numbers, but also the names of the couple (last name, then first name for each one). This lets you scan across your files and find the right couple quickly. You can also create empty placeholder folders for couples that you have not yet identified by name.

Let's look at the *Ahnentafel* in action. In the folder labels of a paper-based system, you can put names before the *Ahnentafel* number, helping you easily see and file the couple's folder in the right place. In an electronic system, name the folders with the number first, so the files will sort numerically. But because computer systems treat numbers in file names as text (not actual numbers), you'll run into a problem if you mix single-digit numbers with two-digit or three-digit numbers as you go further and further back in time. Use leading zeroes in order to make all your *Ahnentafel* numbers three digits long, ensuring your parents and other more recent ancestors will automatically sort to the top. For example, your folders may have to look like *002-003 SMITH-MARTIN* or *002-003 SMITH_George_Thomas-MARTIN_Altha_Corinne*. Note that other than letters, numbers, spaces, dashes, and underscores, it's generally best to avoid all other characters in a file name.

You may wonder why you would want a single folder per couple, rather than a folder for each individual. The downside to separate folders per individual is that you'll come across a number of documents that mention both spouses, such as a marriage record, the birth records of their children, census records, city directories, and so forth. Whose folder do you file that one in? (There is no perfect solution to this problem, of course, since you will also have documents that mention the names of the couple's parents and children.)

Alternatives to the Number System

While popular, do these numbering systems actually work for a filing system? I have my doubts. The numbers tell us, at a glance, which generation we're dealing with, but not much else. A descendancy project may lead to a large number of folders. And because the project will involve both males and females, you'll be dealing with a vast number of surnames to track. Additional complications arise when cousins intermarry. Instead, surnames and geography will often be more useful. Whatever system you adopt will need to keep together family units. And because your research will have a geographic component, consider geography in your filing system.

Let's use my William Boddie research as an example. The earliest generations have only a small number of family units, and those were all from Virginia. Later generations split, with some ending up in North Carolina, others in South Carolina, and many (later, in a major split) in Louisiana. A sensible filing system will keep each of these states together, then sort by generation within those states. For instance, I've labeled folders *1-VA-BODDIE_William*, *3-NC-BODDIE_William*, and *3-SC-BODDIE_John* to group families and states together. (If these were going to be labeled as computer folders, and you have good reason to believe your project will involve ten or more generations, you might use labels such as *01-VA-BODDIE_William* in order to preserve the right sorting.)

This kind of system can be modified if you find that all of the descendants are in the same state: for example, using county names or city names instead. Whatever filing system you adopt, remember the important thing about your system is that it should allow you to browse quickly to the right folder to find the information you need. You're not aiming for the perfect filing system, but instead for a system good enough that you won't waste too much time locating information.

Another issue with a system ordered strictly by *Ahnentafel* number is that it jumps around between different branches of the family as it moves from generation to generation. Would it make more sense to keep folders together for major branches of one's ancestry? Perhaps, and some organizing systems for paper (and electronic) folders try to overcome this shortcoming by using color to distinguish between up to four different branches of the family: the paternal grandfather's ancestors, the paternal grandmother's ancestors, the maternal grandfather's ancestors, and the maternal grandmother's ancestors.

Other Numbering Systems

While the *Ahnentafel* system provides us with a good way to uniquely identify our direct ancestors going backwards in time, it fails to help us if we're going to be working on a genealogical project that involves going forward in time, such as my project for identifying all of the descendants of an immigrant ancestor. No perfect system has yet been created for uniquely identifying descendants, since at each generation a woman may give

Descendants of James Smith

First Generation

1. **James SMITH** was born about 1825 in Ireland. He died on 15 Nov 1872 at the age of 47 in New Jersey.

James SMITH and Mary Ann REILLY were married in 1850 in Newark, Essex County, NJ. **Mary Ann REILLY**[1] was born on 3 Aug 1829 in Cavan County, Ireland. She died on 22 Mar 1897 at the age of 67 in Newark, Essex County, NJ. She was buried on 25 Mar 1897.

James SMITH and Mary Ann REILLY had the following children:

+2	i.	**Phillip SMITH**, born 18 Aug 1853, Newark, Essex County, NJ; died 1899.
+3	ii.	**Patrick J. SMITH**, born 24 Nov 1855, Newark, Essex County, NJ; married Margaret Genevieve RYAN, Aug 1878, Newark, Essex County, NJ; married Catherine MCCLINCHY, 7 Nov 1897, Newark, Essex County, NJ; died 11 Oct 1911.
+4	iii.	**John William SMITH**, born 29 Jul 1857, Newark, Essex County, NJ; married Ellen Elizabeth PHELAN, 11 Dec 1883, Newark, Essex County, NJ; died 4 Jul 1912.
+5	iv.	**Charles Henry SMITH**, born 30 May 1859, Newark, Essex County, NJ; married Mary Ann BANNON, 4 Jan 1880, Newark, Essex County, NJ; died 22 Apr 1906.
6	v.	**James SMITH** was born on 26 Mar 1861 in Newark, Essex County, NJ. He died before 23 Feb 1863 at the age of 1.
+7	vi.	**James Edward SMITH**, born 23 Feb 1863, Newark, Essex County, NJ; married Mary KELLER, 25 May 1884, Newark, Essex County, NJ; died 18 Jan 1901.
+8	vii.	**Thomas Jefferson Davis SMITH**, born 7 May 1865, Newark, Essex County, NJ; died 30 Jul 1958.
9	viii.	**George W. SMITH** was born on 5 Feb 1867 in Newark, Essex County, NJ. He died on 9 Feb 1896 at the age of 29.

Second Generation

2. **Phillip SMITH** (James-1) was born on 18 Aug 1853 in Newark, Essex County, NJ. He died in 1899 at the age of 46.

Jane STEPHENS was born about 1857 in New Jersey.

Phillip SMITH and Jane STEPHENS had the following children:

The Modified Register System (or NGSQ system) may be an appropriate system to model your file organization scheme on.

birth to more than a dozen children (at least one case is claimed to be as high as sixty-nine children) and a man could theoretically be the biological father of hundreds of children. Before we devise a good filing system for a descendant-based research project, let's look at the other existing genealogical numbering schemes for descendants.

Two popular numbering schemes used in producing published genealogies of descendants are the Register System and the similar Modified Register System (also called the NGSQ System for its use in the *National Genealogical Society Quarterly*). The Register System assigns a unique number to only those individuals who have offspring, while the NGSQ System assigns a unique number to every descendant, regardless of whether or not he has children.

Let's explore the NGSQ system (image B) in more detail. The individual (such as an immigrant ancestor) in the first generation is given the number 1, then his children are given numbers from oldest to youngest, continuing in each succeeding generation. So if the immigrant has three children, they are numbered 2, 3, and 4, and number 2's children are numbered starting at 5, and so on. The downside of using such a system during ongoing research is that new children may be discovered at any time, which would involve renumbering everyone later in the system. This type of numbering scheme does, however, work well once research has reached a stopping point and it's time to publish the results.

Two other numbering schemes avoid the massive renumbering that may occur when discovering new individuals: the Henry System and the d'Aboville System. The Henry System identifies the first generation with a single-digit number (1), individuals in the second generation with a two-digit number (11, 12, 13, etc.), and individuals in the third generation with a three-digit number (children of 11 would be 111, 112, 113, etc; children of 13 would be 131, 132, 133, etc.). If an individual has more than nine children and you've run out of numbers to use, you then use X, then A, B, and so forth. (You're on your own if an ancestor has more than thirty-five children!) If you're not fond of the lettering in the Henry System, you can use a Modified Henry System where you use two-digit numbers in parentheses, so that child 19 is followed by child 1(10).

A system that avoids both letters and parentheses is the d'Aboville System, which uses periods to separate the generations, so that person 1 has children 1.1, 1.2, 1.3, and so forth to 1.10, 1.11, etc. While this can be a bit easier to read with the generations separated out, it can make for some long numbers as you go further back in time.

Paper-Based Systems

Paper materials have long been a staple of genealogical research, and genealogists can acquire physical research (records, family trees, etc.) from a variety of places. Whether your documents come from other family members, research repositories, or the Internet, you first have to think about how you plan to use each document. And once you know that, you'll be in a better position to think about how and where you should keep it.

Materials you're working with on a regular basis need to be near at hand, while materials you rarely consult can be much farther away. If you need the paper for one of your ongoing projects, you should be able to sit at your computer desk and reach out your hand to touch the folder or binder that contains that paper. And if the paper is something you're unlikely to need in the near future, it should be out of your way so it doesn't distract you.

In addition to the *Ahnentafel* system already described, you could adopt a paper filing system based primarily on the way in which you are doing your research. Regardless of what system you choose, the goal is to keep together documents that you will most likely want to review at the same time, such as those that refer to the same family group for the same time period in the same geographical area.

Deciding Your Medium:
Paper or Electronic (or Both)?

Genealogists only a few decades ago had no choices in their filing systems: They had to depend entirely upon paper. But the proliferation of personal computers and a dramatic decrease in the cost of digital storage have led to a huge migration from paper to electronic when it comes to filing systems. But what kind of system should you have for your genealogical research? Do you print everything off your computer and use a paper-based system as your filing system? Or do you scan everything and use a purely computer-based system? Or do you go to a hybrid model, with some things in paper and some things digital? How do you decide?

Certainly, a factor here is your comfort level with technology. A well-maintained and reliable electronic system requires minimal familiarity with using computers, although you may have other household members (or willing family members and friends) who can assist you when you have problems and questions. And even if you decide to go completely paperless in your research, that doesn't mean discarding all of your paper documents. Some of those documents are irreplaceable originals or may have significant emotional value, so you'll want to preserve them. And whatever level of electronic filing you use, give strong consideration to backing up your work in paper form (more on backing up for files later).

Paper-based filing has a comfort because it works regardless of your level of technological expertise. In addition, some people prefer to lay hands on a physical folder or three-ring binder on a nearby desk or in a drawer. And though paper copies can be lost or destroyed by fire or water, many find a simple pleasure in laying out papers on a work surface for review and study. However, paper files have no easy backup and can be lost due to misfiling, accidental destruction, theft, and physical disasters. They also can take up a great deal of physical space in your work area.

Meanwhile, electronic data takes up little physical space and can be easily backed up so other threats (computer failures, user mistakes, theft, hacking, or physical disasters) become much less menacing. While it requires some technical know-how, electronic filing is generally faster and more flexible than paper filing.

Given the pros and cons of each system, I recommend you strive for as much electronic filing as you're comfortable with. Make sure your electronic files are as secure as possible from hacking (e.g., by being careful with computer passwords and making sure your system has good antivirus protection), and use external hard drives and cloud servers to maintain computer backups. If you still want a paper-based system, print those copies off from your electronic system and file them according to a consistent system. And if those paper copies are lost for whatever reason, you can print new copies.

For instance, if you're researching ancestral lines, you could create a folder or binder for each surname. If you choose folders, use a large hanging folder for the surname and individual folders for each generation. If you choose binders, use a large binder for the surname, then individual sections of the binder for each generation. On the other hand, if you're researching descendants of an immigrant ancestor, you may want to create large hanging folders or binders for each descendant surname, with separate individual folders or binder sections for specific family groups or generations.

In all cases, consider separating groups of paper documents that are from different geographies. For example, I might have one folder/binder for Boddie in Virginia, another for Boddie in North Carolina, another for Boddie in South Carolina, another for Boddie in Louisiana, and one last one for Boddies anywhere else.

In this section, we'll outline some more organizational and storage strategies for paper filing systems.

Safely Archiving Your Material

Once you've established how important a document or photograph is, make a version you can archive. Always work from a copy of an original rather than the original itself (unless there is something on the original document that copies poorly). By working from only the copy, you lessen the risk of damage to the original. Your original documents should be stored in archival-safe sheet protectors, but copies that are easy to reproduce can be stored in less expensive sheet protectors to minimize tearing or stains. (Note: Don't mix the two types of protectors in the same folder or binder, as the less-expensive protectors may contain material that will harm your original documents). For more on keeping sensitive research materials safe, consult Denise May Levenick's two books: *How to Archive Family Keepsakes* (Family Tree Books, 2012) and *How to Archive Family Photos* (Family Tree Books, 2015), both available at <www.shopfamilytree.com>. Archival repositories also have helpful online guides to preserving documents.

As you make copies of your valuable documents, keep the size of your other resources and your folders and binders in mind. You want all of your papers to be the same size, so even smaller documents should be copied onto standard-sized paper (namely US letter size of 8.5x11-inch paper, the standard size for North America and many parts of Latin America, or A4, a similarly sized international standard). By having as many documents as possible at the same size, you lessen the risk of overlooking or losing a small piece of paper. The biggest exception for US genealogists will be documents that were originally created as US legal size (8.5x14-inch size), nonfragile original versions of which you can usually fold into standard letter-sized folders and binders.

Once you've made standard-size copies of your most important documents and photographs and have stored them in archival-safe storage of one kind or another, make sure to find a good environment in which to store them. If you can afford it, consider storing these items in a safe-deposit box; however, bank vaults can still be flooded, and safe-deposit boxes (while fire-resistant and water-resistant) are not completely impervious to a natural or man-made disaster. If you decide to keep important and difficult-to-replace original documents and photographs at home, remember to keep them in a cool, dry place, since heat and water are the enemies of paper and photos. This may mean avoiding a basement that could flood or an attic that could get too hot. Your best bet may be an otherwise unused, room-temperature closet where you can put things up off the floor.

File Folders or Binders?

Having found a safe and secure place for your material, your next biggest decision will be whether to use file drawers in desks (or, if you have a lot of files, separate two-drawer or four-drawer filing cabinets) or three-ring binders that can be stored along the back of

Binders can provide a durable place to hold your files. However, they can also require significant time to organize and quickly become bulky and heavy.

File folders provide at-a-glance surveys of your files and easy transfer when your research takes you away from your office.

a desktop or (preferably) on a nearby bookshelf. Your choice should be determined by personal preference and available furniture.

One advantage of binders (image **C**) is that they're always visible on a shelf, so you can go directly to the one you need. On the other hand, visibility like that may be something you want to avoid, as you might prefer to have file drawers that you can close and not even think about when you're not engaged in genealogical research about that topic. Another disadvantage of binders is that (with hole-punching and the need to organize its pages in a particular order) they can take a bit longer to file things in, while filing papers in folders (image **D**) can be done more quickly. And if you plan to take papers with you on a research trip, you will probably find that binders (especially when including sheet protectors) are heavier and more cumbersome than file folders (which can easily fit inside a computer bag or briefcase).

Feel free to also use color for folders or binders to visually sort information or just to liven up your workspace—nobody said that all your folders need to be manila-colored or that all your binders need to be white or black! Whichever system you choose, have fun with it. Keep things simple and avoid creating a convoluted system.

Electronic Filing Systems

Whether you're using a purely electronic system or a hybrid system of paper and digital, your computer filing system will be one of the most important decisions you make in regards to your genealogical organizational setup. Increasingly, you'll be downloading document images from websites, receiving images from cousins, and creating digital files from word processing and genealogical database software. Without some thought and planning, you can become overwhelmed by the number of digital files you're trying to manage and frustrated by the inability to find the one you need at any given moment.

Although we aren't handling fragile paper documents or photos, we are dealing with electronic files that run the gamut from temporary and relatively unimportant to unique and critical. As we'll discuss later, some of this data must be backed up for the sake of your own stress levels, while other data can be easily re-created were something to happen to it.

Selecting Your Device(s)

So where can you keep files? Files closest at hand (in a virtual sense) are on your computer's desktop, a special storage area of your computer's hard drive. Beyond that, you can store files elsewhere on your hard drive. You can also have files on an external hard drive, on other removable media (such as USB flash drives and writeable CDs and DVDs), or through a cloud-based storage service.

Each of these choices has its pros and cons, though some are falling out of usage. USB flash drives have increased in storage capacity, but are being used less now that people can more quickly and easily share data via the web. They're a poor choice for long-term storage, not only because they aren't really designed for that purpose, but also because their small size makes them easy to lose. I once misplaced a gray USB flash drive for over a year because it had fallen under my car's front seat on top of the gray carpeting! While I recommend having one handy when you travel, especially when you travel to a repository or a relative's home, a USB drive should serve only as a temporary holding area for files, and the files should be transferred to a more permanent location as quickly as possible.

However, from what I can see, genealogists will be storing files on their computer's hard drives for years to come. While writeable CDs and DVDs have short (ten-year) lifespans and limited storage space, external hard drives have become more and more popular as the amount of storage they can handle has increased dramatically without a significant increase in price. We'll come back to external hard drives when we discuss backup systems, but hard drives (as well as cloud-based services) are clearly your best choice for storing genealogical files.

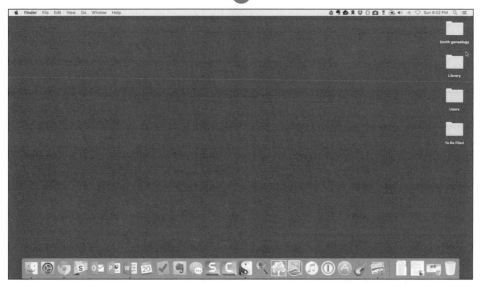

See all the files on my desktop? No? That's the idea. Having a clean desktop helps me maintain focus and stay more productive. Organizing my research into just a few file folders and using cloud-based services like Dropbox help me maintain working versions of my files without cluttering my desktop.

While you may be tempted to put lots of files on your easy-to-access desktop, the bulk of your genealogical working files and reference files should be stored in the normal filing system on your computer's hard drive. Whether those folders are stored only on the hard drive itself, or, as we'll see in the next section, automatically synchronized to a cloud-based service, aim for sending most of your data here. I usually keep my computer desktop empty of files or (at most) with only the one or two files I'm currently working with (image **E**). In some cases, I keep a file or two on my desktop as a visual reminder of what I should be working on.

Naming Your Files

In the first part of this chapter, we discussed folders and how to name them, so let's get to one of the most difficult problems facing the organized genealogist: naming a computer file. Your electronic file-naming system should make it easy to browse for the file you want, just as you would do with paper files. However, with electronic filing, you can also keyword search for information, so you're not limited to your ability to browse in order to find something. Fortunately, on modern Windows and OS X systems, file names can be quite long (generally limited to about 255 characters) and can contain spaces. But as mentioned previously, you should avoid using any non-space characters other than letters, numbers, dashes, and underscores, as these "special" characters won't always translate in other programs. In addition, long file names can be difficult to display, so you should strive for the shortest possible file name that can still provide enough information to identify the file and give a good idea of its contents.

Many of our genealogical files will be images of records or photographs of individuals, and the file name should in some way reflect the name of the person whose record or photo it is. The obvious, immediate problem is when the document refers to more than one person (such as a married couple or a family with children); it's rarely going to be possible to use the file name to identify everyone mentioned in the file.

So if we're going to browse for a genealogical file, what would a sensible name for it be, presuming we'll be unable to name it for more than one person? If the record is primarily about one person, that's the person whose name I will want to include in the file name. But if the record is about more than one person, you'll have to select one to name the file after; for example, I usually select the husband in an opposite-sex married couple or the primary head of household if the record is about a family group. In addition to the name of the key person, I like to also include a date of some kind (at least a year, but it can include a month and day if I have multiple documents for that person from the same year) and the type of event being reflected by the document.

So let's look at an example. Imagine that I have a World War II enlistment record for my father. I would probably name that file *Smith_George-1941-WWII_enlistment*. The advantage of this naming system is that it puts all records for the same person together and sorts them chronologically. If I have more than one event in the same year, I could add months or even dates to the file name like this: *Smith_George-1941-01-06-WWII_enlistment*. In cases where I didn't know the exact year, I could estimate. For instance, if I knew that the event took place at some point in the 1940s, I could name it *Smith_George-194X-WWII_enlistment* and replace the X with a number as I learn the correct year.

Example File Names

Smith_George-1917-birth	*Smith_George-1941-WWII_enlistment*
Smith_George-1920-census	*Smith_George-1943-marriage*
Smith_George-1930-census	*Smith_George-1999-obituary*
Smith_George-1936-SS-5	*Smith_George-1999-SSDI*
Smith_George-1940-census	*Smith_George-1999-burial*

Let's now deal with other problems with this file naming system. For example, what if you don't have a date for the record? Simple: Omit it. Then, the file will sort itself after the items that have dates in their names (as numbers usually sort before letters).

And what if you have more than one person with the same name? In short, you'll need to set up some system of distinguishing two similar ancestors from each other. For example, my naming convention goes

1. name
2. middle initial
3. middle name
4. and so forth.

If I had more than one George Smith, I could add his middle initial (*T*) or, if necessary, spell out his middle name (*Thomas*). And if I have more than one *George Thomas Smith*, I could add another identifying word (such as a state abbreviation) to distinguish the two men from each other. Or if the two ancestors' life spans don't overlap, I could skip adding to the file's name and simply look at the actual record for a date that will identify which ancestor it belongs to.

In a few cases, you may be dealing with a record that refers to a family without naming any particular individuals. If that's the case, you might just use the surname and a dash, and these files will sort after more complete file names (e.g., those starting with the same surname and an underscore). Again, you don't have to have a perfect system, just one that minimizes the likelihood you'll get confused while browsing for the file you need.

Once you've settled on the details of the file naming system you want to use, keep it simple and remain consistent. Then you can refer to those same file names in your other systems, such as Evernote <www.evernote.com> or your genealogy database software. If you're fairly confident you won't be moving your files and folders around on your computer system, you can also link to your files from other programs. Just remember that moving the files to a different location will cause the links to break. Referring to your files in Evernote or your genealogy database software also solves the problem of how to easily find files that refer to an individual whose name isn't part of the file name. You can just search for the person's name in Evernote or in your genealogy software, and use the information there to figure out what file he is mentioned in.

Cloud-Based Systems

One problem many genealogists run into is they want to access their genealogical files from different devices. You may have a desktop computer at home, a laptop computer you take on trips, and mobile devices such as tablets or smartphones that you may have with you almost all of the time. This means that keeping your files, especially the files you are currently working with, only on your desktop computer's hard drive limits your ability to get work done when you're not at that computer.

That's where cloud-based file systems come in. While saving files to a particular hard drive or device can limit your ability to access them, cloud services allow you to sync files amongst multiple devices and access them from anywhere you can log in to your account. In the past few years, cloud-based file services have grown dramatically in popularity. Perhaps the best known of these is Dropbox <www.dropbox.com> (image **F**), which has been around since 2008. Dropbox does have some big-name competitors, such as Google Drive <drive.google.com>, Microsoft's OneDrive <www.onedrive.live.com>, Apple iCloud <www.icloud.com>, and Amazon Cloud Drive <www.amazon.com/clouddrive/home>, but I'll use Dropbox for my examples in this section.

I've been using Dropbox since early 2009, and I can't imagine how I got my work done without it. I use it to synchronize my files between two different desktop computers (one at home and one at work) so I can view and edit the files in either location. I also have Dropbox installed on my tablet and smartphone, which is handy for viewing files when I'm away from my desktop computer. I can also log in to my Dropbox account when I'm out of town or on a friend's computer and download any file I need.

Although the primary purpose of Dropbox is to synchronize files across multiple computing devices, it also can serve as a form of file backup. If I lose a file or accidentally modify it in an undesirable way, I can return to any earlier version of that same file from the past thirty days (and I can access previous versions of files going back a full year if I pay for that feature).

Another big advantage of using Dropbox is that I can quickly and easily share a file with another individual or even the whole world by generating a link to the file that can be e-mailed or published online. This avoids the problem of trying to send extremely large files to others via e-mail, as some e-mail systems place a size limit on attached files. If you're collaborating with another genealogical researcher, this is an ideal way to share access to a document or photo.

Speaking of collaboration, you can also work with other Dropbox users by sharing folders. In a shared folder in Dropbox, you and another user (such as a research partner) can save your discoveries there, and those files are copied automatically to the computers that each of you is using. With this method, professional researchers can share documents with their clients, writers can share manuscripts with their editors, and genealogical volunteers can share society project files with everyone on the committee. If you plan to do this kind of sharing, it's generally a good idea to coordinate who will be updating the

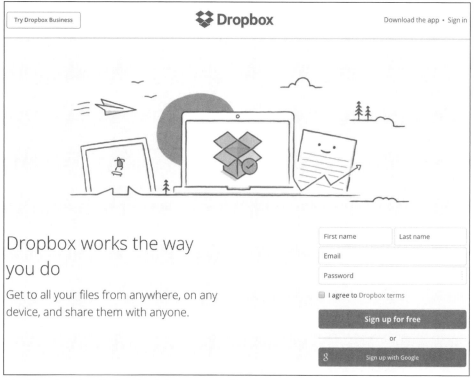

Cloud-based services like Dropbox help ensure your files are preserved, even if your hard drive fails.

document at any given time to avoid having the same document being edited by different people at the same time.

Because a copy of your Dropbox folders normally resides on your computer's hard drive just as any ordinary non-Dropbox folders would, you can use all of the previously mentioned discussion of folder names and file names for your Dropbox-based system. If you're sharing a Dropbox folder with others, you will need to coordinate with them how you will name your files.

Should you put all of your document and photo files into Dropbox? The free version of Dropbox allows for 2GB of storage (with some additional storage if you refer others to Dropbox), which should at the very least give you enough room for your working files. If you pay for Dropbox, you can purchase a plan that gives you 1TB of storage, which is likely to be enough for all of your genealogy-related files. Make the decision based on your needs and your budget.

Electronic File Backup

Nobody likes to think about loss. Just imagine the horror of losing all your computer files to human error, hardware failure, natural disasters, hacking, or theft. But these things can and do happen, and if you aren't prepared for this kind of emergency, you may find yourself heartbroken.

In my early years working for university computer centers, I frequently advised my computer users to backup their important files. Many of these individuals were researchers who had spent years accumulating critical research data, and failure to have good backup systems could undo years of work. But I knew that, at least in those earlier computer days, my advice might fall on deaf ears for some understandable reasons. In those days, it could be a bit cumbersome to backup your files. First, you had to remember to back up files on a regular basis, and it was easy to forget or procrastinate. Second, it used involved keeping all kinds of media, such as floppy disks and (later) writeable CDs or DVDs. More recently, due to the decline in the cost of data storage, many individuals depend upon external hard drives for keeping backup copies of their most important files.

However, many of us live in areas that are still prone to natural disasters, such as floods, earthquakes, and hurricanes, plus house fires that can happen to almost anyone. Depending solely upon a backup that exists in the same physical space as your computer doesn't protect you from those kinds of emergencies, and I know a case in which a desktop computer was stolen with the external hard drive attached to it.

Some individuals solve this problem by e-mailing copies of their most important files to family members or friends. However, involving other individuals in your backup plans comes with its own set of risks and isn't a good option for everyone.

Fortunately, the need for automatic backups to another location has been met by cloud-based backup services. Dozens of companies work in this market, and in our household, we have previously used both Mozy **<www.mozy.com>** and Carbonite **<www.carbonite.com>**. These days, two of the most popular services are CrashPlan **<www.code42.com/crashplan>** and Backblaze **<www.backblaze.com>**. We currently use CrashPlan (image **G**).

Using an online backup service that runs on your computer and regularly makes backups of any files that have changed since your last backup provides several benefits (image **H**):

- You can schedule when backups take place so they can run when you're not actively using your computer, such as overnight. (While you can certainly run backups while you're using your computer, you may find that it slows access to your files.)

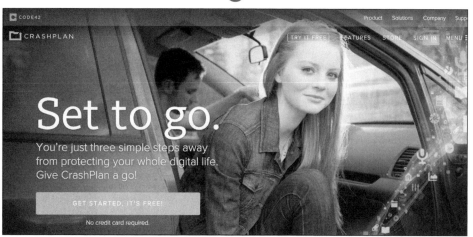

Services like CrashPlan allow you to back up your research, preventing data loss from natural disaster or hard drive failure.

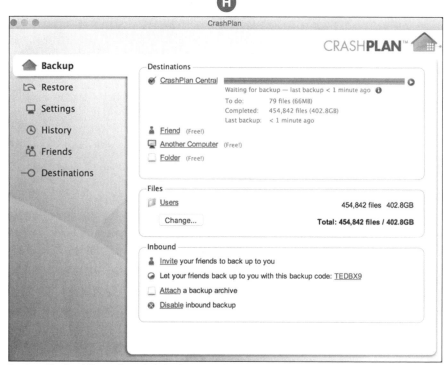

Services like CrashPlan will regularly back up your files, and you can even schedule a backup for when you're not using your computer.

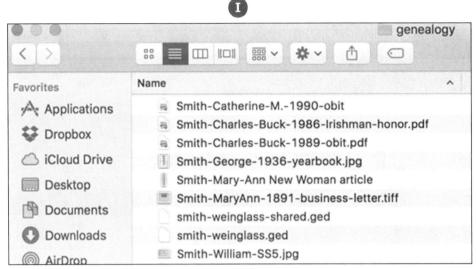

Dropbox will store a copy of your files on your hard drive in addition to in the Dropbox cloud.

- You can quickly and easily retrieve a backup copy of a file that you may have inadvertently deleted or modified, shortening your recovery time should you lose data.

- In the case of a complete loss of all of your files (and if restoring all of those files over the Internet would take too long), you can usually make arrangements (for an extra fee) for a physical copy of your files to be mailed to you so you can copy them to a new computer hard drive. If you digitize all your documents and photos and have them backed up by an online backup service, you can access those files from any Internet-connected device; I can look at my CrashPlan files on my tablet or smartphone.

You may be wondering if you need both a file synchronization service like Dropbox and a file backup service like CrashPlan. First, remember that Dropbox normally saves deleted or modified versions of files for a maximum of thirty days (for free) or for a year (if you pay for the service), so you're out of luck if you realized you've lost a file that's been gone for more than a year. Second, many computer professionals recommend that you keep at least three different copies of every important file. For example, I've got copies of my files on my desktop computer's hard drive (image ❶), Dropbox (image ❷), and CrashPlan. Third, I'm not dependent on a single company for my file storage, so my data will be safe should something happen to one of these companies (e.g., it goes out of business or radically changes its service model or features).

By using cloud-based solutions for your file storage, you can keep your filing system simple and automated while reducing your stress levels the next time you hear about someone else losing their files.

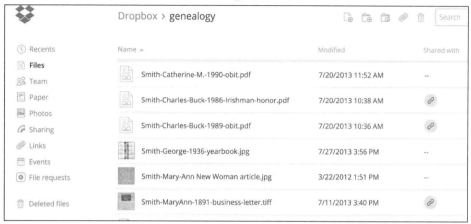

Dropbox stores your files on its own servers so they'll be safe even if your computer hard drive fails or gets stolen.

Drew's **To-Dos**

👉 Examine your research needs to determine the most appropriate way to store your files, such as in a numbering system like *Ahnentafel*.

👉 Understand the difference between searching and browsing and how different kinds of organizational systems help with these activities.

👉 Decide whether your personal filing system should be paper-based, online, or a combination of both.

👉 Determine whether you'll file your papers using binders or folders, and pay attention to the need for long-term preservation of original and sensitive documents.

👉 Choose a consistent, methodical digital file-naming system that works for your research and limits potential problems (e.g., with relatives that appear in your tree more than once).

👉 Subscribe to a cloud-based filing service to enable access to your files from any device and back up your computer files.

DIGITAL FILE NAME CONVENTION TRACKER

With the ever-expanding storage capabilities of hard drives and cloud-based computer software, you might be tempted to just save and forget your digital information. However, consistently naming your data files is just as important as organizing your physical files. Use the table below to keep track of your file-naming conventions so you can create a consistent, flexible digital organizational system. The first row has been filled in as an example. Like the other worksheets in this book, you can download a fillable version of this form at <ftu.familytreemagazine.com/organize-your-genalogy>.

Name convention (example)	Type of file	Location	Notes
Lastname_firstname-year-recordtype (Smith_George-1917-birth)	individual records for the Smith family	external hard drive	• If multiple names are associated with record, save record in both ancestors' folders. • If year is unknown, use X in place of the missing digit (for example: 194X if the record was sometime in the 1940s and 19XX if it was sometime in the 1900s.) • If multiple spellings for a name, use the spelling that appears in the record

6

organizing your research process

I f this book were about cooking instead of genealogy, the first half would have been about purchasing and organizing your appliances and utensils; organizing your drawers, cabinets, pantry, refrigerator, and freezer; planning meals; and organizing your recipes. And if that were the case, you might be wondering if I would ever get around to talking about actual cooking! As this is a book about organizing for genealogical research (and not about cooking), the previous chapters have been about preparing for research without talking about actual research. Now, let's get into the genealogical research process.

Before we begin, remember the lessons from chapter 3 on organizing genealogical goals: Having a well-organized, purposeful, and methodical research process is the key to productive and fruitful research. In this chapter, we'll discuss how you can use research logs, genealogy software, and skills already mentioned in this book to maximize your research time and keep track of your work, data, and results.

Understanding the Research Process

Before you can go somewhere, you need to know where you're going and how to get there. Here, I'll outline the basic structure used by thorough researchers as they seek family discoveries. Throughout this section, I'll use my simplest project as an example: identifying and documenting my eight great-grandparents. As you'll recall from chapter 3, I divided that project into two parts on the basis of geography; I'll be focusing on my father's side in the examples that follow.

1. Articulate Your Questions

First, identify specific questions that you want to answer, as this will guide what you'll be researching. Even a simple project like my eight great-grandparents could involve a large number of questions, so for our purposes I'll limit myself to some basic questions:

- When and where was the person born?
- When and where did the person marry?
- When and where did the person die?
- What were the names of the person's parents?

Your research questions should reflect your current knowledge about your ancestors and experience (if any) with the project. For example, if I were just beginning this project and did not know the answers to all those above questions, I would have to use placeholders instead of actual names as part of these questions. My list of questions, for example, might look like the one displayed in image Ⓐ.

Later we'll talk about tools that help you keep track of these questions (and their answers). But for now, note that you want to explicitly list these questions so you don't accidentally leave one of them out, causing you to return to missed research later.

As you learn the answer to some of the earlier questions, you can edit the later questions to replace the placeholder relationships with the actual name of the individual (though you may want to keep the relationship in parentheses after the name so you can be reminded who the person is and how he fits into your project).

2. Identify and Investigate Sources

Once you've explicitly written your research questions, you can now take them one at a time. Pull together any relevant information you might already have and identify sources you'll want to consult to research the question. Because each question will normally involve some type of personal historical event that occurred on a date and at a location,

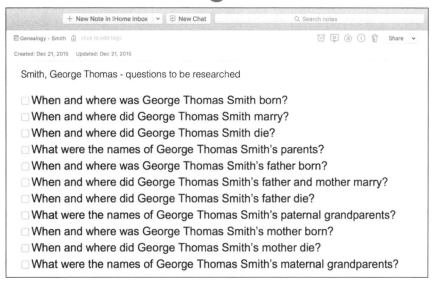

Verbalizing what you want to uncover in your research will give your search purpose and help you stay focused.

The Research Wiki on FamilySearch.org can help you identify and learn about resources to search.

you'll need to take into account at least three things when figuring out which sources to consult:

1. what sources would document that **kind of event**
2. what sources would document an event that took place during the likely **date range of the event**
3. what sources would document an event that took place within the likely **geography of the event**

This means you're going to want to make a list of sources to consult for each question, ranked in order from most relevant to least relevant. For basic life events such as birth, marriage, and death, I like to visit the FamilySearch Research Wiki at <**www.familysearch. org/learn/wiki/en/Main_Page**> (image **B**). By searching for the likely location of the event (such as a country or US state) and the type of event (such as birth, marriage, or death), I can find one or more articles that describe what sources are available and how to access them. I'm also provided with other record types to try if the most direct type is not available.

For a more comprehensive list of types of records that would be relevant to each question in US research, the FamilySearch Research Wiki provides a United States Record Selection Table <**www.familysearch.org/learn/wiki/en/United_States_Record_Selection_Table**> (image **C**). This is worth consulting if you've exhausted the most obvious sources for addressing your research question(s). Again, keep a list of these sources with the specific research question so you can keep track of which ones you've already searched and which you still need to review.

As you consult each source, record the information you find and—just as importantly—the information you don't find. When conducting research, I'm always reminded of "The Adventure of Silver Blaze," a Sherlock Holmes tale by Sir Arthur Canon Doyle in which Holmes points out to a Scotland Yard detective that the dog did something noteworthy... by doing nothing. Holmes notes the dog's lack of barking as evidence. (Spoiler alert for those who plan to read this story: The dog didn't bark because it saw a familiar face stealing and injuring a racehorse in the middle of the night. Therefore, the horse's trainer—not a stranger, as was believed—was the culprit.) In other words: Record negative findings, because they do tell us something, even if they don't directly answer our research question. And many beginning genealogists fail to make note of negative findings. But just as a biomedical researcher keeps careful track of which medicines have a beneficial impact on a disease, she keeps just as careful track of which medicines are not beneficial. This helps prevent unnecessary repetition in your research.

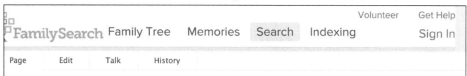

FamilySearch   Family Tree   Memories   Search   Indexing   Sign In

Page   Edit   Talk   History

United States Record Selection Table   Edit This Page

United States ⟳ **Record Selection Table**

This table can help you decide which records to search. It is most helpful for post–1800 research in the United States.

1. In column 1 find the goal you selected.
2. In column 2 find the types of records most likely to have the information you need.
3. In column 3 find additional record types that may be useful.
4. Then look for the record type you need in the Place Search of the FamilySearch Catalog.

Note: Records of previous research (Genealogy, Biography, History, Periodicals, and Societies) are useful for most goals, but are not listed unless they are especially helpful.

1. If You Need	2. Look First In	3. Then Search
Age	Census, Vital Records, Cemeteries	Military Records, Taxation
Birth date	Vital Records, Church Records, Bible Records	Cemeteries, Obituaries, Census
Birthplace	Vital Records, Church Records, Census	Newspapers, Obituaries
City or parish of foreign birth	Church Records, Genealogy, Biography, Naturalization and Citizenship, Societies	Vital Records, Obituaries, History, Emigration and Immigration
Country of foreign birth	Emigration and Immigration, Census, Naturalization and Citizenship, Church Records	Military Records, Vital Records, Newspapers, Obituaries
County origins and boundaries	History, Maps, Historical Geography	Gazetteers
Death	Vital Records, Cemeteries, Probate	Newspapers, Bible Records, Military

The United States Record Selection Table provides valuable information about what popular kinds of genealogy resources to consult when answering research questions.

3. Draw Your Conclusion

The information we derive from sources must be evaluated and analyzed to determine whether it provides evidence to address our research question. At some point, we take the evidence and decide upon a research conclusion. This conclusion is (hopefully) going to include not only the answer to the question, but also documentation of the process of selecting, analyzing, and evaluating the sources, information, and evidence.

Read the last statement carefully: The conclusion is not just the answer to the question, but should also include the documented reasoning behind it. As an organized genealogist, you should use a process to document what you find, how you found it, and what you did with it. This attention to detail will help you defend your findings to other researchers and even offer up new avenues of research. The remainder of this chapter will discuss specific tools you can use to accomplish this level of documentation.

Maintaining a Research Log

Anyone who has watched old movies involving mad scientists may recall that the scientist often keeps a journal of his (they were typically male in those old movies) diabolical research experiments. Perhaps this was your first exposure to the idea of a "research log," some sort of document used to preserve the ideas, processes, and results associated with ongoing scientific research. Of course, even sane scientific researchers keep research logs!

In the July/August 2003 issue of *Ancestry Magazine*, genealogists Terry and Jim Willard wrote an article on the subject of research logs for genealogical research, saying, "It often seems like we get lost in the thickest part of the research 'forest.' But one tool, a good research log, can help to guide us through the dense trees." That advice remains as sound today as it was in 2003, but what has changed is we now have greater computer technology that we can apply to our need for a research log. Whether via smartphones and tablets, new apps, or cloud computing that can sync across multiple devices, we now have many choices for how to keep a research log that moves beyond the original paper-based notebooks.

Certainly, you can use a notebook or binder for preserving your research process, but the disadvantage of such a system is that it isn't instantly searchable and may not be available when you're away from home. This points toward the idea of using some sort of electronic system for your research log. In this section, we'll talk about how blogs and Evernote can help you do this, and (in the next section) we'll discuss software specifically designed to record the genealogical research process.

Blogs

So what tool might serve well as an online, searchable research log? If you had asked me that question a few years ago, I would have pointed to the option of blogging, and in particular to such examples as Ralph Brandi's *Geneablogy* blog **<www.brandi.org/geneablogy>** (especially active between 2000 and 2004) and Steve Danko's *Steve's Genealogy Blog* **<www.stephendanko.com/blog>** (especially active between 2006 and 2012). Blogs are still

Rootsmithing: Genealogy, Methodology, and Technology

Sunday, October 24, 2010

SS-5 and the Grandparents

Let's complete the collection of SS-5 images by looking at the ones for my 4 grandparents. 3 of them were easy to obtain, because three of my grandparents were originally listed in the SSDI.

The 4th, belonging to my paternal grandfather William Henry Smith, required me to use his death certificate as the way to document his death (and thereby obtain his SS-5). Here is his SS-5:

Notes based upon other knowledge: His father's name was Charles Henry Smith, his mother's name was Mary Ann Bannon. (The Bannon surname was sometimes spelled "Bonnon".)

Subscribe To

- Posts
- Comments

About Me

Drew Smith
G+ Follow

I'm an Assistant Librarian at the USF Tampa Library, Chair of the Family History Information Standards Organisation (FHISO), and President of the Florida Genealogical Society of Tampa. I frequently speak and write about genealogy.

View my complete profile

My Podcast and Other Blogs

- The Genealogy Guys Podcast
- Boddie One-Name Study
- Social Networking for Genealogists (no longer updated)

Blogs, like the one that chronicles my own genealogy research, can serve as research logs and as a way to share your findings with friends and family.

an excellent choice if part of your motivation for blogging is to get your research out in front of as many other people as possible. After all, Google **<www.google.com>** and other search engines will normally index blog entries, so anyone using a search engine to look for the name of an ancestor may stumble across your blog.

Blogs (like my blog *Rootsmithing*, image **D**) are extremely easy to set up, easy to post to, and are normally free through sites such as Google's Blogger **<www.blogger.com>**. Not only are they every-word searchable, but they can also include images (family photos, documents, charts/graphs created by genealogy software, etc.). Many blogs allow for the addition of pages that are not part of the usual chronological blog entries. Such pages could be used to list genealogical goals, projects, and tasks. Blog entries can be tagged, making it possible to associate them with particular projects, surnames, locations, or event types. This would allow you to see all the entries for one particular project.

Clearly, a blog can serve well as a research log, but that doesn't mean it's a perfect solution. Normally, all entries will be displayed together in the same chronological stream, even if they are from different projects. And while you can certainly keep your blog private (providing access to only those collaborators you might want to work with), blogs have no easy way to limit access to just a portion of your blog (such as if you were working on different projects with different people). Yes, you could keep a separate blog for each project, but that makes the entire process more cumbersome.

Evernote

My first choice for a general online tool that can serve as a research log today is Evernote <www.evernote.com>. I won't repeat everything I said about Evernote in chapter 4, but I'll focus on how Evernote could be used specifically for the research process.

Having a note for genealogical goals makes sense. Once you've established those, you can then create an Evernote notebook for each of your projects. At that point, you can consider sharing that notebook (and *only* that notebook) with one or more genealogists who may be collaborating with you on the project, as each notebook can have its own set of collaborators.

Within the notebook, you may want to create a note that describes the project and discusses how it relates to your genealogical goals. You may find it helpful to title that note starting with a punctuation mark so it sorts automatically to the top. Or you can create a table of contents note (described in detail in chapter 4) with the project description note being the first listed note.

Create a note listing your genealogical questions (e.g., a to-do list with checkboxes so you'll know which questions you've addressed and which ones remain; image **E**). You can then create a note for each question and use it in a variety of ways to:

- type in your ideas
- list the sources you plan to consult (another to-do list with checkboxes)
- discuss what you find (or don't find) in each source
- add images from research documents
- write an analysis of the information and what evidence it provides
- record the conclusion you draw from the evidence

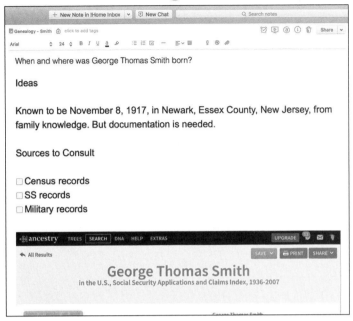

You can start and finish a query in an Evernote note. For example, you can state your research question, hypothesize about its resolution, list possible sources, and even include an image of the appropriate record or search.

In addition to the normal genealogical tags for the note, such as names, locations, and event or document types, you can also tag the note to indicate whether it's a goal note, a project note, or a question note.

The advantage of using Evernote over a blog is that you're not forced into a (primarily) normal chronological sequence for the entire research log. Rather, you can organize the log into the projects and questions that constitute the first stages of the research process. In addition to sharing just those notebooks with the right people to view or edit, you can also create a shareable public link to any note so you can ask for assistance on a mailing list, message board, or Facebook group. And you can use the Evernote Web Clipper <www. evernote.com/webclipper> to add relevant content for a project or question, take document photos with your smartphone or tablet to put immediately into your research log, and forward relevant e-mails into your research log. You also have a powerful system in Evernote that can search for just the content you want to see.

If you're already an Evernote user, you may find that using Evernote as your primary research log will make a great deal of sense. But are some tools designed specifically for genealogists to track the research process? Let's find out.

Evidentia

One of my go-to applications for organizing research—including logging what I've accomplished—is Evidentia **<www.evidentiasoftware.com>** (image **F**; available for both Windows and OS X), a software tool that provides features that support the elements of the Genealogical Proof Standard **<www.bcgcertification.org/resources/standard.html>**.

Once you've identified a list of likely sources to address the research question (perhaps using an online resource such as the FamilySearch Research Wiki), document each relevant source within Evidentia (image **G**), indicating whether it's an original source (Evidentia refers to this as an "Original Record"), a derivative source ("Derived Record"), or an authored work (such as a published family history that presumably relies upon other original or derivative sources). Each source has a unique assigned ID number. Evidentia includes citation templates for the most common source types, plus a way to discuss the source's quality and limitations, which are useful to consider when constructing the conclusion.

F

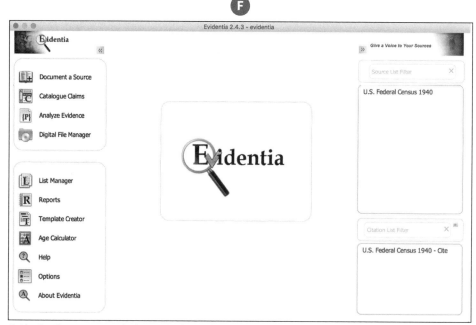

Evidentia allows you to track what you've learned in your research and where you found the information.

In "Catalogue Claims" (image **H**), you can extract specific information from the source, and the program creates a citation listing for each relevant piece of information. You can also record any thoughts about the information that might figure into the final conclusion. You'll then classify evidence as direct, indirect, or negative in "Analyze Evidence" (image **I**). On this screen, you can write the analysis of the evidence and make a summary conclusion for this one item. Finally, Evidentia can create reports that pull together the various conclusions that were based upon each individual piece of evidence. This can serve as the basis of a more complete argument to make a general conclusion based upon the totality of the evidence.

G

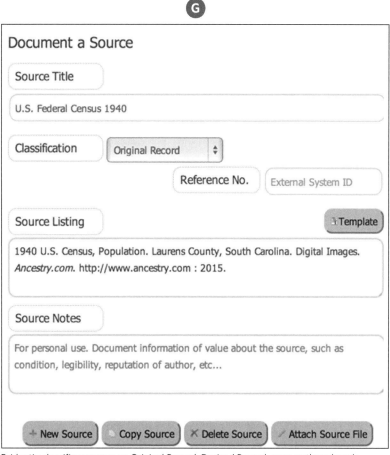

Evidentia classifies sources as Original Record, Derived Record, or an authored work.

Catalogue Claims - U.S. Federal Census 1940

Citation Title

U.S. Federal Census 1940 - Cite

Citation Title for Reports

U.S. Federal Census 1940 - Cite

Citation Listing   Template

1940 U.S. Census, Laurens County, South Carolina, Population, enumeration district (ED) 30-27, 3A, 7, 34, dwelling 216, family 62, Corrine Martin; digital image, *Ancestry.com* (http://www.ancestry.com : accessed 15 March 2015); citing NARA microfilm T627, roll 3821.

Citation Notes

For personal use. Document information of value about the portion of the source referenced by this citation, such as condition, legibility, reputation of author, etc...

| + Add Row | Mini-Editor | Attach Fragment | + New Citation | Copy Citation |

X Delete Citation

Claim	Classification	Subjects
Corrine Martin was the sister-in-law of William C. Tollison.	Primary ⬍	Corrine Martin [relationship]

Make notes about specific records using Evidentia's cataloging feature.

Using Genealogy Software

Just a few years ago, I would have expected almost every serious genealogical researcher to have a desktop genealogy database program. On rare occasion, I might run across someone who used Microsoft Word or Excel to keep track of their family tree or someone who was still entirely paper-based. Those uncommon individuals either began their research prior to the age of personal computers (and had no plans to buy one) or weren't eager to learn how to use a specialized genealogy tool. And when genealogists think about genealogy software, their first thoughts often turn to database programs such as Roots-Magic **<www.rootsmagic.com>**, Legacy Family Tree **<www.legacyfamilytree.com>**, Family

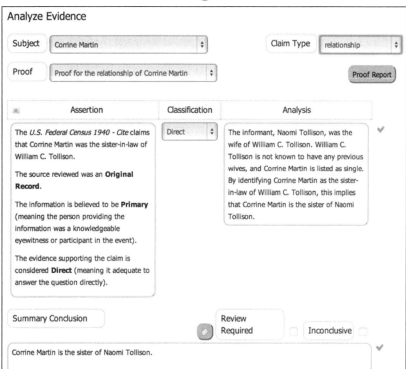

Once you've cited and classified a record, you can use Evidentia to analyze evidence and put forward a summary conclusion.

Other Genealogy Software Programs

The genealogical research process is not limited to the conclusion phase. A number of other software tools have been produced to address other aspects of research. For instance:

- GenSmarts <www.gensmarts.com> is a Windows-based program that looks at your genealogy database, identifies missing data, and makes suggestions as to what sources might be relevant to the missing data.

- Clooz <www.clooz.com> is a Windows-based program that records documents, allows for analysis, and links the documents to specific individuals.

- ResearchTies <www.researchties.com> is an online subscription-based service that provides logs for recording research objectives, intended searches, search results, and links to online records. Records for the same individual can be compared and analyzed.

Tree Builder **<www.myheritage.com/family-tree-builder>**, and Family Tree Maker **<www. familytreemaker.com>**. These tools are designed to focus on documenting and organizing the conclusions of genealogical research, such as life events for ancestors and other relatives and how these individuals are related to each other.

My research history testifies to the variety in genealogy software. As someone who has worked closely with computer technology since his college days four decades ago, I began using genealogy database programs when I first became serious about my genealogical research in the early 1990s. I recognized that I would be lost and confused without recording who I believed was in my family tree and what I believed I knew about them. Because I was a Macintosh user, I began by using the now-obsolete Mac version of Personal Ancestral File (PAF) **<www.familysearch.org/paf>** and obtaining a copy of Reunion **<www.leisterpro.com>** in order to print more elaborate charts, later switching to Family Tree Maker when I replaced my Mac with a PC. Eventually, I settled upon RootsMagic as my primary tool when I returned to a Mac. But because I often presented and wrote on the subject of genealogy software, I continued to familiarize myself with Family Tree Maker, Legacy Family Tree, and Family Tree Builder, plus a handful of other popular programs, some of which are no longer supported.

All that switching around taught me that no one program is "best" for all people (just as no one brand or model of car is best for everyone). Rather, you'll need to select a program and system that works for you (and is compatible with your device's software; see the Software Comparison Worksheet at the end of this chapter). Some programs have less of a learning curve than others and differ in their offering of a support network of fellow users. You can find several good, free options, and several paid versions that cost less than thirty dollars (though some range in the one-hundred-dollar range).

Genealogy software programs have a lot to offer genealogists. They can help you in almost every step of your research, featuring detailed profiles of your ancestors (image **J**) and tools to help keep the best information.

I'm not going to try to persuade you to switch from whatever you're using as your desktop genealogy software to some other product. Rather, in this section, I'll outline how to use genealogy software programs to verify, simplify, preserve, and present your research workflow and results.

Recording Your Findings

While some programs include features for maintaining to-do lists and research logs (which are not quite as elaborate as the to-do list and research log options mentioned earlier in this book), genealogy software developers primarily focus on recording your genealogical conclusions regarding who your ancestors were and the events of their lives.

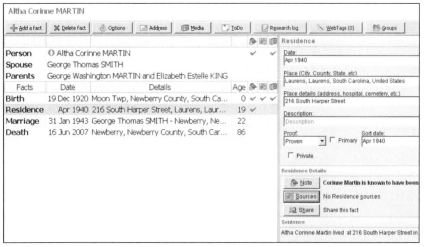

Programs specifically designed for genealogy research (such as RootsMagic, pictured above) allow you to compile your data into thorough person profiles, find potential research mistakes, and create research logs and reports.

By the time you've entered the name of a new ancestor or a fact about an existing one into your program, you should already have identified the sources (the most recent generation of programs provide excellent templates for citing them), examined the information, evaluated the evidence, and come up with a valid argument as your conclusion.

So let's go through this process with a generic genealogy program and see how you would use the program's features to preserve your process and make it accessible to yourself and others at a later date:

STEP 1: SEARCH FOR YOUR ANCESTORS IN RECORDS. In this example, I've searched for my mother's residence in 1940 by using the 1940 US federal census. I find *Corrine Martin* in the household of William C. Tollison in Laurens, Laurens County, South Carolina, and she is identified in that census as his sister-in-law. The informant is William's wife, Naomi. Because I knew my aunt, Naomi Martin Tollison, I'm confident that this *Corrine Martin* is my mother.

STEP 2: ADD INFORMATION TO YOUR ANCESTOR'S PROFILE. I now open my mother's record in my genealogy software and prepare to add a new Residence fact. For the software I'm using, I'm provided with fields for date, place, place details, a description, level of proof, notes, and a source link. I enter that information, choosing "Proven" as my level of proof.

STEP 3: DOCUMENT YOUR SOURCE. I copy and paste my proof argument into the Note field for the fact. I can also either copy and paste the source citation information from the original source (some online services provide this) into a free-form source template, or I can use one of the program's existing source templates and enter each of the pieces of the citation. While the former method is faster, the latter method provides more consistency across all sources, no matter where they came from.

You'll receive many benefits by going through these steps for each of the facts in your genealogy database program. First, they prevent you from entering any fact without giving it some serious thought. Second, you now have useful information to consider when you have conflicting facts without having to redo the research that led you to the contradiction. And third, you're in a great position to defend your research if someone else asks you how you came to a particular conclusion about a fact you've published or shared.

Preventing Research Errors

Having good genealogy software certainly can organize your data entry and, if used to its fullest potential, prevent you from entering conclusions without thoughts behind them. But how else can this software keep you organized?

Many genealogy software programs can prevent you from entering obviously bad or possibly questionable data (image Ⓚ). Trust me, we all have typos in our databases! Some errors the program prevents include:

- a child's birth date when a parent is too young, before the parents' marriage (though, of course, this isn't necessarily an error), or after the mother has died or too long after the father has died
- questionable marriage dates for spouses who are too young
- questionable death dates for individuals who are too old
- duplicate people if your new entry has the same name as someone already in your database

While a good program will catch these things as you enter them, potentially bad data can get into your database through some other means (perhaps by importing data from another source). If so, your program likely has a feature that allows you to run a problem report, looking for these kinds of issues. You may want to put a monthly or annual problem report on your calendar so you can keep your database in good shape. If you find you don't make many errors, an annual report should be sufficient. But if you're regularly guilty of more typos than you would like, you may want to make this a monthly ritual.

Typos can result in not only bad dates being entered into your database but misspellings of names and places. You may also be missing helpful geographic divisions in your data, such as a city and US state with no county given. Again, the ideal software will provide you with a tool to search your databases for any inconsistencies in names and places, and you can make this part of your monthly or annual cleanup.

Problem Search

Select the types of problems to search for

☑ Individuals without sex entered   ☑ Birth before parent's birth

☑ Proper order of events   ☑ Birth after father's death

☑ Birth before parent's marriage   ☑ Birth after mother's death

☑ Age at death should be less than   [100 ⬍]

☑ Age at marriage should be between   [14 ⬍] and [70 ⬍]

☑ Father's age should be between   [14 ⬍] and [70 ⬍]

☑ Mother's age should be between   [14 ⬍] and [50 ⬍]

[OK]   [Cancel]

Software programs can also help you find potential research mistakes.

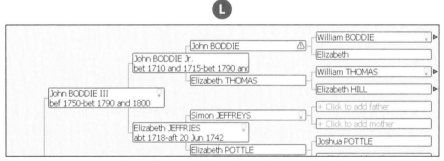

Some software programs will provide research hints that may be a match for that ancestor (indicated here in RootsMagic by a light bulb).

Identifying New Leads and Hints

Once you've entered well-supported facts into your database and eliminated the typos, the program's can identify online records that may also pertain to the individuals in your database (image L). This relatively new feature of genealogy database software is due to either companies owning both online record collections and desktop software (MyHeritage **<www.myheritage.com>** with Family Tree Builder) or partnerships between organizations or companies and online record collections and companies with genealogy software (FamilySearch <**www.familysearch.org**> and Ancestry.com <**www.ancestry.com**> and MyHeritage with RootsMagic).

Ideally, you should examine each of these hints, marking them in such a way that indicates whether or not you have accepted them or rejected them. As with anything else, proceed in an orderly way that's appropriate to your current goal. For instance, if your project involves going back in time, start with the most recent generations and work backwards one generation at a time. If the project involves an immigrant or distant ancestor and all of their descendants, start with that most distant ancestor and work forward in time one generation at a time (from the oldest child to the youngest). By using this system, you may discover an error early in your project that could prevent a lot of unnecessary research work on the wrong individuals.

Visualizing Your Data: Charts, Reports, and Lists

Another major set of features that an organized genealogist will want from her genealogy database software is the ability to create a variety of lists, reports, and charts (image **M**). Let's examine some of these options and how they would keep you organized (we'll come back to some of these when we talk about online research and research trips in chapters 8 and 9).

The first two kinds of published genealogy documents that a typical genealogist encounters are the pedigree chart and the family group sheet (sometimes called a family group record). These two document types were common even in the days of paper-based genealogy, and software programs tend to reproduce them on-screen for obvious reasons. The pedigree view displays the individual's ancestry, and the family view displays the family unit within which the individual tended to interact the most. You can find a family group sheet in this book's appendix and both forms online at <**www.familytreemagazine. com/article/freeforms**>.

Beyond these two common views, most genealogy software also offer an individual view (the person and all of his associated life facts) and a view of someone's descendants (often depicted as a list from oldest to youngest, indented by each generation). Each of these views provides a different level or way in which to view an individual or collection of individuals: the individual view, the family view, the ancestral view, and the descendants view.

They serve the organized genealogist as a microscope or telescope would, zooming in for details, and out for the big picture. At different levels, you can observe the relationship of one personal event to another, one person to another, or one family to another. Modern programs may provide additional views, such as timelines that add events that go beyond the individual (for instance, birth/marriage/death events for parents, siblings, and children) or maps that display the geographical relationship between events. As an

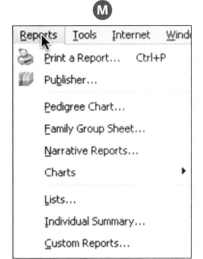

You can use software programs to export your research in a variety of forms, charts, and reports.

research tip

Choose the Best Report

Decide which report to export your research as by considering what you need the report for. Pedigree charts and family group sheets are good for getting a quick glance of your research, while narrative reports share large information without having to provide direct research data. Charts visualize data and are more appropriate for display, while lists help identify inconsistencies in your data and group together events for a particular time or place (especially useful for research trips).

organized genealogist, you should explore all your program's views to see how they might aid in your research.

The beginning of chapter 5 discusses different organizational schemes, and genealogy database programs that can produce lists and reports using those schemes, such as *Ahnentafel* lists, ancestor reports, or descendant reports. Once you have enough information in your genealogy database, experiment with producing each of these lists/reports and see which ones provide you with the most helpful way of displaying your research project's conclusions.

Both lists and charts can be helpful in directing your future research. They may visually highlight omissions (missing numbers from an *Ahnentafel* report, missing individuals from a fan chart, etc.). In some cases, an error within your data may be easier to spot on a report or chart than it would in your program's regular display screens.

While lists and reports are most helpful to those who like to view information in textual form, charts may be more helpful for those who like to visualize how one person is related to another. Of course, if you're planning to give a decorative research gift to a relative, you can create a framed chart that will undoubtedly be appreciated and proudly displayed on a wall.

Because giving others direct viewing access to your desktop software's data can be difficult (unless you synchronize that data to an online family tree), reports and charts are also helpful when publishing research online or sharing it directly with others. This may generate feedback in the form of corrections or additions.

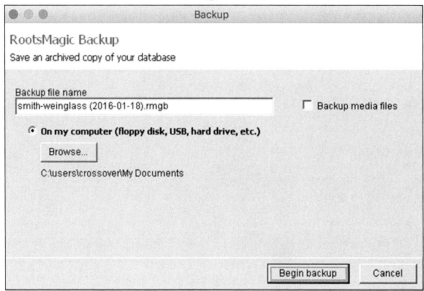

Software programs like RootsMagic will back up your research, preventing you from losing data.

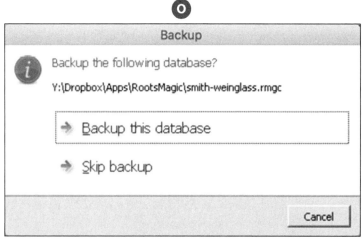

RootsMagic allows you to automatically back up files, such as when you exit the program.

As you collaborate with cousins or other researchers, you may want to ask them what form they would prefer to see your data in. Some may ask you to export a data file that they can import into their own software for viewing and analysis, but others—especially those who don't have their own genealogy software—will be better served with a standard report or chart.

Backing Up Your Research

Finally, no discussion of organized use of genealogy database programs would be complete without mentioning backups (image **N**). Although the previous chapter discussed the importance of backing up your computer's most critical data, such as your photos and digital genealogy documents, you should also be aware of what features your genealogy database program provides you for backing up its own data. Even if you're already backing up these files as part of your system backup (which you may be doing every night; image **O**), consider making database backups whenever you're significantly changing your database.

Some programs are clever enough to ask you if you want to do a backup each time you close the file (if you have changed it), and your answer should normally be "yes." Deciding how often to back up will always come down to how much work you're willing to redo in case of a hardware failure, software crash, or accidental user error. At the end of chapter 1, I suggested standing every hour and taking a brief break from your research was a good idea, so perhaps you can incorporate an automatic backup into your hourly routine. This would limit any data loss to a maximum of an hour's work.

No matter how often you back up your program's data, keep in mind where you're storing your backups. Having them on the same hard drive as your main genealogy database may not help if your computer experiences a hard drive crash. Consider using at least an external hard drive, if not a cloud-based solution.

Drew's **To-Dos**

👉 Learn each of the important components in the research process: goals, questions, sources, information, evidence, and conclusions.

👉 Maintain a research log to track your progress and preserve your ideas.

👉 Use a tool such as Evidentia to organize your research process into a step-by-step procedure.

👉 Record your genealogical conclusions in your genealogy database software to best record, visualize, and back up your research.

RESEARCH PLANNING WORKSHEET

As detailed in the Understanding the Research Process section, the research process has multiple stages, beginning with articulating your questions and ending with drawing conclusions. Account for all of these stages with a form like the table below to keep track of your research. You can also find a downloadable version of this form at **<ftu.familytreemagazine. com/organize-your-genealogy>**.

Research Question	Sources to Consult	Conclusion

SOFTWARE COMPARISON WORKSHEET

You have many genealogy software programs to choose from. Check out this comparison guide that displays the major software programs available to genealogists on both Windows and Macs. For user ratings, visit **<www.gensoftreviews.com>**.

For Windows

Name	Price	Multiple views	Reports	Syncs with FamilySearch.org	Syncs with Ancestry.com
Ancestral Quest <www.ancquest.com>	free "Basics" version; $29.95 (download); $19.95 (upgrade)	●	●		
Brother's Keeper <www.bkwin.org>	$45 (CD); $24 (upgrade)	●	●		
Family Historian <www.family-historian.co.uk>	$46.50 (license); $32.29 (upgrade)	●	●		●
Family Tree Maker <www.mackiev.com/ftm/index.html>	$69.95 (download); $29.95 (upgrade from FTM 2012 or earlier)	●	●		●
Genbox Family History <www.genbox.com>	$29.95 (license)	●	●		
Heredis 2015 for Windows <www.heredis.com/en/heredis-2015-for-windows/>	$29.99 (download) or $19.99 (upgrade)	●	●		
Legacy Family Tree Deluxe <www.legacyfamilytree.com>	free "Standard" version; $29.99 (download); $39.95 (CD with manual); $21.95 upgrade	●	●		
RootsMagic 7 <www.rootsmagic.com>	free "Essentials" version; $29.95 (download); $19.95 (upgrade)	●	●	●	●

For Mac

Name	Price	Multiple views	Reports	Syncs with FamilySearch.org	Syncs with Ancestry.com
Ancestral Quest <www.ancquest.com>	free "Basics" version; $29.95 (download); $19.95 (upgrade)	•	•		
GEDitCOM II <www.geditcom.com>	$64.99 (license) or $19.99 (upgrade)	•	•		
Family Tree Maker for Mac <www.mackiev.com/ftm/index.html>	$69.95 (download); $29.95 (upgrade from Mac 2 or earlier)	•	•		•
Heredis 2015 for Mac <www.heredis.com/en/heredis-2015-for-mac>	$49.99 (download)	•	•		
iFamily for Mac <www.ifamilyformac.com>	$29.95	•	•		
Reunion 11 <www.leisterpro.com>	$99 (download/CD) or $54.95 (upgrade)	•	•		
RootsMagic 7 <www.rootsmagic.com>	free "Essentials" version; $29.95 (download); $19.95 (upgrade)	•	•	•	•

7

organizing your communication

One of the great things about genealogy is that it's collaborative. You'll find yourself corresponding with other researchers, chatting up newly found cousins, and requesting records from archives. But like everything else in this field of study, all that communication can become too much to handle over time, especially as your volume of research grows. In this chapter, we'll discuss how to systematically handle various kinds of communication you'll make in your research, including paper mail, e-mails, and posts on message boards and Facebook **<www.facebook.com>**.

Handling Paper Mail

I find it a fun mental exercise to think about what genealogical research must have been like prior to the days of computer communication and even before the telephone. Setting aside the possibility of doing genealogical research via telegraph, it's reasonable to assume that most serious genealogical research before the twentieth century was accomplished via postal correspondence, occasionally coupled with visits to libraries, archives, and other repositories.

Today, genealogical researchers will rarely use mail to correspond with other genealogists or distant relatives. But you still may need to mail copies of documents to others, and it's even more likely that you'll receive physical copies of genealogical documents from repositories and other researchers.

Although we discussed handling paper material in chapter 5, here's an important reminder: Whenever possible, scan any paper documents you receive and file them using both your computer's hard drive and a cloud-based filing system. This could be some combination of using Dropbox <www.dropbox.com> (for the scanned files) and Evernote <www.evernote.com> (for comments about and links to the file images). If the original paper document would be expensive or time-consuming to replace, first preserve it using archival-safe storage mechanisms and keep it in the safest possible storage area, such as a cool, dry, dark area of your home.

Whenever you order documents—either paper copies or digital—use a Waiting category in your to-do list system and indicate when you made the request and when you expect to receive the results. Check this list on a regular basis (weekly or monthly) to see if anything is overdue. And if you receive what you were waiting for, remember to mark it as received. For overdue items, make a to-do for yourself to follow up, but be sure to read the organization's instructions on how long you can expect to wait to receive your order if you're dealing with an organization rather than an individual.

Exchanging correspondence (paper or electronic) with another individual can be a bit trickier than with an organization, as the latter is normally interested in providing good customer service and responding reasonably quickly. In the case of an individual, unless that person is a professional genealogist (and you're dealing with something you've paid for), temper your expectations. After all, the other person is a hobbyist like yourself, who has many other, higher-level priorities that can interfere with responding quickly to your request. To increase your chances of hearing back from an individual via paper, be sure to enclose a stamped, self-addressed envelope. Anything you can do to reduce the hassle of writing back is going to smooth the way for a quick and cheerful response. You may also want to provide your e-mail address and phone number in your postal request in case the other person is more comfortable responding in one of those ways.

Also keep track of your correspondence in your research log (as described in the last chapter), as it provides another way to see how you're making progress toward your research goals.

Handling E-Mail

E-mail is both a blessing and a curse. In my earliest days of using e-mail back in the 1980s, I was delighted with the speed I could send a message to anyone in the world (at no cost to myself) and receive a response within minutes. Corresponding via e-mail means you don't have to worry about expensive long-distance phone calls, disturbing people while they're sleeping or busy doing something else, or having one's words misheard due to a poor phone connection or heavy accents.

But it wasn't long before the dark side of e-mail appeared. Strangers filled my e-mail inbox with spam and even possible computer viruses (if I was so foolish as to open the wrong message's attached file). Friends and acquaintances sent absurd chain letters, inappropriate humor, and the kind of nonsense that would later result in the creation of the Snopes website. Individuals accidentally sent e-mail to the wrong address, analogous to dialing the wrong phone number, but with the added embarrassment of including content that was not meant for anyone else but the intended recipient to see.

Selecting an E-mail Address

If I were starting fresh with using e-mail in my genealogical research today, I would seriously consider having a unique e-mail address just for genealogy to keep my genealogical correspondence separate from my general, personal e-mail. This makes it less likely that you'll lose an important piece of e-mail from a newly discovered cousin amidst the mess in your inbox.

When I got serious about genealogical research, I didn't have an e-mail address that seemed to work well with genealogy. I quickly learned that it would be best to use something based upon my own name, which would provide an extra measure of trust in those who received my e-mail. For many years I used *drewsmith@aol.com*.

I eventually transitioned my primary e-mail service from AOL to Gmail. In fact, I adjusted my old AOL account's settings so it forwards any messages to my new Gmail address, though this process only works if you still have access to your older e-mail address. If you can no longer access the old account, you may have to make sure you let people know elsewhere online that your old address has now been replaced with a new one (and hope they can find that message if they Google for your old e-mail address).

That process can work just as easily for you—keeping your personal and genealogical lives separate (or even just moving to a more genealogy-friendly e-mail address) can help you better organize that correspondence.

Both the benefits and drawbacks of e-mail exploded with the introduction of electronic mailing lists, where a message could be sent to a single address and automatically re-routed to hundreds if not thousands of recipients, nearly all of whom were unknown to the original sender. Now all of the bad kinds of e-mail could be shared more easily than ever. It wasn't long before all of us tried to remember what it was like to look forward to opening our e-mail inbox instead of dreading what we might find.

Today, while we're still inundated with a combination of spam and desired communications, technology has made great strides in helping us to delete the stuff we have no interest in, file away the stuff that might prove useful someday (but not now), and display the remainder consisting of immediately important e-mail.

I strongly recommend that you use e-mail desktop software or online services that will give you a lot of important features beyond the normal "delete," "read," "reply," and "forward." But which e-mail tool will give you the features you need? Unsurprisingly, the most popular and feature-rich e-mail tools are from the biggest companies currently in the technology world: Google (Gmail) <mail.google.com>, Apple (Apple Mail) <www.apple.com/support/mac-apps/mail>, and Microsoft (Outlook) <www.microsoft.com/en-us/outlook-com>. Because I'm most familiar with Gmail, I'll use that for the remainder of the examples in this chapter.

Useful Account Settings and Features

The starting point for organizing your e-mail is reviewing your e-mail settings to see which will help you be the most organized and productive. As I look at Gmail's Settings, I see a number of things in the General category that are important (image Ⓐ). For instance, your Default reply behavior should be set to Reply rather than Reply All, as it is far more problematic to accidentally send a response to multiple individuals when that response was intended for only one, than vice versa. (You can always later resend the message to others who you might have accidentally omitted.) I'm also a big fan of Gmail's Conversation View, which groups all of the e-mails together in the same thread (i.e., an original message together with all of its replies, all having the same subject line). This reduces the number of different lines in my inbox and helps me avoid overlooking someone's response in a thread.

Gmail also provides me with the ability to "star" a message with one of twelve different kinds of markers (such as different colors and punctuation marks; see image Ⓑ) to make it stand out from the rest. While you don't want to overcomplicate your e-mail system, feel free to use a red star to note an e-mail that requires extra attention (as long as you're consistent and can remember why you starred the message). For instance, you could use the star to mark an e-mail requiring a response or that needs to be forwarded

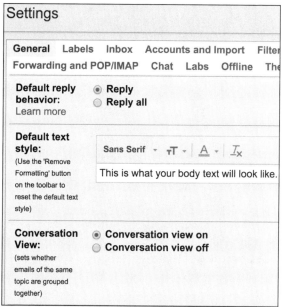

Gmail allows you to toggle several features—such as default reply behavior, text style, and conversation view—to suit your organizational needs.

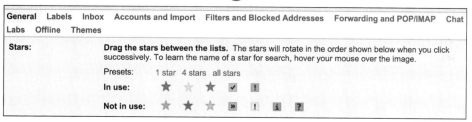

Various annotations like stars, checkmarks, and numbers can help you mark important e-mails.

to someone else, an e-mail that creates a to-do that should go into your to-do system, or an e-mail you want to save for future reference, either within Evernote or within Gmail itself. Once you have used one of these star indicators, you can have Gmail display only those messages that have stars.

Another general setting that Gmail provides is the Snippets feature (image **C**), which gives a portion of the beginning of an e-mail message. This can be handy since so many e-mail senders are not as skillful as they might be when choosing informative subject lines (*Help!* and *Question* are both poor—but not uncommon—subject lines). When you

| General   Labels   Inbox   Accounts and Import   Filters and Blocked Addresses |
| Forwarding and POP/IMAP   Chat   Labs   Offline   Themes |

Snippets: ⦿ **Show snippets** - Show snippets of the message (like Google web search!).
　　　　　　　◯ **No snippets** - Show subject only.

Selecting Show snippets allows you to see a brief portion of the e-mail, allowing you to more easily sort
e-mail at a glance.

| General   Labels   Inbox   Accounts and Import   Filters and Blocked Addresses |
| Forwarding and POP/IMAP   Chat   Labs   Offline   Themes |

Personal level　◯ **No indicators**
indicators:　　⦿ **Show indicators** - Display an arrow (›) by messages sent to my address
　　　　　　　　　　(not a mailing list), and a double arrow (») by messages sent only to me.

Indicators can visually distinguish e-mail sent just to you (>>) from e-mail sent to you and others (>).

turn the Snippets setting on, Gmail will display the snippet right after the subject line of
the e-mail, giving you a much better idea of what the e-mail is likely to be about.

Another general setting that is useful for organizing the way you read your Gmail is Personal level indicators (image **D**). If you turn this feature on, Gmail will mark e-mail sent to
you (and only you) with a double arrow (>>), and e-mail sent to you and others (but not to a
mailing list) with a single arrow (>). This often influences the order in which I process my
e-mail, since I can look first at the double-arrow messages, then at the single-arrow ones,
and finally at everything else (which is usually stuff that was sent to a mailing list).

The sections below detail some more of Gmail's account settings and how they can
help you sift through genealogical-related e-mail.

NOTIFICATIONS

E-mail software can generate notifications when there is new mail (image **E**), but don't
necessarily take advantage of this feature. Whether it's a Gmail notification in my browser
or an Outlook notification on my computer, I've decided to turn off notifications. Remember from the discussion of triggers in chapter 1 that notifications are intended to alert you
to acting in a certain way (e.g., your alarm clock's alarm is a notification that you should
wake up or your coffee maker's beep is a notification that the coffee is ready and may turn
cold unless you do something with it). But what happens if you get a notification each and
every time you receive a new e-mail?

Since the days when AOL's voice first told us "You've got mail!", many of us have
become addicted to checking e-mail, but it's a worthwhile habit to break. After all, we

Desktop Notifications: (allows Gmail to display popup notifications on your desktop when new email messages arrive) Learn more	Click here to enable desktop notifications for Gmail. ○ **New mail notifications on** - Notify me when any new message arrives in my inbox or primary tab ○ **Important mail notifications on** - Notify me only when an important message arrives in my inbox ◉ **Mail notifications off**

While desktop notifications for e-mail can be helpful, they can also create unnecessary distractions while you work.

could be talking about more than a hundred notifications per day, interrupting you while you're searching for a genealogical record or analyzing evidence and creating a conclusion. Even if the notification is silent, a visible notification in the form of an icon somewhere on your computer's desktop is still a form of distraction.

While I won't rule out that you may sometimes need to instantly know about an incoming e-mail, I'll argue that such occasions are not common enough to justify being distracted by new e-mail notifications the entire time you're on your computer. (If an e-mail is actually that critical, you should arrange for the sender to text message or call you when it's sent.)

In short, turn off your e-mail notifications and only check your e-mail inbox two or three times a day.

AUTOMATIC SIGNATURES

Another popular e-mail feature is the automatic signature (image **F**). Unless you're using a specific e-mail address just for genealogical purposes, it may be difficult to create an appropriate e-mail signature (beyond just your name) that will suit all of your outgoing e-mail. Of course, if you're a professional genealogist who uses a specific e-mail address for your business, you'll include your name, company name, phone number, and possibly a website URL. (People should be able to use your website to find your postal address as well.) If you're an officer of a genealogical society and are given access to a unique e-mail address for that role, you may want to have a signature for that, too. Note: You generally don't need to include your e-mail address itself in the signature, since the recipients of your e-mail will already have access to that in the e-mail header.

I have mixed feelings about the vacation responder feature of e-mail software. While I understand that it's designed to explain why someone may not be able to get back to me in a reasonably timely manner, I find that it often responds inappropriately, such as when e-mail is sent to a mailing list. And why would I want to let strangers who

General Labels Inbox Accounts and Import Filters and Blocked Addresses
Forwarding and POP/IMAP Chat Labs Offline Themes

Signature:
(appended at the end of
all outgoing messages)
Learn more

○ **No signature**

◉ Drew Smith <drew@ahaseminars.com>

| Sans Serif ▾ | ₸▾ | **B** | *I* | U | A ▾ | ⊖ | 🖼 | ≣ ▾ | ⅔≣ | ≣ |

☑ Insert this signature before quoted text in replies and remove the "--" line
that precedes it.

E-mail signatures are useful shortcuts for when you're responding to many e-mails per day. Make sure your signature is appropriate for the kind of correspondence you're sending.

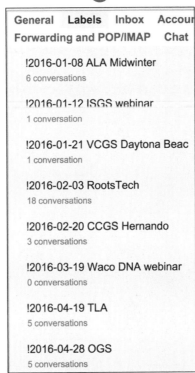

General **Labels** Inbox Accour
Forwarding and POP/IMAP Chat

!2016-01-08 ALA Midwinter
6 conversations

!2016-01-12 ISGS webinar
1 conversation

!2016-01-21 VCGS Daytona Beac
1 conversation

!2016-02-03 RootsTech
18 conversations

!2016-02-20 CCGS Hernando
3 conversations

!2016-03-19 Waco DNA webinar
0 conversations

!2016-04-19 TLA
5 conversations

!2016-04-28 OGS
5 conversations

Labels, such as labels about upcoming events, can help you organize your e-mail by topic or keyword.

e-mail me know how long I may be out of town? As a result, I personally avoid using vacation responders.

LABELS

Just as Evernote lets you tag notes to provide another way of organizing them, Gmail lets you create labels and apply them to e-mail messages for organizing and searching (image Ⓖ). In some ways, this is like filing e-mail in folders, but the advantage of labels over folders is that folders normally only allow messages to be in one folder at a time, while a Gmail message can have as many different labels as you want. This means you could create Gmail labels for the people or organizations you correspond with, events that the e-mail is about (such as conferences, webinars, or research trips), surnames you're researching, or research projects you're engaged in.

Because Gmail sorts labels alphabetically, I use a punctuation trick to force certain labels to the beginning of the list. This means that my most important labels begin with an exclamation point or even multiple exclamation points. I also use a trick to force information about my upcoming speaking and other events to the top. For instance, if I know that my local genealogy society is having an event on October 1, 2016, I will create the label *!2016-10-01 FGS Tampa* and apply it to any e-mail that relates to that event. This means my alphabetical list of labels shows me all of my planned events in order of occurrence, which is just what I need since I'll refer most often to the events coming up next rather than the ones a long time away. (By the way, I use the exact same system for creating computer folders for any documents related to those events, again using punctuation to force those to sort to the top of my list of file folders.) Once the event has passed and I've dealt with anything relating to that event, I rename the label (such as *FGS Tampa 2016*) so it moves down my list of labels but is still available for archival purposes.

Once you've set up your original set of Gmail labels (though you can certainly keep adding new labels as you need them), you're ready to think about how to process your incoming e-mail. Eventually, you'll want to categorize the incoming e-mail as something to be deleted, something to be saved for reference, or something to be acted upon.

Let's discuss each of those categories. E-mail to be deleted falls into a number of categories, the first of which that comes to mind is spam. Fortunately, your Internet service provider (ISP) is probably catching a lot of obvious spam so you don't even have to see it, but the rest may be sent to your e-mail software. Gmail puts what it thinks is spam in your Spam folder, where it remains for a maximum of thirty days before being automatically deleted. Unfortunately, some non-spam will make its way into your Spam folder. Even so, you may want to set up a schedule (say, every two weeks) to see what is in there and pull out anything that isn't spam. Once you've removed the non-spam, you can delete

Gmail has a number of default inboxes that can help you sort your e-mails by sender.

everything else in that folder. If legitimate e-mail from one of your correspondents is frequently ending up in your Spam folder for some reason, you can minimize the number of times this is likely to happen by being sure your correspondent is in your e-mail contacts.

After dealing with spam, you can look quickly through your e-mail to delete other categories of items that require no further processing. These may be notifications of events that you have no plans to attend, ads for products you're not interested in, or simple "thank you" messages for things you have already dealt with. If you find that you're getting a lot of commercial e-mail, open one of the messages to see if it provides you with the option to unsubscribe at the bottom of the message. If not, and you know that you'll never want to deal with that particular company, consider putting the commercial sender on a blocked list so that you'll never see e-mail from them again.

Now it's time to turn attention to the regular inbox. Gmail provides an option to divide your inbox into a number of sub-inboxes, with your normal one labeled Primary and the others labeled Social, Promotions, Updates, and Forums (image). The advantage of this system is that it puts lower priority e-mail away from immediate viewing, but you can still tell at a glance if there is something new in each of those tabs.

OTHER FILTERS

If you don't like the way Gmail sets this up, would prefer more control over how you separate your e-mail, or if your own e-mail software doesn't have this feature, take a look at your e-mail software's filtering features. When combined with labels, filters provide you with the ideal way to automatically categorize your incoming e-mail.

A filter (image) is a feature that lets you create a rule that says what happens to incoming e-mails that match a certain set of criteria. For instance, you might want to filter all e-mail sent from a particular person (say, a fellow researcher), all e-mail sent to

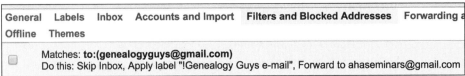

In addition to Gmail's default filters, you can have your mail sorted using customized rules.

a particular mailing list you subscribe to, all e-mail that has a particular subject line, or all e-mail that contains or doesn't contain certain words. For example, if you're working with two other researchers on a genealogical project (and all the e-mails you'll receive from them will be about that project), you could set a rule/filter for each of those e-mail addresses that states all e-mails from those two addresses will be given a label you've created for the project.

Filtering is also a good way of dealing with genealogy mailing lists you're subscribed to, since you don't want to have those mixed in with your personal e-mail. By creating a "lists" label (or something similar) and filtering those messages, you can automatically redirect those messages so you can read them at your leisure instead of when you're trying to deal with more important e-mail.

Note: The filtering rule can also automatically archive messages so they aren't in your inbox, mark them as read, or even star them so they're marked as important. You also have options to set up a filtering rule to automatically delete e-mail that matches your rule, but use this one carefully.

Sorting E-mail

If your e-mail filters have been set up reasonably well, you may find that your regular e-mail inbox isn't quite so daunting. Even so, you'll now need to go through that inbox on a regular basis (as mentioned earlier, perhaps no more often than two or three times per day) and make some decisions.

First, look at the subject lines and figure out which e-mail you can safely delete without even opening the message (e.g., e-mails about events you aren't interested in). Once you've eliminated the obvious discards, you can begin to open the remaining messages and read them. For each message, your first decision is whether or not to delete the message (maybe you couldn't tell just from the subject line). If the message has no relevance to you, delete it. If the message does have some relevance, but doesn't require you to do anything, you'll want to file it in some way. If it just contains useful content, you may want to forward it to your Evernote system (if you don't have a paying Evernote account, you can still use the Evernote Web Clipper <www.evernote.com/webclipper> to save the content of the e-mail).

Depending on what the content is, you may also want to keep a reference copy of the e-mail in your e-mail system. I do this when I have received some sort of acknowledgment for something I have purchased or reserved, or when another person has received something from me. In this way, if a question comes up about this at a later date, I can then re-forward that message back to the organization or individual as evidence.

The remaining messages are ones you need to act on in some way. This may mean putting something on your calendar, adding a to-do into your system (you may be able to forward the e-mail to your to-do system as a quick way for this to happen), replying to the sender of the e-mail, or simply taking some action that won't require more than a few minutes and isn't worth the time to add to your to-do system. How you respond to the e-mail will determine the message's fate. When an e-mail requires me to add something to my calendar, for example, I usually delete the e-mail after editing my calendar (though I may archive it if it contains additional information about the event).

Even if the nature of the e-mail causes you to put it into your Evernote, calendar, or to-do system, keep a copy of the e-mail in your archive if there's a good chance you'll need to reply to it. For instance, an e-mail might be from a fellow researcher asking you what you have learned in the past week about your joint project. You might forward that to your to-do system and add a brief item to your calendar to summarize that research and send a reply. You can then safely archive the message, knowing that your calendar and to-do system will remind you to respond. One thing I often do is immediately let my correspondents know when they can expect to hear back with the details so they won't be left wondering if I got their original message.

It's not always possible to achieve the ultimate goal of "Inbox Zero," but regularly following the e-mail practices described in this section can get you pretty close.

Handling Mailing Lists, Message Boards, and Facebook

The rise of social networking services has had a dramatic impact on the way many genealogists communicate. I've been known to argue that genealogists were among the first users of social networking, as they adopted mailing lists and message boards back in the 1980s, years before there was a World Wide Web (let alone Facebook)! Speaking of Facebook: Given its impact on society, it may be difficult for anyone to believe that Facebook is just ten years old.

So if the Internet boasts more than thirty thousand genealogy mailing lists, approximately two hundred thousand genealogy message boards, and more than five thousand genealogy Facebook groups and pages, how is an organized genealogist expected to keep up with this deluge of information?

Although mailing lists, message boards, and Facebook groups are excellent places to go for advice on all kinds of genealogy-related questions, we'll focus here on using them to ask questions directly related to your research. This could be, to name a few examples: locating a difficult-to-find town or cemetery; discovering a source of records to answer a question; or asking someone if she can do local research when it is impractical to travel to the place yourself.

Track Queries with a Research Log

Use your research log to track your use of mailing lists and message boards. You can even create good subject lines, save them in your research log, and re-use them on other lists and boards if they seem useful. Also, the more you standardize how you approach subject lines, the quicker and easier it will be for you to create new ones.

1. Decide Where to Ask Your Questions

Once you've convinced yourself that your question has not yet been asked (and answered) on any of the social media sites, formulate a research plan for your question. First, consider which lists, boards, or groups would be most relevant to your question. For typical research questions, you'll be dealing with a surname or location (or both), and you can find many lists and boards for many surnames and places (at least down to the county level in cases of US research).

To find a relevant RootsWeb list, search using the Find a mailing list search box **<lists. rootsweb.ancestry.com>** or browse using the Browse mailing lists link (image 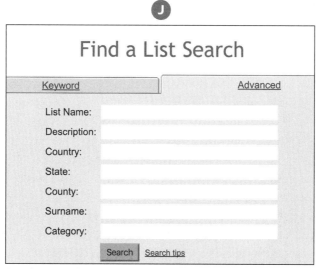). For the Ancestry Message Boards, search using the Find a board about a specific topic search box at **<boards.ancestry.com>** or browse using the surnames and categories links.

J

Find a List Search

Keyword	Advanced
List Name:	
Description:	
Country:	
State:	
County:	
Surname:	
Category:	

Search   Search tips

Search RootsWeb for mailing lists that are relevant to your research, as the people on them may be able to answer your questions.

Facebook hosts several user groups for genealogists, allowing you to connect with other family historians and help answer research questions.

Archives Search Engine

| Keyword | Advanced |

Body:

Subject:

From:

(email address of poster)

List:

(limit search to one mailing list)

Date:

(e.g. 10 Jun 2005, Jun 2005, or 2005)

Search | Search tips

RootsWeb has a search engine that searches past posts, allowing you to quickly find relevant material.

To find relevant genealogy Facebook groups, use the main Facebook search box at the top of the page (image **K**). An alternative is to browse through Katherine R. Willson's categorized list of genealogy Facebook groups and pages, which she links to from her "Genealogy on Facebook List" **<www.socialmediagenealogy.com/genealogy-on-facebook-list>**. Before posting in any Facebook group, be sure to read the group description and any pinned post that might provide guidelines as to which postings are appropriate and what etiquette to follow. Based on that reading, you may discover that your genealogy question isn't relevant to that group after all.

Another thing to consider is that you want to use a list, board, or Facebook group with a large and active group of participants. With lists and boards, it's difficult to know how many other people are using the same list/board, though you may be able to browse the archive to see how often people post to that list or board. With Facebook groups, you can see the numbers of group members when you're searching for relevant groups. Small or inactive forums may not be of much help to your question, although your question might be overlooked in extremely large and busy forums that have a tidal wave of information. (We'll get to some tips on how to make sure your message gets noticed.)

Once you've identified the relevant places to post your query, consider posting to multiple locations. Avoid posting the same question to too many lists or boards at the same time. In particular, if you have a question involving a US state but don't know which county your question pertains to, don't post the same question to every county list or board in that state. Instead, look for and use the appropriate state-level list or board.

2. Search for Previously Answered Questions

To save yourself and everyone else some time, search the list, board, or group archives to see if your question has already been asked and answered. (And, of course, be sure to track what you're doing in your research log!)

The vast majority of genealogy mailing lists are hosted on Ancestry.com's free RootsWeb site **<lists.rootsweb.ancestry.com>** and are archived, so search their archives for relevant content (image **L**). If you use the search page provided by RootsWeb, you can search across all of the lists at the same time or limit your search to a single list. If you want a bit more control over your archive search, you can use Google **<www.google.com>** instead, since the contents of the list archive have been incorporated into the Google database. When doing the Google search, you can use *site:archiver.rootsweb.ancestry.com* as one of the search terms, together with whatever names, places, or other keywords you're using in your search.

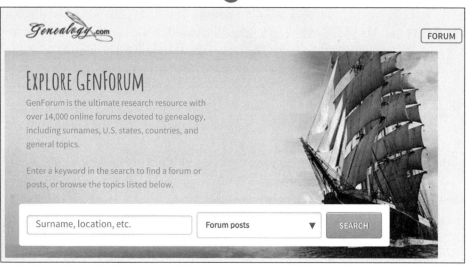

Genealogy.com's massive GenForum hosts questions and answers from thousands of genealogy forums.

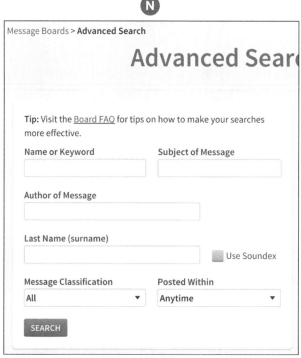

You can search for Ancestry.com message boards by a variety of fields, giving you flexibility in finding forums for your research questions.

Find a board about a specific topic

Surnames or topics

[   ]   [GO]

Surnames

A B C D E F G H I J K L M N O P Q R S T U V W X Y Z

If you already know of an Ancestry.com message board that has the answers you need, you can browse for it or search by surname or topic.

| Discussion | Members | Events | Photos | Files | Search this group 🔍 |

Search an individual group's Facebook page to see if your question has already been asked and answered.

The two primary genealogy message board systems, both owned by Ancestry.com, are also archived. The read-only GenForum boards found on Genealogy.com **<www. genealogy.com/forum>** can be searched on its main page (which searches across all the boards; image **M**) or within each board. Again, if you like the control that Google gives you, you can use *site:genealogy.com/forum* as part of your Google search to locate the posts you want. The other major message board collection is Ancestry's Message boards, located at **<boards.ancestry.com>** (images **N** and **O**).

Finally, while you can't search across all genealogy Facebook groups for relevant posts at once, you can search within each group by using the search box at the top that says Search this group (image **P**) search.

3. Craft a Meaningful, Descriptive Title

Mailing lists and message boards are alike in one way, which is also a way they differ from Facebook groups: Mailing lists and message boards let you create a subject line for your post. As an organized and productive genealogist, strive to use well-crafted, informative subject lines. Poor subject lines may cause your question to be ignored, while good subject lines may be quickly noticed and responded to. This is true in personal e-mail, mailing lists, or message boards. Your subject line should include enough information that readers will know whether there's a chance they can help you, but not so much information that the key words are lost in a long sentence (very long subject lines may be cut off in the software's display).

On a list or board dealing with a particular surname, focus your subject line on details such as locations, first names, and time periods. On a list or board dealing with a particular location, focus your attention on surnames, specific locations, and time periods. For instance, a post on the Smith mailing list or message board will need a subject line that indicates that your Smiths are from Newark, New Jersey, in the 1840s and later. This allows those Smith researchers whose Smiths are from other places or time periods to safely ignore your question while simultaneously attracting the attention of those researchers who might have something to share with you. In the same way, a post to an Essex County, New Jersey, mailing list or message board would need to indicate that your question is about Smiths specifically in Newark in the 1840s. In any case, remove unnecessary words from the subject line, such as *help*, *question*, or words that merely repeat the name of the list itself.

4. Ask Your Question and Record the Response

Once you've gotten past the subject line, focus on the content of your query. Avoid rambling and share only relevant information. Ask a clear question and tell people what you already know (and how you know it) and where you've already looked for help. In this way, people will less likely ask you to clarify what you're trying to find, tell you things you already know, or point you to resources you've already checked.

As your question gets tracked, remember to save responses using Evernote so you can easily find them later. Also remember to keep track of the source of the information so you can both cite it in your genealogy software and make contact again if desirable. If you do get something you can use, state your appreciation publicly or privately so the person who helped you knows you received the information.

Drew's **To-Dos**

☞ Process your paper-based correspondence by discarding what isn't needed and scanning the important items.

☞ Handle your e-mail using a step-by-step method so important questions are responded to in a timely manner and other, valuable messages are preserved for reference.

☞ Know and take advantage of your e-mail's settings to maximize your inbox's organizational potential.

☞ Use genealogical mailing lists, message boards, and Facebook groups in a structured way (e.g., researching places to post and if your questions have already been asked) to have the most success in getting answers to your questions.

8

organizing your online research

n chapter 6, I discussed the importance of using a research log to document your research process, and in particular, to record your research goals, project plans, and questions arising from those projects. I pointed out that some aspects of this could be done as a blog (especially if you have relatives or other researchers who want to follow along with your research) or using Evernote **<www.evernote.com>** (a great way to record and tag what you are finding) or Evidentia **<www.evidentiasoftware.com>** (to take you through the best practices of genealogical research step by step).

However, one aspect of modern genealogical research that can be tricky to organize and record is the search for online records. (Searching physical record repositories will be discussed in chapter 9.) While organizing physical objects that you can touch and move around is simple enough, online records and searches present a whole different set of problems for researchers.

One fact that makes this kind of searching especially challenging is that online record repositories are a mix between extremely large company or organizational websites (such as Ancestry.com **<www.ancestry.com>**, FamilySearch.org **<www.familysearch.org>**,

Findmypast <**www.findmypast.com**>, and MyHeritage <**www.myheritage.com**>), and relatively smaller genealogy-relevant sites maintained by other groups: companies; national, state, and local governments; national, state, and local genealogical and historical societies; and individuals. This means that the sheer number of websites possibly relevant to our research can be daunting to use, let alone keep track of.

The second aspect of online research that can cause problems for the organized genealogist is that, for a given website, new collections can be added at any time, existing collections may be augmented with new records, or collections that were once only images that needed to be browsed may now be partially or totally indexed (and even if collections are indexed, indexing can be poorly done or not include records that may be of interest to us). As a result, a search of a website today that leads to a negative outcome may tomorrow lead to a positive outcome, and you might never know if or exactly when it will happen.

Another challenge to online research is that each website may have its own idiosyncratic user interface, and that interface may change over time. This means not only spending time to initially learn how to get the most out of the site, but also spending time in some cases relearning how to use the site after a change has been made.

In this chapter, we'll identify ways of countering these and other shortcomings of online research.

Planning Your Online Search

The organized genealogist will want to be as exhaustive as reasonably possible to identify all of the relevant sites, visit each one, learn how to use it to its fullest capacity, track exactly what it's for and how it's being searched, and document the positive or negative results of each search. This may be especially important if the site is linked in some way to a physical repository, as you don't want to waste valuable time at the repository itself doing research that could have been done online without leaving home (a theme we'll return to in the next chapter). Thorough and well-documented online searching also permits the researcher to provide useful information when corresponding with other researchers and with repositories.

In this section, I'll walk through the three steps you'll need to take to ensure a successful online research session.

1. Identify Record Types and Collections

The first step is to examine your research question, as the question suggests the types of records that will be relevant. You may find it helpful to keep a master list of fact types

FamilySearch   Family Tree   Memories   Search   Indexing   Sign In

| Page | Edit | Talk | History |

Choose a Record Type

Edit This Page

Principles of Family History Research ➲ *Step 3. Select Records to Search* ➲ **Choose a Record Type**

Now that you know whether you need genealogical records or reference tools, and have selected the category of records (compiled, original, background, or finding aids) to search, you need to determine which record type will best help you meet your objective. The following tables can help you choose a record type.

Contents [hide]

1 Sources Useful to Genealogists
   1.1 Compiled Records: Choices
   1.2 Original Records Choices
   1.3 Background Information Choices
   1.4 Finding Aids Choices
2 Other Tools for Choosing a Record Type

Sources Useful to Genealogists

• Family History Library Catalog Locality Search Classification System

Names *in a record*	Records *in a collection*	Geography *of places*	Instructions *related to conducting research*	History *of places or groups*		Culture *religious, social or ethnic*	Facts *about places or groups*	Language *and handwriting*
• Indexes	• Inventories, registers, catalogs	• Gazetteers	• Handbooks, manuals, etc.	• History	• Jewish history	• Religion and religious life	• Almanacs	• Language and languages
• Names, Personal *(etymologies)*	- *inventories*	• Maps	• Periodicals *(articles)*	• Church history	• Buddhist history	• Social life and customs	• Statistics	• Handwriting
– *Query files[1]*	- *catalogs*	• Historical geography		• Encyclopedias and dictionaries	• Hindu history	• Ethnology	• Heraldry	• Encyclopedias and dictionaries
	• Bibliography	• Postal and shipping guides		• Military history	• Islamic history	• Folklore	• Names, personal	
	• Archives and libraries	• Description and travel		• Minorities	• Shinto history		• Politics and government	
	• Directories *(of organizations)*	• Names, geographical		• Centennial celebrations	• Chronology		• Occupations	
	• Church directories			• Laws and legislation	• Yearbooks		• Dwellings	
					• Migration, internal			

Some online sources, like FamilySearch.org and its Research Wiki, will help you identify sources to consult when solving research questions.

together with the types of records that would be most relevant. One good example of this is the "Choose a Record Type" article on the FamilySearch Research Wiki **<www.familysearch.org/learn/wiki/en/Choose_a_Record_Type>** (image), similar to the resource discussed in chapter 6. Additional potential resources could be identified by using Cyndi's List **<www.cyndislist.com>** (image **B**).

If you're using Evernote for your research log and you have a note for the specific research question, make a checkbox list at the beginning with each of the record types

Cyndi's List has links to thousands of genealogy websites.

you'll need to consider. Don't worry if it turns out later that one of the particular record types is unavailable for the dates and/or locations relevant to your question. You'll still want to check that record type off the list and make a notation in your research log as to why that particular type of record is a dead end for your question.

As an example, imagine that I am working on my first project (identifying my eight great-grandparents) and my question is "When and where was my great-grandfather, Charles Henry Smith, born?". I may make a list including compiled sources, census records, cemeteries, government birth records, church baptismal records, and obituaries. The specific order may be determined based upon my previous knowledge of the family (for example, when and where they lived, what religion they were), ease of obtaining the records, and so forth. The list is not fixed. I may add to it later depending upon what I learn from initial research and from communicating with repositories, librarians, or other researchers.

Once you have the list of record types and begin working your way down the list, you'll want to identify online and physical sources for that type of record. Again, the FamilySearch Research Wiki is a good starting point, as it has articles organized by type of record and geography. Within those articles, you'll usually find a chronological list of date ranges that identify whether or not the records exist for a given year, and if they do, whether they are online, available only at a physical repository, or completely unavailable due to privacy laws.

In the case of Charles Henry Smith, who likely resided in the Newark, New Jersey, area in the late 1800s and early 1900s, I used the FamilySearch Research Wiki to look for articles about New Jersey births, and found "How to Find New Jersey Birth Records." Within that article is a section entitled "1848 up to 100 years from present year" (image). This identifies three online collections: two that are free to search at FamilySearch. org and another on Ancestry.com. You can also find a link to an article that identifies substitutes for US birth records, some of which might be relevant to my particular question (examples such as records for death, census, cemetery, church, military and family Bible).

C

Births from 1848 up to 100 years from present year

STEP ONE: Find Birth Information

The New Jersey Department of State houses birth records from May 1848 up to 100 years from present year. For births during this time period try the following databases. Try each link.

New Jersey Births Databases – Includes Index Only

Try 1st:

1660–1980, New Jersey, Births and Christenings ⊠	**Free;** Name index to birth, baptism and christening records from the State of New Jersey on FamilySearch Historical Recor‹ Collection ⊠

Try 2nd:

1848 to 1867 New Jersey statewide indexes to births and deaths ⊠	**Free;** Births from 1848 through 1867 are indexed in the International Genealogical Index (IGI) online at FamilySearch Historical Record Collection ⊠

Next try:

Ancestry database: Includes Index Only

Choose one of the following:

1660–1931 New Jersey, Births and Christenings Index– use Ancestry	**Free at FamilySearch Centers and Libraries;** Find your local FamilySearch Center ⊠

The FamilySearch Research Wiki breaks down the first and second resources you should check to find your ancestors' information, suggesting potential databases.

2. Scout Your Sources

The next step in any online research process is to visit the website and learn as much as possible about it, including:

- What is its stated scope of record coverage? Beware of taking this at face value, as I've seen cases in which new records were added to a collection but the range of years was never updated to reflect it in the record set description.

- What is the source of the records? If there's an index, what on the record is being indexed (e.g., only a key name, other names, or every name)?

Clicking the Learn More link on a FamilySearch.org database's page will bring you to an in-depth article on the FamilySearch Research Wiki, detailing the database's coverage and other related resources.

- Is it only an index, or does it have images that can be viewed?

- What are the ways in which the search can be conducted?

- Is there both a basic search interface and an advanced search interface? I'm partial to using the advanced search interface whenever I do online research because it gives me better control over the search.

- Is there an online help document that explains how to format searches and provides examples?

Some of the information from online collections should go into your research log, such as the identifiable range of years and locations for the collection being searched. As you do the search, you'll also want to record exactly how you formatted the search (spellings, truncations, name variations, etc.).

For my Charles Henry Smith, I'll take on the first listed database, "New Jersey Births and Christenings, 1660–1980." A Learn More link gives detailed information about the collection, including how many records there are for each county (image **D**). In this case, the database has 156,218 birth and christening records for Essex County, where I would expect to find my great-grandfather. The description indicates that the collection is an index created from another source, and that there is an issue with the year listed for some calendar months. A separate "Known Issues" document for this collection provides details about the information and where to go for more content. Without clicking to read more information, I might have the wrong impression about any information I discover on this page.

3. Conduct Your Search

It's now time to enter data into the search interface. Generally, make the initial search as broad as possible so as not to accidentally miss relevant information. But depending upon the initial results, you can repeat the search with additional delimiters. For instance, I'll search for *Charles Henry Smith*, of any gender (in case that field was in error), born in Essex County, New Jersey, between 1850 and 1865. (Note that if I don't find anything relevant with this search, I can replace the middle name with an initial or remove it entirely.) I'm rewarded with two essentially identical hits at the top, although it appears that the first one has omitted Charles' surname from the index and has only his first and middle names. While this is only an index, the source for these particular index entries are identified as the same specific church record, providing a lead for my next set of research actions.

What if I had not found a good piece of information relevant to my question for Charles Henry Smith? I would have needed to note my negative findings in my research log, then continue to work my way down the list of record collections for the given record type and down the list of record types relevant to my question.

You may exhaust the likely types of records that can address your question but feel that you haven't yet been able to obtain enough information to support a conclusion. In that case, consider putting your research question out in front of others, as described in the previous chapter when referring to mailing lists, message boards, and Facebook groups. Use your documented checklists of record types and websites to communicate where you have already looked so others won't suggest the same record types or online repositories you've previously considered or visited. If you feel that any of the suggestions make sense, add them to your existing checklists and return to the research. Make a note in your checklist of who offered the suggestion so that, if it pans out, you can go back and thank them!

Don't despair if your online searching leaves you empty-handed. After all, not everything is online (many things never will be in our lifetimes), and new content appears online every day. But your documented online searching will give you some peace of mind that you've looked in all the right places and that, if you didn't find your answer online, it wasn't for lack of trying.

Organizing Your Bookmarks

One of the challenges of using online information for any purpose is being able to return to the same information later. When doing online research, we often find that we return again and again to the same set of online resources. This holds true for both major online genealogy record websites and the lesser-known sites run by societies, government agencies, and individuals. As none of us like searching for these sites or typing in URLs, we depend upon our browser's ability to bookmark the sites.

However, if you're not careful, you may find yourself facing an enormous and growing list of bookmarks, some of which may not even have helpful titles. Not only that, but the bookmarks may be tied to a single computer, giving you problems if you find yourself using multiple devices as part of your research.

So how do we address the problem of managing large numbers of random, poorly titled bookmarks so they are well organized, named, and available on multiple devices?

Name Your Bookmarks Carefully

Before we worry about where to put our bookmarks, or even how to arrange them, let's begin by talking about how to name them. While it's true that a website has a particular

Browser bookmarks can be handy, but they can easily become unruly if you don't name and organize them carefully.

title associated with it, we're not talking about the title that appears at the top of the page within the browser's window, but instead the title that appears displayed within the browser's tab. (For those of you who enjoy knowing a bit of HTML, the tab title is taken from the title tag of the HTML code.) It is this title that is normally automatically saved with the URL when the web page is bookmarked.

However, the page title is not written to best serve our research. For example, I may use the Newspapers.com site **<www.newspapers.com>** frequently, but its official title, *Newspapers.com—Historical Newspapers from 1700s–2000s*, is too long for my purposes (image **E**). Rather, a shorter and just as informative title would be *Newspapers.com (1700–present)*. Similarly, the main page for GenealogyBank **<www.genealogybank.com>** provides a title of *Genealogy Search and Family History Records—GenealogyBank*, but if I'm interested specifically in its newspaper archive, I may want to bookmark its newspaper search page directly and replace its automatic title of *Newspaper Archives—GenealogyBank* with *GenealogyBank Newspapers (1690–2010)*.

As a general rule, make the first word of your bookmark the one you're most likely to use when looking for the site, followed by other information that can help you determine whether or not the site will be helpful. Group similar sites together into named folders (in this case, I would name my folder *Newspapers*) and list them alphabetically within the folder unless some other order would make more sense.

Select the Best Tool

Although you can certainly set up a folder structure for bookmarks within your browser (and in some cases, have browsers on multiple machines synchronize your bookmarks so you can access them in more than one place), it may not be your best bookmarking solution.

You can choose from several web-based solutions for bookmarking, especially if you have any interest in sharing your genealogy bookmarks with the greater genealogical community. I have previously tried out Delicious **<www.delicious.com>** and Diigo **<www.diigo.com>**. Both sites let you add bookmarks and tag them so you can find them in a number of ways. However, I have concerns about the long-term sustainability of a site that focuses only on bookmarks. And because you'll find so many other ways to share good websites with others, I don't see the added value of the social aspects of these bookmarking-specific sites. Nor do I need to pay something additional just to keep track of my bookmarks. (Diigo requires a paid plan for certain social features and for more than five hundred "highlights," or links.)

THE EVERNOTE WEB CLIPPER

I already have a great pair of tools installed on my system to manage my bookmarks: Evernote and its Web Clipper. So how can we best make use of Evernote to manage our bookmarks? Certainly, we'll want to install the Evernote app on all of our devices, and if we're using someone else's computer, we can sign on to the Evernote website under our own account for access. We'll also want to make certain that we have Evernote Web Clipper installed on all of the browsers on our desktop and laptop computers, so that it's ready to capture any website we regularly use for our genealogical research.

One way to organize your bookmarks in Evernote is to create an Evernote notebook just for that purpose. Once you've created your Bookmarks notebook, visit each of your most-used genealogy websites and use Web Clipper to save the URL of each one. Edit the name at the top as previously discussed, choose Bookmark as the type of clip, indicate you want the bookmark to go into your Bookmarks notebook, and add the most appropriate tags you would likely use to find this website again. (Since I'm likely going to use this same system for things other than genealogy, I would normally want to include *genealogy* as one of my tags.)

research tip

Clip Copies of Your Material With Evernote
You can also use the Evernote Web Clipper to make copies of helpful images and photographs, documents, and articles, as web clippings include the URL of the site the item was clipped from, which can be helpful if I'm looking for similar information later. This way, even if the online version is deleted or simply moved to a new location, we would still have our own copy to refer to.

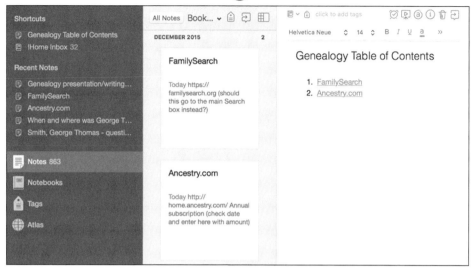

Evernote can help you track your bookmarks and even create a Table of Contents to help you easily navigate to your note with bookmarks.

After you have saved the bookmark into Evernote, you may want to visit the new note and edit out any extraneous content you don't want. You can also add comments to the note, such as the scope of the website or anything else you might want to know before you click on the link. If working on a subscription site, you can use the comment area to note when your subscription expires or what your ID is for logging into the site.

Once you've bookmarked the most common websites you use for searching, you can do additional organizing by using Evernote's Table of Contents feature (image). Select all the notes in your Bookmarks notebook (this is where using a *genealogy* tag comes in handy for having different tables of contents notes for different topics). Click the Create Table of Contents Note button, then edit the new note as you see fit, such as by rearranging the order of the bookmarks in it or even grouping them into categories based on their function (major search sites, newspapers, geographical, etc.). If you're managing both genealogical and non-genealogical tables of contents, rename this one *Genealogy Table of Contents*, then make it a shortcut so it always appears at the top of your Evernote left-side menu.

Got all of that? Congrats! Now you've got a highly flexible and organized bookmarking system that's available to you on all of your devices, and you don't have to worry about losing it if one of your devices fails.

Scheduling Return Searches

Let's return to an issue that was briefly discussed at the beginning of this chapter: the changing nature of online repositories.

If there was ever a difference between the printed books in your local public library's genealogy collection and the websites that contain genealogical information, it's that the books never change. Yes, sometimes new editions of genealogy books are published, but that's more common for reference books and how-to books than it is for family histories or books that index a set of records. This means that when you check a family history book or a book that has indexed a set of records, you can check it once (for that name) and never have to go back to it.

Websites, however, are trickier. An online collection of data can be modified (to fix errors) and added to (when additional records are scanned or indexed). Even if you've checked the particular online data collection once, the record you need might not have been there when you checked but will appear at a later time.

Online research, then, can be of a different—and in some ways, more challenging—nature than research into printed materials and microfilm. There's a good reason that some citation formats used by historians, such as MLA and Chicago, provide for citing the date of either the last update to the website or the date on which the website was accessed. This allows the user of the citation to recognize that the cited source may have changed since the time the researcher accessed it. The older the date of access, the more likely this could be.

The organized genealogist needs to keep track of the date on which an online repository was searched (or, if available, the date that the online repository was identified as being last updated). This can be done as part of the research log, perhaps in your checklist of completed searches and those that haven't been completed, together with whether the search gave positive or negative results. If your research question remains unanswered, and some of the sources you consulted were online sources that came up empty, these are the sources you may have to return to in case new information has been added or older information corrected.

But before you do that, you may want to be even more precise in your research log as to the nature of the source. Some online sources are fixed in much the same way as a print source. For instance, a digital copy of a print book can be treated in the same way as its print counterpart, and (barring a missing page) shouldn't require returning to if the information wasn't found during the first search.

What if your source is a set of document images? If you browsed that set and didn't find what you were looking for (and the source description gives no indication that the images are being added to), it's unlikely you're going to need to return to it. But what if you used an index instead of browsing the images? Because individuals can update the indexes when they find errors at many online resources, you may have reason to return at a later date to repeat your search.

A good example of this kind of record is the US federal census. If you use these censuses primarily with indexes, be aware that some names have errors that may lie undiscovered for years. Updates and corrections to the index might result in more or better matches for your ancestors. However, if you've personally browsed all the relevant pages and still have no valid results, you don't need to worry about the index for that same location. (Though, of course, you need to make a note in your research log as to whether you used only the index or instead browsed the pages.)

Once you've identified which resources you should revisit, make a note on your calendar to do another search at some point in the future. You might set yourself a standard of returning in one year if you know the site is being regularly updated or returning in two or more years if your only hope is that a bad index entry has been corrected. And if you get to that date and realize you've already answered your research question successfully, you can delete the calendar entry and re-celebrate a job well done.

Drew's **To-Dos**

☛ Plan what you will be searching for and when in online records, learning what you can about the resources so you can make the most of your research time.

☛ Track your online search activities (including when you last accessed a source) in your research log.

☛ Bookmark the most useful websites to make it easier to return to them quickly, shortening or making their names more specific if necessary.

☛ Schedule yourself to return to those websites that are updated with new information to repeat past searches.

RESEARCH DATABASE WORKSHEET

Most online resources are constantly being updated, with new records added and indexes updated to include user-submitted corrections. As a result, you may have different results when searching the same database at different times. You can download a Word-document version of this form at **<ftu.familytreemagazine.com/organize-your-genealogy>**.

Collection Title and Record Coverage Dates	
URL	
Date Searched	
Search Terms/Criteria Used	
Notes (e.g., found record, next steps)	

Collection Title and Record Coverage Dates	
URL	
Date Searched	
Search Terms/Criteria Used	
Notes (e.g., found record, next steps)	

Collection Title and Record Coverage Dates	
URL	
Date Searched	
Search Terms/Criteria Used	
Notes (e.g., found record, next steps)	

9

organizing
your research
trips

The speed at which print and microfilm genealogical records are being scanned and published online is astounding, but what has already been published is still a drop in the bucket when compared to the swelling ocean of records relevant to our research that are still offline. Sooner or later, you'll have to seriously consider a research trip to a library or archive, especially if you would like to visit that location to spend time with relatives or see where your ancestors lived.

When going on a research trip—by plane, car, train, boat, or some combination—avoid going to the repository only to find that it's closed or that the records you want are already available online (or worse: that they aren't accessible at all). Careful planning can turn what would have been disappointment into a productive and positive research experience.

This chapter will discuss how to best plan and organize your genealogy research trip before, during, and after your journey, as well as how to create a mobile office.

Before Your Trip

Some steps and precautions to take before embarking on a research trip are necessary, whether you're driving downtown to a public library or navigating a complex network of flight patterns, highways, and subway connections in Europe. Let's examine what you need to do before you leave home.

1. Research the Repository and Its Holdings Online

Be sure to do as much online research in advance as you can. If one or more of the big online genealogical record repositories has some of the records you need, complete as much of that research as possible before you hit the road; with careful digging online, you might find that a trip to an archive isn't worth your time and money after all. And as you do this online research, make notes if you find that the online collection is incomplete, either because not all of the records have been scanned or the online collection is only an index to physical records at a repository.

If you'll be visiting a library or archive, spend as much time as possible visiting its website to search its catalog or to read its finding aids. You can search most libraries' catalogs to see exactly what materials are held and where in the library they are located (image **A**). Pay close attention to whether the materials are in a generally available set of open stacks or part of a special collection, which will normally have closed stacks and require you to make requests of the staff to pull materials you want. In addition, if you want information that's stored off-site, you'll likely need to schedule some lead time during which someone at the archive can pull the records and transport them to the facility for your use.

In addition, carefully read the organization's website for useful information about the facility's hours of operation and any mention of upcoming closures due to holidays

---

research tip

Consider Hiring the Pros

Depending on your circumstances, you might be better off hiring a professional researcher than doing the research yourself. Although you may consider professional researcher fees to be expensive, they can cost far less than traveling to a distant location yourself. If the records are difficult to read or in a language you don't speak, a professional who is already familiar with the record collection or who is fluent in the language may save you time and effort. And nothing says you can't hire a professional at his most minimal fees to do some exploratory research work, then follow up on the professional's research with a personal visit to your homeland.

Most libraries and archives will have an online catalog or list of available resources you can browse before visiting. This will save you valuable time on the ground at repositories and libraries.

You may have to contact an organization in advance to access certain materials, like those in special collections or that are only available for a limited time. Note that special collections may have different operating hours than the full archive or library.

or renovations. If you're visiting a library, note that its special collections area may have more restricted hours than the general collection, so don't assume the special collections area is open on evenings and weekends just because the entire building is on that schedule (image). And even when a facility is *scheduled* to be open during the days and hours you need, the city around it may experience some special event that interferes with access to the facility or parking. Skim the town's calendar or e-mail someone working at the library/archive to see if any such disruptions might occur when you're visiting. (I'll discuss communicating with the archives in more detail later.)

Another problem that can relate to accessing materials held by special collections units of libraries is that some materials are under access restrictions. Some materials have been deposited with the special collections unit under an agreement that limits access to academic researchers, or the special collections unit may restrict access due to the materials' fragility. The finding aid for the collection, which will normally be published online, may inform you if these restrictions exist.

After you've verified that a repository has materials you want to see and will be open for the dates and times you'll be there, read everything you can find about the repository's

BEFORE YOU VISIT

Special & Digital Collections welcomes researchers, students, and community users and encourages the use of its collections in a safe, secure, and productive manner. The department has developed the following policies and procedures in concert with best practices developed by ACRL, RBMS, and SAA. Please see **their joint statement** for more information.

1. All patrons are required to register via Aeon prior to using materials.
2. All materials must be consulted in the reading room. Place requests via an Aeon account or ask the desk attendant for assistance. A staff member will retrieve all items requested; archival collections will be retrieved five (5) boxes at a time.
3. Appointments are not required, although some patrons, particularly those traveling some distance or seeking an in-depth research consultation, may find it helpful to make advance arrangements for their visit with a member of the staff. A list of the staff and their subject expertise may be found here »
4. Personal belongings, including briefcases, backpacks, purses, and notebooks, must be placed in a locker. Please ask the desk attendant for a key.
5. Food, drink, and chewing gum are prohibited in the reading room.
6. Patrons may use pencil and paper, laptop computers, or mobile devices to take notes. Pens may not be used. Pencils and paper are available upon request.
7. Patrons are encouraged to wash their hands prior to using rare books and archival materials. Gloves will be provided for handling some photographic materials.
8. Please do not place any items (e.g. writing materials, laptops, note cards, arms, jewelry, archival boxes, etc.) on top of materials. Book supports and snakes are available upon request. Please maintain the original order of manuscript and archival materials and do not remove fasteners.

Libraries will likely have their own rules about what you can and can't bring or do in their buildings, such as these from the University of South Florida's Special Collections. Learn as much as you can about restrictions prior to visiting to maximize your time in the archive and avoid potential pitfalls.

use. Many repositories will post a "before you visit" page on their site with a list of rules (image **C**). Look for what you may and may not bring into the facility (the most common no-no's will be food, drink, and gum) and whether or not you'll have access to lockers to place any personal items (such as backpacks, briefcases, purses, or notebooks); otherwise, you may need to leave these items safely locked in a car trunk or back at a hotel room. Look for any restrictions regarding laptop computers, mobile devices, cameras, and in particular, when you can or cannot take photos of documents. If you find any of these rules unclear, call or e-mail the facility in advance to clarify.

To save time, look for options to request materials in advance (e.g., via an online form). Otherwise, bring a list of the items you need and info about where they might be located, such as a library call number or a special collections collection name, box number, and folder number. This will save you valuable research time inside the archive.

2. Contact the Resource

As mentioned earlier, consider e-mailing a repository in advance. In addition to confirming information you find on a library or archive's site, you can also explain your research question to staff members. Should they respond, you can save yourself a lot of time by having them identify if and why their records are the ones you need and potentially refer you to a different repository that will be more helpful. They may even suggest additional records in their holdings that you didn't know about or hadn't considered, and you can add these records to your checklist for viewing when you arrive.

In addition, contacting a repository ahead of time can save you time in the archive and help you plan your trip by allowing you to make an appointment in advance. Take advantage of this service if available, especially if you'll be traveling to an archive far away and want additional assurance that someone on the library's staff will be available to help you.

3. Create an Itinerary

Once you have your list of repositories to visit and records to search, decide how much time you'll need at each stop and create an outline for each day of your research trip. Here are some things to consider when putting together your itinerary:

- Look for ways to change the order of visits or make use of more time at a different repository when you finish early at another one.
- Build some planning time into your schedule, either early in the morning before the facility opens or in the evening before bed.
- Avoid overbooking yourself so you don't exhaust your mental energy.

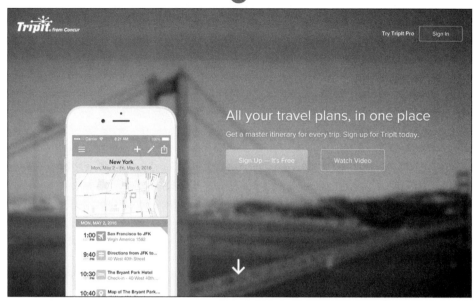

Apps like TripIt will help you plan, schedule, and organize information about your trips abroad.

- Alternate indoor and outdoor activities to provide some variety (e.g., a library one day, a cemetery the next).

- Allow for sufficient travel time from place to place, and include time for meals and breaks.

- Create a plan B in case something unexpected turns up, such as a repository being unexpectedly closed.

Keeping track of a travel itinerary can be as simple or as complex as you like.

One tool I've used for many years for all kinds of trips is TripIt **<www.tripit.com>** (image **D**). The web-based service has both a free version and a paid Pro version (forty-nine dollars per year) that gives more information during air travel and doesn't have ads on the mobile app version.

Regardless of its version, TripIt allows you to enter details of your trip, including air travel, airport shuttles, hotels, car rentals, and appointments. Because your information is stored on TripIt's cloud server, you can access your travel itinerary from any device (desktop, laptop, tablet, smartphone, or smartwatch) and make these plans available to fellow travelers or nontraveling friends and family.

You can link TripIt to your e-mail account and allow TripIt to monitor that account. That way, information such as confirmation e-mails from airline ticket purchases and

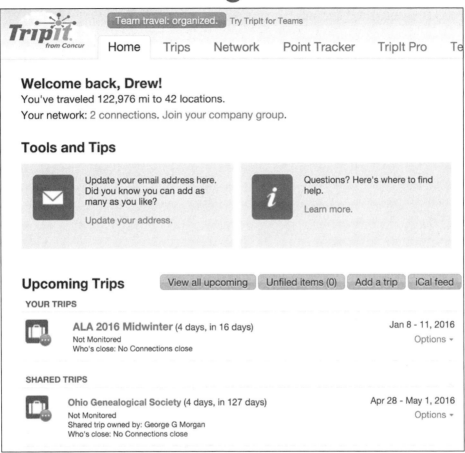

TripIt allows you to plan upcoming trips, and you can even automatically add trip necessities like car rentals, flights, and hotel reservations by forwarding e-mail confirmations to your TripIt account.

shuttle, car rental, and hotel reservations, will automatically go into your itinerary, including those all-important confirmation numbers (image **E**). Even if you don't permit TripIt to monitor your e-mail account, you can still manually forward copies of your travel correspondence into TripIt, and that data will be added to the appropriate spots in your itinerary.

4. Make a Packing List

Once you've established your research itinerary, turn your attention to a list of what to take with you. In the next section, we'll focus on the mobile research office, but what about packing in general?

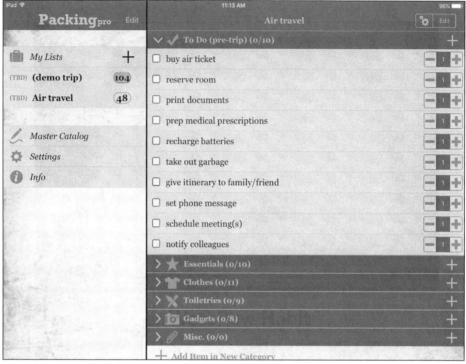

Worried about forgetting something on your trip? Apps like Packing Pro will remind you what to bring based on how you're traveling (e.g., by car or by plane). You can also customize these lists to suit your needs.

What you pack will obviously depend upon where you're traveling, how long you'll be there, and how you're getting to your destination. You may want to create different types of lists for different types of travel, such as air travel versus car travel. Set up another list for travel outside the country, as that is bound to require additional items not otherwise needed. All these lists should be set up as templates, then copied for each trip so you can delete items you won't need or add items for just those trips that need them.

Several apps on your smartphone or tablet are designed specifically for packing, although you could probably get by with a packing template created in Evernote **<www.evernote.com>** and copied to a new note for each trip. If you go the Evernote route, you can use the checkbox feature to make sure you check off each thing as you pack it.

My personal favorite when it comes to a packing app is Packing Pro **<www.quinnscape.com/PackingPro.asp>** (image), an extremely popular iOS app that will set you back less than three dollars. (Android users can purchase Packing List **<play.google.com/store/apps/details?id=com.dotnetideas.packinglist&hl=en>**, a similar app, for about $1.50.)

Packing Pro allows you to store your data using Apple's iCloud so you can synchronize it across multiple devices. This means that it may be easiest to set up the list on a larger tablet but use a smaller smartphone as you actually pack and check items off the list.

Whatever tool you use for your packing list, keep your list organized by dividing it into categories. In most apps, you can set up one category in your packing list app for pre-trip activities, including buying your air ticket and making reservations for airport shuttles, rental cars, or hotels. Remember to include making appointments (if needed) at repositories and pre-ordering materials. Other pre-trip activities may involve giving a copy of your itinerary to family and friends or notifying work colleagues of your plans. Don't forget to arrange to fill any needed prescriptions, set up your voicemail messages, charge any rechargeable batteries you're taking on the trip, and take out the garbage. If you'll need printed documents for the trip, put *print documents* on your pre-trip activities list, too.

Another separate category will be clothes, and of course this will vary according to the expected weather, the length of the trip, and whether or not some activities will require more formal attire. If you plan to visit any cemeteries, include clothing that will allow you to walk outside in grassy areas and protect you from any outdoor pests.

Next, include your toiletries category with whatever you would normally take on a trip. Be sure to include sunscreen for outdoor activities, as well as pain medication and cough drops to get you through long days of sitting and working in repositories.

Create a packing checklist category for other such travel essentials as your driver's license and/or passport, your tickets (if you print them), any printed reservation documents, business cards, financial items (wallet, cash, credit cards, and debit cards), and finally the larger items such as suitcases and computer bags. You'll also need a category for your electronic gadgets and their accessories, but we'll get into those details in the next section.

5. Create a Mobile Research Office

In the previous section, I discussed having a packing list app to keep track of everything you're going to bring on your research trip. Most of what I described would also work perfectly well for any non-business trip you might take, but successful research trips depend heavily on a number of items that you might leave at home for other trips. Having the appropriate portable gear when visiting libraries and archives is just as important as the pre-trip tasks I've outlined above. Some of this gear includes:

- a laptop and appropriately sized travel bag
- a portable charger
- paper and pens
- mobile devices

- charging and power cables
- USB flash drives
- a digital voice recorder
- headphones
- a VGA adapter and/or HDMI cable

In this section, I'll discuss each item in more detail so you can assemble the perfect mobile research office.

LAPTOP AND TRAVEL BAG

Although you will likely have one or more ordinary pieces of luggage that will be part of your travel for your clothes and toiletries, a research trip will generally require some sort of travel bag that can contain electronic devices, accessories, and other items needed for referring to information or for taking notes (image G). The size of this bag will depend upon the primary computer device you travel with, whether it's a laptop computer or a large tablet. Although I have sometimes traveled without a laptop computer, I generally find that I miss having the full-sized keyboard and a screen large enough for me to review digital documents or run my genealogy database software on it.

When I do take a laptop computer with me on a trip, I like to have a sufficiently large travel bag that will protect the laptop (especially during air travel) and can be used to comfortably include the associated charging cable and even a portable mouse. Whether or not I take the laptop with me when I visit a repository will depend a great deal on the repository's usage rules. Otherwise, I may need to leave the laptop locked safely in my car's trunk or back in my hotel room. Or you can invest in a sturdy locking cable so you can safely leave your laptop out of your sight for brief periods while you're at a repository.

PORTABLE CHARGERS

Another important item is a portable charger. These devices, essentially portable batteries, usually look like heavy rectangular blocks. They come with a charging cable that plugs into a normal outlet, and once they are charged, they can allow you to plug one or more devices into them for recharging on the go. They're especially useful when you're somewhere that regular outlets may not be handy—such as in airports, airplanes, or repositories—and you've noticed that your tablet or smartphone is getting low on power. Because you have many different models of these devices to choose from, I can't recommend a particular one. But you can generally expect to pay between fifteen and one hundred dollars for a good one. In general: The more you pay, the faster it is able to recharge your devices and the more devices it can recharge before it runs out of power itself.

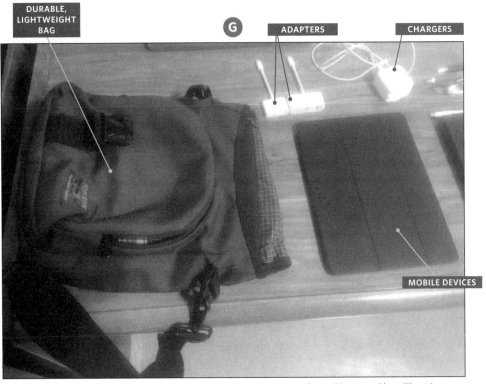

DURABLE, LIGHTWEIGHT BAG

G

ADAPTERS

CHARGERS

MOBILE DEVICES

Be sure to bring along a research bag that you can take with you into archives. Your travel bag (like mine pictured above) will likely contain a small laptop or tablet, portable chargers, and some pens/pencils and notebooks. Again, review what you can and can't bring to the repository on the organization's website.

PAPER AND PENS

There's still much to be said for packing paper and pens in your travel bag. My current favorite notebook is a Moleskine **<www.moleskine.com>** that is designed to work well with Evernote. I also pack a few good pens as well as several cheap ones (usually picked up from hotel visits). The good pens are for me, while the cheap pens are for lending to anyone at a repository who has forgotten their pen, as I won't mind if they don't return them. In addition, before I traveled with laptops, tablets, and smartphones, I packed paper copies of my genealogy documents, such as pedigree charts and family group sheets. Now, I have these documents available to me in digital form, so there is no need to print them. But if you do decide to bring paper documents with you on a research trip, bring only copies and never original documents, to avoid loss.

MOBILE DEVICES

For a number of years, my most important travel device has been a tablet, currently an iPad Air. It's well suited for displaying easy-to-read information, and I can include a

The Flip-Pal scanner is designed for 4x6 photos, but you can scan larger documents or photos by piecing portions of the documents together using the scanner's software.

special case for the tablet that includes a physical keyboard if I don't have a laptop computer along for the trip. I also have a smartphone that can be used to look up information no matter where I am (such as when I'm walking in a cemetery).

Although your tablet or smartphone may serve as an adequate tool for scanning the documents and photos you'll be looking at on your trip, you may decide to bring more specialized scanning equipment. If you'll be visiting relatives who have family photos that you would like copies of, you may want to invest in a portable scanner that is small and light enough to easily fit into your luggage or computer bag.

Perhaps the best-known example from recent years is the Flip-Pal mobile scanner <www.flip-pal.com> (image Ⓗ), which is specifically designed to scan color photos up to 4x6 inches in size. However, it can accommodate larger photos and documents if you scan portions of the larger item and use the included software to stitch the pieces together. If you use this type of device, be sure to have enough SD cards with you to avoid running out of storage for the scanned images, at least until you can safely copy those files to your laptop computer.

On the other hand, if you expect that you will more likely be scanning original documents or pages from books and magazines, you may want to invest in a flatbed scanner that can scan an entire letter-sized document at once. The CanoScan family of scanners made by Canon <www.canon.com> is a good example of this type of device (image Ⓘ).

If you feel you can make do with your smartphone, you may still want to obtain a table-top tripod that would allow you to mount the smartphone so it will remain steady as you take photos of documents.

Regardless of which kind of scanning device you decide to purchase and bring with you on a research trip, check the scanning rules that each repository may have in place.

Flatbed scanners like those made by Canon will better scan larger resources like books and magazines.

CHARGING AND POWER CABLES

With all of these mobile devices, it's critical to remember to pack the appropriate charging cables and cases. I find that if I can afford it, I have multiple charging cables, and some of them remain permanently in my travel bag. Also, if you're traveling to a part of the world that requires a different electrical plug than what you have at home (e.g., Europe), you'll need to pack the necessary electrical adapters and/or voltage converters. You can learn more about adapters and converters at **<www.rei.com/learn/expert-advice/world-electricity-guide.html>**.

Hotels (and the homes of your relatives) vary widely in their ability to provide enough electrical outlets to charge all of your mobile devices. Fortunately, newer or renovated hotels have gotten better at accommodating electrical charging and may have plugs in USB cables. To prepare for hotels and homes that don't have enough outlets or USB ports, invest in a portable power strip that can also provide surge protection. I recommend the one I've have been using for years and is still highly regarded among travelers: the Belkin SurgePlus **<www.belkin.com/us/p/P-BST300>**. The Belkin provides not only three regular outlets but also two USB charging ports, which should suffice for the mobile devices used by two travelers in the same room. It can swivel (especially useful when trying to fit it

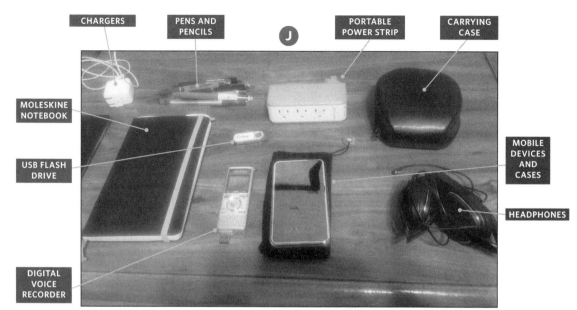

CHARGERS

PENS AND PENCILS

J

PORTABLE POWER STRIP

CARRYING CASE

MOLESKINE NOTEBOOK

USB FLASH DRIVE

MOBILE DEVICES AND CASES

HEADPHONES

DIGITAL VOICE RECORDER

You'll likely want to add more resources to your travel bag, such as those labeled above.

into tight spaces in a hotel room) and is small and easy to pack, and you can usually buy it online for less than its thirty-dollar retail cost.

OTHER ITEMS

Depending on your research needs and where you'll be going, you might consider adding several other items (image J).

USB flash drives are not as necessary for travel as they used to be, but you may still run into a few cases where they provide the only way to easily copy information you acquire on your trip. For example, my library has several book scanners that can scan images onto a USB flash drive, but those scanners also provide the option to e-mail the images to any address. If you're visiting a relative, you may find that transferring files from their own computer to a USB flash drive is the easiest way to acquire the information. The downside to USB flash drives is that they're easy to misplace and can sometimes fail without warning, losing whatever data they have stored. Bring one along with you when you travel, but use it only in those cases where you have no alternative.

If I'm planning to conduct any interviews of relatives during the trip, I'm sure to pack a small digital voice recorder, such as one of the models sold by Olympus <**www.getolympus. com/us/en/audio/digital-recorders.html**>. The model I use can double as a USB flash drive, meaning I can omit packing a separate USB flash drive.

Another useful electronic accessory is a good pair of headphones. I have a pair of noise-cancelling headphones that I find especially helpful during air travel, and it also allows me to listen to educational podcasts and videos as I travel. If you think you'll be using some sort of audio/video communication during your trip (such as Skype **<www. skype.com/en>** or Google Hangouts **<hangouts.google.com>**), you may want to pack a USB-connected headset that can be plugged into your laptop.

Because I often travel to make presentations to groups—and often present using my tablet instead of a laptop—I also pack adapters that can connect my tablet to a projector: one for a VGA connector and one for an HDMI.

During the Trip

If you've done your pre-trip work in an organized fashion and packed everything you need in your luggage and your mobile research office, you should find that much of the work of on-site research will be easier than it would have been otherwise. You won't find yourself on the road discovering that you've forgotten to take care of some matter that needed to be done before you left or are missing an item you will need for the research.

But even with all of the best-laid plans prior to the trip, you can't afford to be disorganized during the trip itself. When you wake up each morning, remind yourself what you plan to accomplish that day, but be ready to make adjustments during the trip if you get finished early at a repository or you need more time at a repository than you had originally planned.

As you visit each repository, your primary work will be looking for and examining documents. Remember that you'll need to take good notes as you search each record collection, indicating not only what you have found but also what you didn't find. Also take notes from any conversations you've had with staff or other researchers, as these may provide clues for future research.

If you discover a useful document and choose to scan it, your work is still not quite done. You'll also need to record any information you need for an accurate citation. For instance, if you scan the page of a book, remember to scan the title page as well. Also in the case of a book, scan any relevant index pages, as you may find the book has too many pages to review in one sitting but still want to keep track of all the pages you need to review.

The same situation occurs when you're using part of a printed or microfilm record collection that consists of both an index and the documents to which the index refers. Again, scan the relevant index pages first, followed by the pages to which the index points. Also scan any early pages that will help to identify the record collection. If the records are held in a bound volume, take a photo of the outside cover or spine, and, if in a microform box or sleeve, take a photo of the box/sleeve to preserve its identifying information.

Whether during the day or in the evening, take advantage of any opportunity to copy what you've scanned to at least one other form of storage, such as a second electronic device or to whatever cloud storage service you are using. Ideally, you should make it a daily habit to transfer your newfound information to an online backup area so an unexpected loss of your computer equipment or its storage won't lose all your hard-earned research discoveries.

And as mentioned earlier in this chapter, be sure to schedule regular breaks during the day for food and rest to keep your mind sharp. If your itinerary permits it, and you find yourself getting mentally foggy during a particular repository visit, consider cutting your day short or switching around your activities so as to remain mentally fresh.

If you can't complete everything you need to accomplish at a repository before you have to leave, make detailed notes about what remains to investigate so you can either return to that same place at a later date or make a request online for a volunteer to check into something for you. Or if you've exhausted the collections at a given repository but still have unanswered questions, see if the repository staff can offer any suggestions about collections you may not have originally considered. And if you do make good progress on your research, take a brief moment to thank the staff for their assistance and for maintaining the facility. You will often make their day!

At the end of each research day, review your findings and notes. If you would still have time to revisit the same repository the next day, pay special attention to anything you may have forgotten to do during your first visit. In some cases, what you find or don't find may directly impact your research at other local repositories or on later stops on your research trip, so be sure to record notes for yourself on new ideas to pursue when you visit the next stop.

After the Trip

When you return home from a research trip, it can be tempting to collapse from exhaustion and put aside everything you found for several days. However, you should power through a couple key steps while the trip is still fresh in your mind:

1. Review your packing list template to see if you want to add, modify, or remove items. If you wait to do this just prior to your next trip, you may find yourself unable to remember what it was that you should have taken on the trip but have now forgotten, or that you packed but really didn't need.

2. Go through your luggage and computer bag with a fine-tooth comb, looking for anything you might have forgotten to unpack. I know that I have sometimes discovered

things when pulling out an old piece of luggage that I had previously lost because I had somehow overlooked them when unpacking.

3. Once you've unpacked and stored away the usual travel items and dealt with the dirty clothes, pull together everything you collected or used on the trip of an information nature, such as SD cards, USB flash drives, business cards, and mobile devices. If you haven't already copied everything off the SD cards and USB flash drives to more permanent storage, do that immediately, even if it is to put it all into a temporary To Be Filed folder on your computer's desktop. (It's ok to do the filing at a later time as part of your normal filing procedures.) Scan business cards or copy the information on them into your contacts list, then discard the cards. If you've taken handwritten notes, scan copies of those, too, and add those images to your files needing to be filed. You may even want to start a manual backup of your computer's hard drive to your cloud-based backup service.

4. Review the images you have brought back from the trip. Do this in a block of time when you're mentally alert and not rushed so you can carefully examine each image and make notes that will go into your usual research process. Remember to file the items according to the system you have set up.

5. Having taken stock of what you've accomplished and found, begin a new list for your next research trip, including any unfinished items remaining from your previous trip and adding any new questions that may have resulted from your work.

6. If a particular repository stuck out in your mind as being especially helpful during your trip, e-mail a quick thank-you directly to its manager (if you grabbed the manager's business card before you left or if you can find the manager's e-mail address online) or to the general repository e-mail address.

Drew's **To-Dos**

☞ Plan ahead for your research trip by learning all you can about each repository online, setting up a to-do list, using TripIt to maintain your itinerary, creating a packing list, and syncing your files.

☞ Set up your mobile office with the right equipment and documents.

☞ Scan and upload documents to your cloud-based filing service as you travel.

☞ File documents, review results, and make a list of future to-dos after you return home.

RESEARCH TRIP PACKING LIST

As we've discussed earlier in this chapter, you'll need a variety of gear to have a successful research trip. Make sure you at least consider packing the following:

- ☐ paper or tablet device for note-taking
- ☐ pencils and pencil sharpener or mechanical pencil with plenty of refills
- ☐ smartphone and/or tablet, along with charging cables
- ☐ laptop computer with copies of your files
- ☐ camera (and/or camcorder), flash, tripod and batteries; consider investing in a close-up lens for copying documents (ask permission before photographing in archives)
- ☐ appropriate, comfortable clothing, including comfy and durable shoes (preferably thick-soled shoes that can stand up to cobblestone streets)
- ☐ maps
- ☐ change for photocopiers
- ☐ lists of what information you want to find and where it is in the repository
- ☐ business cards with your name, address, and e-mail address to leave behind
- ☐ file folders or light binders containing the necessary research to reference
- ☐ magnifying glass
- ☐ tape recorder for dictating notes or for taping an onsite translator (if not already on your mobile device)
- ☐ handheld scanner (such as a Flip-Pal or Canon)
- ☐ gloves and trowel for clearing around tombstones, plus a plastic trash bag to kneel on
- ☐ umbrella
- ☐ USB flash drives
- ☐ a voice recording device
- ☐ headphones

If you're traveling abroad, consider the following objects as well

- ☐ passport and/or visa and a photocopy of each
- ☐ local currency and/or prepaid credit cards, plus change for photocopiers
- ☐ plug adaptor and/or voltage converter (see **<www.worldstandards.eu/electricity/plug-voltage-by-country>**)
- ☐ little souvenirs or postcards from home you can leave as thank-you gifts

10

organizing
your learning

W e're always learning; it's just a matter of what and how that changes as we grow older. When we're young, we have little control over what we learn in school, having perhaps a few more options once we reach high school. We may be encouraged to spend time with a guidance counselor who can advise us on how to prepare ourselves for the time and expense of pursuing higher education. And once we're in a college degree program, we usually have access to academic advisors who can suggest which courses to take and the order in which to take them, so as to minimize the cost and time needed to graduate.

Unless you're pursuing a college degree in genealogy (and yes, such a thing exists), your genealogical education (which will not normally be as time-consuming or expensive as a college education) requires you to be more proactive than traditional learning and takes serious thought and planning. Back in my earliest years as a genealogist (in the early 1990s), I had no digital books, no online periodicals, no blogs, no podcasts, and no webinars. My options were limited to print books and periodicals, seminars offered at public libraries and local genealogy society meetings, and national and state genealogy conferences. I visited as many local bookstores as I could, looking for every book I could find on the subject of genealogy. My only goal was to have a general understanding of genealogical methodology.

Today, the educational options available to new and experienced genealogists are vast. You can be easily overwhelmed, wondering where to start when it's all too easy to spend unnecessary money and time on educational products and services that aren't that helpful for the problems you're facing. What might happen instead if you treated your educational needs like a genealogical project?

I've worked in some sort of educational environment my entire working life. Whether it's writing helpful documentation, teaching a for-credit course at a college, presenting a one-hour workshop, or writing books and articles, I spend a great deal of time thinking about my audience and how I can best help them learn what they want to know so they can accomplish their goals. In this chapter, I'll discuss how to organize your genealogical learning to continue your education throughout the years.

Making Learning Goals

To really teach yourself a skill (be it how to change your car's tire or how to speak or read a new language), you need to develop a plan to learning the skill to best ensure your success and complete understanding of the subject. Genealogy is no different. In this section, I'll outline how to successfully identify your educational outcomes.

Begin by figuring out where you are now in terms of your genealogical knowledge and skills, then determine where you would like to be. If you consider yourself to be a true genealogical beginner, then it would make sense for you to set a goal of having a basic overall understanding of genealogical methods and resources. If, on the other hand, you've been engaged in genealogical research for some time and have had some good success, then perhaps your needs are geared either toward achieving a better understanding

research tip

Make Specific Learning Goals

Make sure your learning goals reflect your research goals and are specific enough to be actionable, since goals that are broad or exceedingly difficult will be too daunting or complicated to accomplish. For example, you don't need to be fluent in Latin to decipher seventeenth-century church records. Rather, you just need to learn some key vocabulary words and know enough about the language's structure to get by.

Keep Your Projects in Mind

Consider your current or future genealogical projects when identifying educational goals. For instance, if you'll be linking an ancestor back to the ancestral homeland in Ireland, learn whatever you can about doing *Irish* research. If you're struggling with a brick wall involving finding a woman's maiden name, look for information specifically on researching women ancestors.

of a particular record type, or obtaining an introduction to a particular state or country and its unique genealogical records and problems.

You may find, for example, that you need to learn more about a certain technology such as DNA to break through brick walls, or you need assistance collecting and preserving information, such as scanner technology. Perhaps you need to study a foreign language to better work with records from a particular country. You may feel a need to improve your research methods, such as dealing with incomplete or conflicting evidence, or creating accurate source citations.

You'll need to assess where you are now, then prioritize those types of education that will get you to where you want to be. Focus on one kind of educational topic at a time so as not to be too distracted and disorganized. If you find yourself getting bored or losing interest in a topic, it's ok to move to a new subject and come back to the first at a later date.

Don't Be Stressed by the Best

It's okay to be new and inexperienced. When starting out in genealogy, you might be intimidated by experts, especially if you meet them face-to-face at a seminar or conference. They might act confident and field seemingly any question they're asked. You may even think there's nothing they don't know about genealogy.

But the reality is that all genealogists, no matter how experienced, can't know everything, and even the very best spend a great deal of time and effort trying to learn more. The only difference between a beginner and an expert is that the expert has put more time and effort into the learning; the expert was once a beginner, too.

There's nothing wrong with being impressed by experts, but don't feel intimidated by them. When they write or speak about genealogy, they want to help you learn as much as you can, but they're not elitists who are disdainful of those with less education and experience. Just as they learned from the experts who preceded them, they want to turn around and pass it on to the next generation of learners. Be open to what they offer, and you'll be amazed at your own progress.

You can also combat subject fatigue by using some variety in your educational activities, mixing reading with listening to audio files, watching presentations and webinars, and traveling to conferences and institutes.

As you set your educational goals for the next twelve months, you'll also want to think about your budget, how much time you have available to learn, and how soon you need results. Is there a particular time frame for when these resources are offered or available? If so, when can you view them? And are the educational resources free (such as blogs, podcasts, and some webinars), somewhat expensive (such as books or some presentations at a local society), or pricy (such as online courses or conferences and institutes)? Set aside a portion of time (and perhaps money) each month for some sort of educational activity, regardless of format.

No matter how you learn, take notes and reflect on your learning experiences. You may discover that learning about a new method or a new set of records leads to sudden awareness of other gaps in your skills and knowledge. Or you may become fascinated with a particular topic and want to seek out everything you can possibly find on the subject. You'll take pleasure in mastering some aspect of genealogical research, then starting all over again with a new area to explore.

Obtaining and Organizing Books

We may be in an Internet age, but books (like this one!) are still essential to genealogists, and I wouldn't be much of a librarian if I didn't own any books myself. When I moved from South Carolina to Florida in 1990, the moving company had to deal with something like twenty boxes of books. And when my spouse and I bought our first house together in 1995, the next moving company had to deal with as many as thirty boxes of books. In recent years, I've downsized by giving away many to student club used book sales, instead purchasing more digital books. My genealogy books (image Ⓐ) constitute only a small percentage of the thousands of books I own, but they're the ones I'm least likely to part with. (If I've given away any older genealogy books, it's because they are older editions of reference books that have been replaced by newer editions.) Even so, this means that I have hundreds of genealogy books, covering a wide variety of topics. Without keeping track of my book collection, I might buy a genealogy book only to find I already own it.

As it happens, I've found a tool that prevents this: LibraryThing <www.librarything.com> (image Ⓑ). While LibraryThing is not the only online service designed to help users catalog their personal book collections, it *is* one of the oldest, having been around since 2005. Approximately two million book owners keep track of their personal collections using LibraryThing. Although you can use it for free for up to two hundred books, you'll

More and more resources may be online, but some of the most valuable resources for genealogists can still be found in books. My personal genealogy library, for example, is pretty expansive.

With LibraryThing, you can catalog and organize all your books.

almost certainly exceed that amount within a short period of time. You'll then need a paid subscription, either ten dollars per year or twenty-five dollars for life to catalog as many books as you own (I sprang for the latter years ago).

Over the years, I've met genealogists who used a spreadsheet or word processing document to keep track of their books. However, you generally have to type everything about the book into the system, including the title, author, year of publication, edition, format (hardcover or paperback), and number of pages. Many genealogists would be immediately put off by the thought of how long it might take to enter all of this information for hundreds or thousands of books.

Fortunately, LibraryThing takes nearly all of the effort out of the equation. Once you have set up your LibraryThing account, you can begin entering books in several easy ways. For relatively recent books, you can type just the ISBN from the book, and LibraryThing can look up all of the rest of information and add it to your personal catalog.

This may work fine for popular books published since 1970, but what about older books that were published before ISBNs existed or more recent books that were self-published by genealogists who didn't bother to obtain an ISBN? LibraryThing allows you to add books by typing in either a title or an author, which then is searched in either Amazon or in the Library of Congress. If you see the right book in the search results, you can just click on the title to add it to your online catalog. Using these methods, you can go through dozens of books in an hour. You may even discover that you already own a book that you forgot you had!

Once you've entered your books, you can sort them by title, author, publication year, or publisher. However, LibraryThing has one more key feature that is relevant to our current discussion of educational activities: Each book in your collection can be tagged using whatever terms you find helpful (like *genealogy*; see image **C**). For instance, you might tag every book related to Irish genealogical research as *Irish*, and every book

---

research tip

Know Your Copyrights

You can legally make a copy of one article from an issue for your personal research or educational use. (If you need more articles from a single issue than that, you may want to contact the publisher to see if they can sell you a back issue.) And if the work was published before 1923, you can copy the work in its entirety. When possible, make a digital copy (rather than a photocopy) that you can add to your personal files, but remember to never share a copyrighted article with others without permission from the copyright owner.

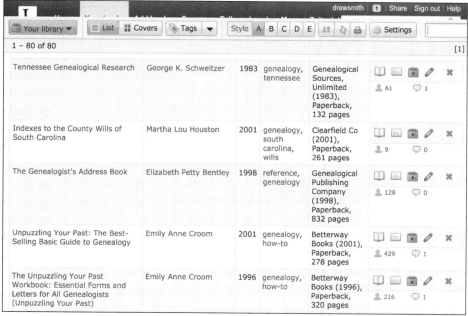

LibraryThing allows you to add tags (such as *genealogy*) to your cataloged books, making them easy to find by subject.

related to South Carolina research as *South Carolina*. You can give multiple tags to the same book, so a book about early Irish immigrants to South Carolina can be tagged using both tags. This way, you can quickly identify every book you already own on that particular subject, perhaps putting relevant titles on an easy-to-access bookshelf near where you plan to use them.

Once you've figured out exactly what books you have and have cataloged them, you can decide whether or not you need to augment your book collection with additional books (or newer editions) on the subject of interest. But before you spend money on new books, see if your local public library (or even a local academic library, if it allows public access) has books you don't own. This can save you a great deal of money, especially if you borrow the book and discover that it doesn't really meet your needs.

Also check online genealogy book collections, such as the FamilySearch collection of over two hundred thousand books **<books.familysearch.org>**. Most of these will be older, public domain books instead of current how-to books, but they still may be of value in your research and are worth a look.

If you decide you need more books, set yourself a reasonable budget for planned acquisitions. Then make a list by browsing Amazon **<www.amazon.com>** as well as online genealogical publishers like Family Tree Books **<www.shopfamilytree.com>**. Prioritize your list based on the relevance of each book to what you are trying to learn. If you know you'll be visiting a state or national genealogical conference in the near future, you can expect one or more genealogy book vendors will attend, giving you the opportunity to skim books of interest before you buy them. Regardless, look for online reviews of the books on your list, especially if they tend toward the expensive side.

Whether you buy one new book or a dozen, be sure to set aside adequate time to read the books you buy; nothing is sadder than a huge stack of unread or partially read books. In some cases, you'll need to move slowly through the book or re-read it several times, especially if it's trying to teach you a more advanced type of research methodology. One good way to integrate a book into your education plan is to set up a reading schedule. Allot enough time each week to read a chapter and put into practice some of what it is trying to teach you, not unlike how textbooks are read and used during a fifteen-week college course.

Finally, consider locating one or more study group friends, either in your local area or online, who would like to work through the same book. You can then get together on a regular basis in person or in an online chat room to discuss what you read the previous week or ask each other questions about anything you found confusing. Group learning is both motivating and fun!

Organizing Magazine and Journal Articles

Genealogy periodicals have been in the United States since the *New England Historical and Genealogical Register* quarterly was published in 1847. Nearly 150 years before the advent of the Internet, those early journal readers must have felt that new information was arriving at a leisurely pace. As national, state, and local societies came onto the genealogical social scene, they produced more journals, magazines, and newsletters, eventually joined by popular genealogical magazines unaffiliated with specific genealogy societies. By this time, the typical genealogist might have begun to feel a bit overwhelmed by how much was available to read and keep up with.

Today, although web-based communication has somewhat diminished the need for printed or even electronic newsletters, both society-based and commercial periodicals in the journal and magazine formats continue to be produced (image **D**). These periodicals, usually published either quarterly or bimonthly, are full of useful how-to articles and overviews of genealogical resources. When compared with books, periodicals have the

Journals (such as the *National Genealogical Society Quarterly*) and magazines (such as *Family Tree Magazine*) continue to be valuable resources for genealogists.

advantage of coming out on a more timely basis and with a variety of topics in each issue (although some are themed issues with multiple articles on the same topic).

So how should genealogical journals and magazines fit into your educational planning, and how do you decide which are right for you? Begin by visiting the nearest public library that has a decently sized genealogical collection to see which periodicals they subscribe to. Ask the librarians for recommendations (based upon your research needs). Spend time browsing a few issues to see if you like the content, and make copies of some articles so long as you abide by copyright laws.

If you'll be attending an upcoming national or state genealogical conference, you may find that national or state genealogical societies, together with some of the commercial magazine publishers, may be exhibiting. Either the societies or the publishers may have sample copies of their older publications for you to browse or even take. This will also give you an opportunity to see if they're selling specific back issues of interest.

And whether or not you're planning a trip to an upcoming genealogy conference, investigate which national, state, and local societies fit most closely with the kinds of research you're doing now or will be doing in the near future, and join those whose benefits include publications that may assist you with that research. Spend time on both the societies' and the publishers' websites to learn about their publications and see if they have sample issues or articles that you can view online.

In some cases, joining a society may provide you with digital access to all (or at least some) of the group's past issues. Commercial magazine publishers may provide you with both print and digital options or a package deal that provides both. You have an advantage by using the electronic version of a periodical: It won't take up any room on your shelves. You may also find it easier to search across digital copies of an issue—or even multiple issues—to locate content you want.

If you're receiving a print subscription, scan articles that you find personally relevant to your research and education, and file them on your computer in folders identified by research topic. If you pay for an Evernote account, create a note and attach the PDF of the scanned article so Evernote will perform OCR (optical character recognition) to the article and make it findable during an Evernote search. Evernote won't scan the contents of an attached PDF file if you're using the free version of the software, but you should still create a note and attach the file. Make sure to type some keywords in the note itself to make it easier to find the article as well.

As with books, set aside some regular time on your schedule to read through the periodicals that have become available to you since the last time you read. If your time is limited, simply skim the periodical to see if you want to spend more time with specific articles. In the case of print periodicals, mark the articles with tape flags so you can easily return to them, then place the periodicals on a "to read" shelf. If you instead have a digital article, save the file in a to-read folder on your computer (in Evernote, this can be a to-read notebook or note).

Organizing Blog Reading

In the previous section of this chapter, I referenced genealogy society newsletters and suggested that their production and usage has diminished during the last few years. One of the problems facing newsletters is that, as sources of news, they cannot easily compete with the spread of information now possible via the web. By the time a monthly newsletter is compiled and disseminated, much of its information is old news. Although electronic newsletters are faster at moving through production than a newsletter requiring printing and mailing, they still lag time if news has to wait for a particular date in the month to be sent out. Blogs provide a more immediate way of communicating with an audience and providing information.

One advantage that blogs have over books and periodicals is they allow you to comment on an article and receive additional information from the blogging author. Bloggers usually appreciate thoughtful comments and questions, which may lead them to write follow-up articles on related topics. If you comment on a blog article and are given the option, you may want to have yourself notified via e-mail if users reply to your comment or add comments to the same article.

Popular Genealogy Blogs

- The Ancestry Insider **<www.ancestryinsider.org>**: The latest information about megasites Ancestry.com **<www.ancestry.com>** and FamilySearch.org **<www.familysearch.org>**
- Eastman's Online Genealogy Newsletter **<blog.eogn.com>**: Long-time genealogist Dick Eastman curates genealogy news from across the Internet
- GeneaBloggers **<www.geneabloggers.com>**: Resources for genealogists, including deals on genealogy products and lists of even more blogs
- Genealogy Gems **<www.lisalouisecooke.com/blog>**: Genealogy guru Lisa Louise Cooke posts key research tips, resources, and news
- Genealogy Insider **<www.familytreemagazine.com/insider>**: Diane Haddad and the rest of the editorial team at *Family Tree Magazine* share their musings and the latest news from the genealogical community
- Genealogy Guys **<www.genealogyguys.com>**: Experts George G. Morgan and Drew Smith (yes, the same Drew Smith from the book's cover!) share notes and highlights from their Genealogy Guys podcast

Furthermore, more and more content creators are choosing blogs as their medium. In other words, some genealogy articles that might have once appeared in a newsletter are now found online in blogs. Blogs about genealogy have been around since at least 2000, but those with a more "news" flavor have become prominent in the past ten years. Today, you'll find news-oriented genealogy blogs on almost any general topic you're interested in, whether about a certain country or ethnicity, a certain US region, research methodology, technology, or DNA. And part of a good genealogy education is keeping up with the genealogy news, as this may alert you to new resources now available, new products and services, upcoming events, and other educational opportunities.

And there's seemingly no limit to genealogy blogs, as many of them are about more than just news. They may provide opinion pieces about some aspect of the genealogical community or detailed how-to explanations for using a particular resource. You may even find a well-written case study taken from the blogger's personal experience, which can enlighten you on how to solve a similar problem with your own research.

So how do you find genealogy blogs of interest? The most current and extensive list of genealogy-related blogs can be found at the GeneaBloggers site **<www.geneabloggers. com/genealogy-blogs>** (image Ⓔ). Enter a keyword in the Search box, and you'll likely find dozens of blogs that focus on an area your area of interest. See the Popular Genealogy Blogs sidebar for some of the most frequently visited genealogy blogs.

Genealogy Blog Roll

Here is our blogroll with OVER 3,000 genealogy and family history-related blogs.

Show [100] entries   Search: ireland

BLOG	TYPE
A Light That Shines Again	Family, Ireland, Irish, Massachusetts, New England
A Rebel Hand	Australian, Family, Ireland, Irish
A Twig In My Tree	Canada, Canadian, Ireland, Irish, Scotland, Scottish
Ancestor Chasing	Australian, Family, Ireland, Irish
Black Raven Genealogy	Family, Ireland, Irish

Thomas MacEntee's GeneaBloggers site has collected a master list of genealogy blogs that you can search when looking for new resources.

Discovering blogs of interest, as you can see, is easy. Figuring out how to keep up with them, however, is a bit trickier. After all, while you could go visit each blog every day or every week, you can imagine that this wouldn't be a very productive use of your time, as some blogs are updated frequently while others may go days or weeks (or longer) without anything new to see.

This is where you need a blog reading tool (most often called a "feed reader"), which keeps tracks of which blogs you're interested in and then displays anything new from those blogs that you haven't yet seen. For many years, my go-to feed reader was the now-defunct Google Reader, but I switched to one of the most popular alternatives: Feedly <www.feedly.com> (image **F**).

Using Feedly, which is available on the web for desktop and laptop computers and as an app on both iOS and Android tablets and smartphones, I can subscribe to and view updates to hundreds of blogs at the same time and organize them by major topics. For instance, I subscribe to approximately 250 blogs, about fifty of which are in the Education category. Another fifty sites are in my Libraries category because of my full-time job as an

Podcasts: Blogs for Your Ears

Let's not forget to mention podcasts, which are like the audio equivalent of a text-based blog. Because audio recording, editing, and publishing are typically more technical and labor-intensive than blogging, you're not going to find more than a handful of podcasts focused on genealogy, and you can find most of these using iTunes (or just by searching Google for *genealogy podcast*).

The wonderful thing about podcasts for an organized genealogist is that they easily fit into an already crowded schedule; you can usually listen to them while busy doing something else, such as commuting, exercising, or engaging in household chores. I subscribe to podcasts on my smartphone and play them through my car's stereo system while I commute between home and work.

If you hear something useful on a podcast, create an audio or written reminder to yourself to visit the episode's show notes at a more convenient time and follow-up on whatever item attracted your attention.

And while a back-and-forth is a little more difficult to facilitate in their medium, podcasters often enjoy getting questions from listeners, as they may provide content for future episodes.

The Genealogy Guys Podcast

George G. Morgan and Drew Smith discuss genealogy.
This is the longest-running, regularly produced genealogy podcast in the world!

Tue, 15 December 2015

The Genealogy Guys Podcast #298 - 2015 December 14

In this themed episode, George and Drew discuss desktop genealogy software. The episode begins with Drew's quoting from the Ancestry.com announcement about retiring Family Tree Maker. George and Drew discuss what programs they have used over the years, and Drew provides a history of the Family Tree Maker product. Drew and George explain what GEDCOM means and why it is useful, and discuss issues involving syncing of any kind of data. Finally, the Guys make recommendations as to what genealogists can do going forward.

The Genealogy Guys
Drew (l) and George (r)

Search

[Search]

Direct download: The_Genealogy_Guys_298_-_2015_December_14.mp3
Category:Genealogy -- posted at: 11:01am EST

Contact Us

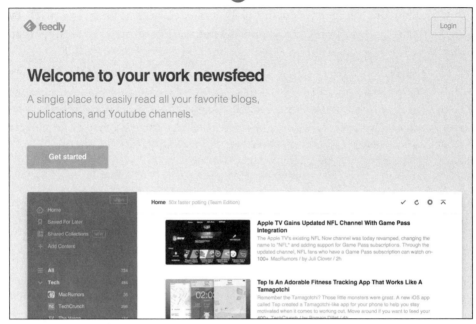

Feedly allows you to view all your blogs/publications and YouTube channels in one place.

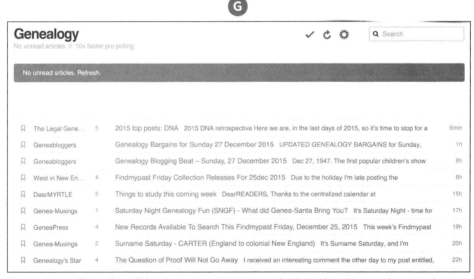

You can create different lists of blogs so you can view your saved websites by subject, such as genealogy.

academic librarian. I also have about fifty blogs in my Genealogy category (image G). By categorizing blogs in this way, I can devote different segments of the day to keeping up with different categories of information.

While Feedly is free, it also has a Pro version for five dollars per month or forty-five dollars per year. In my opinion, the biggest advantages of the Pro version are that it allows me to keyword search across all my subscribed blogs and send blog articles I want to preserve directly to Evernote, OneNote, and/or Dropbox. You can click the link for going to the blog's own website, then use the Evernote Web Clipper in your browser to copy and save the blog article. (This also gives you the added advantage of specifying some tags to accompany the clipped article.)

With Feedly, you can choose either a category to read or view all your categories at once, and the program will display the titles and opening words of any new blog articles. I usually skim through those quickly, much as I might skim through a long list of e-mails. I open only those links that appear useful, and after dealing with those few, I mark the rest of the category as read so I won't be shown those unread articles again.

When you open a blog article in Feedly, you'll usually be able to read the entire article in your Feedly window, though some bloggers have set up their blogs so you can read only the first part of the article without going to the blog itself. You can also tag certain articles as Saved for Later and view only these articles together (similar to tags or categories in an e-mail account).

Planning for Presentations and Conferences

We don't know when someone first stepped up in front of a gathered audience to deliver a lecture about doing genealogical research, but today's genealogists enjoy a wide variety of educational opportunities that are provided in some sort of presentational format, such as:

- single presentations provided by a local genealogical society or public library
- webinars from state genealogical societies and companies
- all-day workshops sponsored by local societies (image H)
- multi-day conferences hosted by state and national societies
- week-long, all-day institutes that resemble intensive college courses

The educational options you choose will be influenced by your available time and budget. But in this section (later broken up by type of event), we'll focus on how to locate these opportunities, how to prepare for them, how to make best use of them during the event itself, and what to do after the event is over.

In-person presentations, like this all-day event hosted by the Florida Genealogical Society, can greatly enhance your genealogical learning.

While different strategies will be the most useful for specific kinds of educational events, certain steps to having a thorough and well-organized experience are common to all:

STEP 1: IDENTIFY AND SCHEDULE EDUCATIONAL EVENTS. If you're a member of any local, state, or national genealogical societies, you'll hear about their meetings, conferences, and webinars (image). You should add these to your calendar as soon as you know about them, even if you don't know yet whether you plan to attend. This will prevent you from scheduling another activity at the same time, only to realize you do want to attend the genealogy event but now have a conflict.

STEP 2: EVALUATE THE PRESENTATION'S RELEVANCE TO YOUR RESEARCH, AND DECIDE IF YOU'LL ATTEND. If planned well, the lecture or webinar will have a widely applicable topic, and the sponsor will feature a nationally known speaker. But is the topic relevant to your current genealogical goals? While it's tempting to go to a session you think might be useful at some point in the future, you're more likely to forget much of what was presented unless you can put it into practice immediately. Because the same topic may be available in other formats (book, article, blog post, or webinar), skip a session that isn't really all that helpful to what you're doing in your research today. Instead, use the time you

Florida Genealogical Society (Tampa)

Serving the Needs of the Genealogical Community for Over 50 Years

Filter by Category: All

Timeframe: Within 12 months

Search: Event Title   For:

Listings Per Page: 50

Records: 1 to 5 of 5

Saturday, January 2, 2016
January 2016 Meeting (FGS Tampa Monthly Meetings)
11:00 am to 12:30 pm
John F. Germany Public Library, 900 N. Ashley Drive, Tampa, FL

Join us for our January meeting with **Maureen A. Taylor**, the well-known Photo Detective, in a live webinar titled "The Perfect P.O.P.: Photo Organizing Plan." Basic photo organization will be explained in the first half of the lecture, the rest is open to audience participation.

- Traditional Library Organization for the Real Stuff
- Three Ways to Deal with Your Digital Photos? download, caption/keyword and share

Saturday, January 23, 2016
Finding My Family Tree (Tampa-Hillsborough Library)
10:30 am to 12:00 pm
John F. Germany Public Library, 900 N. Ashley Drive, Tampa, FL

The Tampa-Hillsborough County Public Library presents a genealogy program titled **Finding My Family Tree**. If a tree exists, how do I know it's accurate? If none exists, what do I do? Learn how to locate or research a branch of your family tree.

The presentation will be held on Saturday, January 30, 2016, in the auditorium of the John F. Germany Public Library, 900 N. Ashley Drive, in downtown Tampa.

Organizations such as the Florida Genealogical Society in Tampa, Florida, host a variety of events their members (or the general public) can attend.

would have spent at the meeting to study a more relevant topic using one of the methods described earlier in this chapter.

STEP 3: CAREFULLY LISTEN TO THE SPEAKER AND TAKE NOTES. Before you go to the presentation, write down your goals for attending the event. Make a list of the main questions you want answered, and check them off during the presentation if your question is answered. If one of your questions isn't addressed during the session (but you had hoped that it might be based upon the presentation topic's description), use an appropriate means to ask your question of the speaker. Make notes to yourself of the answers given, and if more questions occur to you, write them down, too.

STEP 4: INCORPORATE THE INFORMATION INTO YOUR RESEARCH AND MAKE FUTURE PLANS. Were all of your questions answered? If not, note if you have an opportunity to ask the presenter additional questions.

In the sections that follow, we'll discuss how to make the most of your time at specific kinds of genealogical educational events.

Conferences

The multi-day conference (image **J**) is more expensive and more time-consuming than face-to-face options mentioned earlier, but it's a good option if you can budget for it and you have the time to travel and attend. If you're a member of a state or national society, you'll probably be notified of these types of opportunities, which are usually annual events held around the same time each year. While a state conference will usually be driv-able from where you live, a national conference may require flying to a host city.

Study the conference's website to see which topics are being offered and who is presenting. If you have previously read a book, article, or blog posting by one of the speakers on a topic that you found extremely helpful, you may be encouraged to travel to see them present on the same topic so you can ask questions. Note that, because conferences feature multiple speakers and each speaker is unlikely to give more than two talks in the same day, you'll have many more opportunities to encounter the speakers during the conference and ask them your questions. Just be sure to check the speaking schedule so you're not bothering them on their way to their next presentation.

Check to see if the conference will be providing a printed syllabus containing all of the speakers' handouts, as some conferences are no longer doing this or are only making it available for an extra cost. Download the handouts from the website if you can, then carry them along with you to the conference on your laptop or tablet; if you prefer, print them at home to take with you to the conference.

The state or national society may provide an app to make it easier to keep track

Federation of Genealogical Societies Conference 2016

August 31 - September 3, 2016   Springfield, Illinois

TIME TRAVEL
CENTURIES of MEMORIES

#FGS2016

TIME TRAVEL: CENTURIES OF MEMORIES

A Conference for the Nation's Genealogists

FGS and local host the Illinois State Genealogical Society invite you to join genealogists and family historians from throughout the world for some innovative time traveling experiences in Springfield, IL! Learn from exceptional speakers, network with other researchers, stroll through a large exhibit hall filled to the brim with vendors, and take in the amazing sites and sounds of Illinois' capital city.

Conferences hosted by societies can give you access to helpful presentations and experts—and provide you with an excuse for a vacation!

of your conference itinerary. But whether or not it does, you can use the TripIt app <www.tripit.com> (discussed in depth in chapter 9) to keep track not only of travel activities but also of the sessions you are planning to attend.

As you plan out sessions you want to attend, keep these five key points in mind:

1. **Have a backup choice for each session** in case you get to the room for your preferred session and it's already full (or in case you hear a few minutes of it and decide it's not what you were expecting). If you quietly leave the first session and enter a second session that has already begun, do your very best to enter at the back of the room as quietly as possible to avoid distracting the speaker or the other attendees.

Be a Conscientious Questioner

Keep other attendees' (and the presenter's) time and interest in mind when asking questions at an in-person educational event. If you're asking a question that would likely be of interest to other attendees, feel free to ask it during the appropriate time either during the session or at its end. But if your question is very specific to your own research, wait until after the meeting is over to approach the speaker with your question. Also examine the speaker's handout for additional educational resources on the topic, such as books, articles, and blogs, which may be listed in a bibliography section at the end of the handout.

2. **See if the sessions are being recorded** if you're having trouble deciding between two sessions that are being offered at the same time. If only one of the two sessions you're considering is being recorded, attend the non-recorded session and consider purchasing the recording of the other session at the end of the conference.

3. **Pace yourself by not planning to attend so many sessions** that you become mentally exhausted, and be sure to leave plenty of time for meals. If the host city has research repositories you would find useful, block out some time to visit those, especially if you check the speaking schedule and see several hours without any sessions you find interesting. If the local research repositories are going to require long blocks of time, consider extending your trip to the conference by one or more days either before or after the conference. Also check the conference website to see if they have arranged for extended hours for the local repositories.

4. **Visit the exhibitor space** to browse and shop for books and magazines. If possible, make at least two blocks of time: one early in the conference to quickly see what books and magazines are available, and one later in the conference to spend more time with specific vendors. If your last visit to the exhibitor area is late enough (usually early on the last day before the exhibitor space closes), you may find that exhibitors are offering sales to entice buyers so the exhibitor doesn't have to spend money shipping home any leftover inventory.

5. **Be social** and feel free to add any of the conference's social events to your itinerary. Networking with presenters and other researchers can be rewarding and can help you get the most bang for your buck at conferences. Of course, don't feel obligated to do so if you'd rather spend the time relaxing with friends or alone in your hotel room.

Don't forget to manage the free giveaways you receive for attending the conference. When you show up for the conference to acquire your registration materials, you'll likely receive a conference badge, a syllabus containing all of the handouts (either print, CD, or

USB flash drive), and often a conference bag containing miscellaneous materials. If you were unable to access the syllabus online prior to the conference (or if this was not an option), you may be able to take the CD or USB flash drive to the hotel business center to upload the syllabus to your Dropbox account, then download it to your laptop or tablet. If you already have a favorite computer bag or other bag you would like to carry around with you during the conference, you can take the conference bag up to your room and leave it there. Go through the materials stuffed in that bag and discard the ones of no interest. Keep any remaining items to use during the conference (exhibitor coupons, for instance) or for saving for after the conference.

Genealogical Institutes

The last common format of face-to-face genealogical education to consider is the week-long annual genealogical institute. These institutes include the Salt Lake Institute of Genealogy (SLIG) in Salt Lake City, Utah, the Genealogical Institute on Federal Records (Gen-Fed) in Washington, DC, the Genealogical Research Institute of Pittsburgh (GRIP), and the Institute of Genealogy and Historical Research (IGHR; image 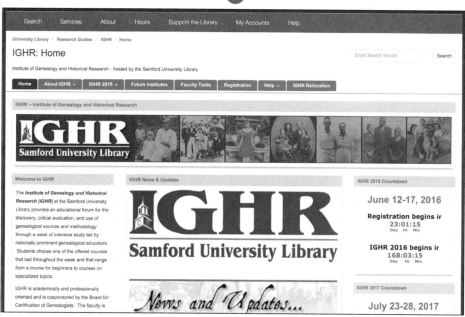), which for

While not as common, genealogical institutes such as IGHR bring together experts and genealogists.

many years has been held near Birmingham, Alabama, but is moving to Athens, Georgia, for its 2017 offering.

Each of these exceptional genealogical institutes offers its attendees a unique educational experience. For example, SLIG provides convenient access to the resources of the Family History Library, while Gen-Fed is affiliated with the National Archives and is an ideal setting for any research in Washington, DC, repositories.

Institute courses are usually geared toward non-beginners, with a heavy emphasis on research methodology, record types, and particular geographies and ethnicities. More recently, institutes have also added courses related to technology and DNA. Courses tend to be hands-on for the attendees, with assigned educational activities in class and as homework.

The very nature of a genealogical institute provides the attendee with some of the best access to genealogical experts, as well as an ongoing and supportive environment for learning among fellow students. Attending an institute is worth giving serious consideration to as part of your educational research plan once you have mastered the basics, though if one thing needs to be said about attending one of these institutes, it's this: anyone who plans to do so needs to be ready to register as soon as registration is made available, as courses quickly fill.

Because an institute is one of the most structured forms of genealogical education, the institute will help you prepare for presentations and how to get the most out of the event. Certainly, you should be clear about what you hope to achieve; before you go, make a list in your own research log about your objectives for attending. If you are already dealing with specific problems in a certain record type or a certain geographic area, write down everything you can about your research issues, so you can see if they're being addressed during the institute classes.

Make use of one-on-one time with the instructors throughout the week to discuss your own research (if related to the topic of the course you are taking). You'll have time to discuss your questions during meals and other breaks. Don't neglect using your fellow students as resources, as they can help shed light on similar problems. Write detailed notes each day and review your notes at the end of the day, creating a summary if possible.

After the institute, spend some quiet time re-reading your course materials and your notes. Try to put what you've learned into practice as soon as possible, while it is still fresh in your mind. Otherwise, you may forget some of the things you have learned.

Webinars

All of the discussion in this section has been about face-to-face educational options (with the exception of purchasing recordings at conferences to listen to at a later date). But the

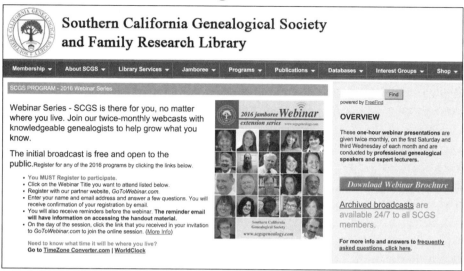

Some research repositories, archives, libraries, or genealogical societies sponsor webinars for free or at a discount to their members. The Southern California Genealogical Society and Family Research Library, for example, offers a webinar series.

development of high-speed home connectivity to the Internet has made a new educational option available: the webinar. From the relative informality of a Google Hangouts **<hangouts.google.com>** to the more structured webinars hosted by Adobe Connect **<www.adobe.com/products/adobeconnect.html>**, GoToMeeting **<www.gotomeeting.com>**, and WebEx **<www.webex.com>**, you can now sit at home and enjoy live genealogical presentations, and in many cases, view a recording if you couldn't attend it live or want to review the live performance again. In some cases, these webinars will be free, or at the very least, free to the members of the society hosting the event, and the recordings may be available for free to society members.

While many webinars have been sponsored by state and national genealogical societies (image **L**), genealogical companies have been attracted to this area and are now providing webinars. In some cases, the company may also provide entire online courses over a several-week period, with greater access to the instructors.

Because webinars need to communicate audio and video to your home computer over the Internet, I would generally not recommend this option to those with ordinary dial-up access. Regardless, test your home computer setup to make sure you're able to receive the webinar before you buy it. In the case of webinars hosted by online software, be sure to join the webinar at least thirty minutes in advance so you can download and install any needed client software on your own computer. You may be given the opportunity to test the audio and video at your end before the webinar begins. Another good reason to enter the webinar as early as possible is to obtain help from the individuals hosting the webinar in case you run into audio or video problems. Otherwise, you may be disappointed if you wait until the last minute to join the webinar and find that something isn't working right.

Study whatever information is provided online about the webinar to see how you obtain a copy of the handout. You may be able to download the handout in advance, so you can print it out or display it on a tablet while you watch and listen.

During the webinar, pay close attention to the instructions for how to ask questions. You may need to submit questions using a particular place on the computer screen (these usually go directly to those running the webinar) or through a chat window where you're encouraged to share questions that can be seen by everyone attending. Recorded webinars and presentations are not interactive like their real-time counterparts, meaning that you won't be able to ask the presenters your questions. However, they do have the advantage of fitting into your schedule whenever is best for you.

Drew's **To-Dos**

- Design a learning plan by figuring out at what level your skills are now and where you want them to be.

- Obtain copies of needed books and organize them using a tool such as LibraryThing.

- Read and scan articles from genealogical magazines for future reference, obtaining digital (i.e., searchable) copies if possible.

- Use a blog reader such as Feedly to keep track of numerous genealogy blogs.

- Determine which presentations, webinars, seminars, and conferences will be of the most benefit to your immediate research and only attend those that are relevant.

ONLINE EDUCATION TRACKER

You'll find all sorts of educational material that can teach you more about genealogy. Use the table below to keep track of the different educational offerings you encounter. You can also download a Word-document version of this form at <ftu.familytreemagazine.com/organize-your-genealogy>.

Name	Kind (webinar, conference, etc.)	Price	Date(s) offered	Topic(s)	Sponsoring organization(s)

organizing your volunteering

t usually starts with that first "yes." You've been regularly attending meetings of your local genealogy society, then someone notices and asks if you would be willing to help with a particular committee or project. After all, it's only fair to give back if you've been getting benefits by being a member of the society, right? (Give back more than just the annual dues, that is.) Before you know it, you're chairing a committee (or two) and being asked to run for an office. At some point, you may get noticed at the state society level, and it happens all over again until you're a state society officer. Then you're working at the national level.

But I'm getting ahead of myself. One of the great things about the genealogical community is its reliance on collaboration, so you'll likely find yourself volunteering your time and energy into assisting genealogical societies or projects. In this chapter, we'll discuss some organization tactics that will help you plan and keep track of your genealogical volunteering, whether you're a one-time volunteer indexer or the society's president.

Defining and Managing Projects

In chapter 3, I spent some time discussing personal genealogy research projects. Those types of projects are typically centered around finding specific sets of ancestors or descendants. They're defined according to our whims and availability, usually with self-imposed deadlines (unless being completed for a particular anniversary or family reunion), and are almost always one-person operations (even if the genealogist solicits some help from cousins or professional researchers).

In this section, I want to talk about a different kind of project: one that is sponsored by a genealogy society. Even so, much of what I'll be talking about will apply to all kinds of projects undertaken by all kinds of organizations, both non-profit and commercial. These projects will have well-defined results, deadlines that may be set by people who will not be doing the actual work, and involvement from multiple individuals (or in the case of society projects, teams of volunteers).

For example, your society may hold an annual all-day seminar, perhaps bringing in a nationally known speaker to present at a venue different from the one normally used for the monthly meetings. Planning for this event would then include:

- having a group decide upon a speaker
- setting a date
- finding an appropriate venue
- choosing the speaking topics
- arranging food choices with a caterer
- deciding upon the cost of the seminar to members, non-members, and walk-ins
- getting photos and a bio from the speaker
- advertising the event in a variety of ways
- obtaining copies of the handouts from the speaker and putting them together into a syllabus
- arranging a printer to produce the copies

I could go on, and I haven't even touched upon the things that need to go on during or after the event itself. But I think the litany above suggests this is far more complicated than a simple monthly meeting, involving a lot more people, different expenses, intermediate deadlines of all kinds, and multiple meetings over a year or more just to ensure that everything is on schedule.

And an all-day event isn't the only kind of project that genealogy societies engage in. They may agree to do work with a local cemetery, cleaning it up and taking photos of all the stones. Or they may pitch in by digitizing or indexing a set of genealogical records. They may move the society's online presence to a new website, produce a local history book, or fundraise for a particular purchase for their local public library. In each of these cases, many different people may need to be involved over a period of time.

And it's easy for these kinds of projects to go wrong. The project may be poorly defined, resulting in confusion as to when the project is to be completed or participants losing focus or interest in what is to be achieved. Instead, clearly identify your project's desired outcome and completion date. In many cases, these aspects of your project may be obvious. Producing and publishing a local history book, for example, can have a clearly defined outcome and completion date; the ongoing marketing and sales of the book are not part of the project, as they have no end date. Likewise, collecting enough money to purchase something for a library and presenting those funds has a clear outcome and completion date.

During the time that I was president of my local genealogical society, the society completed a number of projects, including transcribing eight volumes of cemetery surveys into an online searchable database, indexing thousands of local naturalization records, and scanning many decades' worth of county marriage records. In each case, someone was willing to act as the project manager.

If you find yourself to be the project manager for one of your own society's projects, keep reading. (If you're not the manager—but instead someone who is working on the project itself or someone on the society's board—you might keep reading as well, as you can suggest some of these techniques to the project manager.)

At the very beginning, it's critical to have a clear project definition. In some cases, the society's board will decide what this is, but it may turn out that the board isn't the best group of people to engage in this. If the board has a vague idea of what it wants to accomplish, the proposed project should be turned over to a group of volunteers (the ones who will be working on the project), with the volunteers' first step being to define the project and decide on its completion date. If the project is going to require expenses on the part of the society, they're going to need to come up with a budget as well. The project proposal containing a very clear definition, completion date, and requested budget can then be submitted to the board for approval. In this way, everyone will be in agreement on what is going to be produced, how long it's going to take, and how much it's going to cost (if anything other than volunteer time).

Although I've found society-based projects are among the most fun and rewarding volunteer activities I've engaged in, you might want to volunteer for other kinds of genealogy projects. For instance, some individuals find it easier to volunteer for a website that needs people to engage in transcribing or indexing large sets of records, or to respond to requests for cemetery photos or records in local repositories.

Non-society volunteer projects, because they are normally run at a national level, will require the volunteer to be more of a self-starter, with less overall supervision. There may be pages of guidelines to read and understand; these can be copied and saved into Evernote for easy reference as needed. You may or may not have specific deadlines for these projects, allowing you to pick and choose how much or how little to contribute, and how often (even so, look to see if the project does have an overall expectation of how quickly to respond to requests or to deal with an assigned set of records to transcribe or index).

Start slowly with these volunteer projects, so as not to be overwhelmed. Take on additional work only as you gain experience and know what is to be expected. If you find the work no longer interests you, look at the guidelines on how to notify the project leaders that you will no longer be volunteering for that particular project.

One reason I like these non-society projects is that I can go to them when I'm feeling a bit frustrated about lack of progress in my own research. The progress in the volunteer project puts me in a better mood and makes me ready to return to my own work.

Tracking Your Progress with Trello

If you're going to manage a project of any type, you'll need a way to keep track of the project, ideally something that everyone involved in it can view and update. While it's certainly possible to use e-mail and phone calls to contact project members and find out what they've done so far, it would be better if each member's accountability was tied to a highly visible project management tool. In other words, just as you may be using a to-do list tool to manage your personal projects, you and the other project members should use some sort of shared tool that can visibly display the status of the project and each of its components at all times.

As you might expect, many tools can fulfill this role, and many of them offer a free set of basic features for relatively small numbers of participants. Let me suggest a popular free tool that you and your project team will enjoy using: Trello **<www.trello.com>**.

Trello is a visual tool, consisting of a set of boards that are made up of cards. The boards represent projects, while the cards represent tasks (image Ⓐ). Within each board, the cards can be arranged into lists, so each list can represent a sub-project or phase of the project. Click on a list to see the tasks/cards assigned to it (image Ⓑ).

When you first get into Trello, you'll see a display of all your boards. You can "star" a board so it appears in its own section at the top, ideal if you have a mixture of active projects and future projects or if you want to highlight one or more projects as being especially important. You can also close a board for archival purposes if you've completed the project (though you can always look at it again later, which may be helpful if you want to start a similar project). More importantly, you can also add members to the board so they can view and edit its contents.

Your first use of Trello may be to brainstorm as you work with your team to define the project or what sub-projects and tasks will be needed. As project manager, you might

Trello, available for Mac, PC, iOS, and Android, allows you to create boards (projects, such as making a brochure for a genealogy library) and various lists (collections of tasks, such as writing and editing text, laying out the brochure, and printing and distributing the final publication).

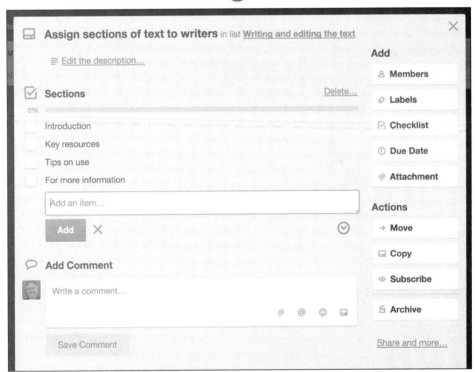

You can add several features to each task (card), such as a due date, an attachment, comments, and (perhaps most important) another member to whom the task is assigned.

want to create some lists to get started, and have your team members create cards to put into each list.

Trello's card system allows for you to change your mind as the project evolves. Existing cards can be edited, deleted, or moved between lists. And even when you get to the card level, you can decide which members will be linked to that particular card and assign each card its own due date and time, an excellent way for everyone to keep important deadlines in mind. Think of this as assigning particular people to accomplish a task. You can label cards with a color code and decide what each color means (for instance, priority or urgency). In addition, each card can have its own checklist, a way for you to decide the specifics of what needs to be done and by whom. When planning a genealogy society project, you could have a checklist for completing each row in a cemetery or each box of records in a transcription project.

Finally, you can attach files to the cards from your computer or from such file sharing sites as Dropbox **<www.dropbox.com>**, Google Drive **<drive.google.com>**, and OneDrive **<www.onedrive.live.com/about/en-us>**. If you attach a file from one of the file sharing sites, the attachment is just a link to where the file is stored. If you instead attach a file from your own computer, a copy of the file is uploaded to Trello. You have no limitations as to how many attachments each card can have or how much storage all attachments might take across your entire account (although for the free version of Trello, an individual file cannot be larger than 10MB).

How might you put Trello into practice for your society project? Certainly, you could set up the Trello account and invite team members to create their own accounts (all for free). Once you yourself have learned to use Trello, have a face-to-face session where everyone has a desktop computer or a laptop and can go over the basic features.

Do something relatively fun (without time pressure), such as the previously mentioned brainstorming activity, when you first introduce Trello to the group. This will get your team members used to using Trello and bring to light any questions they might have. Once everyone is comfortable using it, and you've decided on your project's definition, due date, and budget, begin defining the lists that go into the project. The first list could just be project reference material, with a card for the project definition and due date, a card for the budget (which you can update as you make expenditures), and a card with team members' contact information. The remaining lists could be the sub-projects; give each list a name, and include its own due date to make it highly visible.

As the project gets underway, you can move the lists around as each sub-project is completed. On each card (task), you can encourage all team members to comment if they have questions or problems.

Finally, you can have Trello notify you and the other team members when certain changes are made to the Trello board. This way, you won't have to ask about a task's status, since this information will already be visible to everyone. E-mail notifications are one option. Chrome, Firefox, and Safari browser users can also get desktop notifications within their browser. To receive any type of notifications about an item, the member would need to subscribe to a particular card or list or to the board. The member would also get a notification if he's mentioned in a card's comment or in a card's checklist or if he's been added to a card or board.

If you're the project manager—and even if you have notifications being sent to you automatically when a project's tasks are being complete—set aside some time on a regular basis to review the project's status. How often you do this will be based on the importance of the project, how quickly it's being acted upon, and how soon the deadline is. For instance, planning an all-day seminar event may begin as early as two years before the event, requiring only a monthly or every-other-month review the first year, then reviews every week or two as you get closer to the event. Then a few weeks out, you may be checking the project's progress every day until the day of the event.

Organizing Shared Files, Schedules, and Notes

Whether you're working with a group on a society's committee or managing a genealogical project team, you're going to need to share information with everyone else (and they with you). Other sections of this chapter address agendas, minutes, and project tasks, but we often have a need to share other kinds of things:

- drafts of documents
- final reports
- photographs of people and events
- scanned documents
- calendars
- random notes

Furthermore, in some cases you'll want everyone to have read-only access to the information, while in other cases, you'll want some people to be able to edit the information. You may even want to make some of the information available for viewing by the general public. How can you handle all of this?

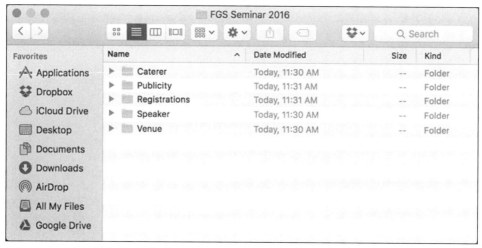

In Dropbox, create a folder for each of your projects, then a sub-folder for each aspect of preparation.

File Sharing

First, you'll need a way to share working files with your fellow volunteers. Because your committee or project team's members may not all be using the same computer operating system, avoid tools that are more familiar to users of just one operating system, such as Microsoft OneDrive or Apple iCloud. Instead, look into using something like Google Drive or Dropbox. While Google Drive provides 15GB of free storage per user and the ability to collaboratively edit documents (such as word processing files, spreadsheets, and presentations), Dropbox provides more ways to integrate itself with other online tools that you and your team may be using. For each committee or project, you may just need to poll your members to see which tool they would prefer to use.

Once you've decided upon a common system to use, you'll need to agree on the folder structure and the way you'll name files. Set up the folders by creating an overall folder named for the project (for instance, *FGS Seminar 2016*), then subfolders for the different aspects of the project (*Speaker, Caterer, Venue, Registrations, Publicity*; see image Ⓒ). The sub-folders can have short names as in the examples, as they'll be visible within their parent project folder.

But when naming the individual files within this shared system, use complete names (such as *FGS Seminar 2016 Speaker bio*), as these files may end up being copied to a different location where they would lose their identifying context. If there are different versions of the files, don't depend on the date stamps that are automatically associated with the files. Instead, append the date in YYYY-MM-DD format to the end of the file name so you'll all be assured that you're working with the right version of a file.

Avoid saving any file in a format that not all team members can use. For instance, don't save files as Microsoft Publisher if not all of your members have that application. If the file is a document primarily for reference viewing and isn't intended to be edited, use a popular format such as PDF that will automatically prevent unintended editing.

Be clear when identifying which documents are to be viewed only by members of the team (such as drafts) and which can be freely shared with others (such as final versions). One way to do this is to include a few words in the file name (such as "internal use draft") if the document should not be shared.

No matter what kind of file sharing system you use, be sure to arrange for a regular backup of the files. The more individuals who have the ability to edit or delete files, the more likely it is that someone will change or delete something that was unintended.

Scheduling

In chapter 1, I described the need for good calendar tools for scheduling your personal genealogical activities. Here we need to think about how we can best set up shared calendars in support of a committee or project team. Only one free and easy-to-use tool is sufficiently popular and well-supported to give serious consideration to: Google Calendar <www.google.com/calendar> (image D). Let's focus on its ability to create calendars that can be shared among a group of people.

While it's true that everyone will need to have a Google account in order to edit the shared calendar, the shared calendar can also be made public for viewing by anyone. Those who have a Google account can display both their personal calendar together with any calendar they have shared access to. Another advantage to this is that the Google Calendar can be displayed on a variety of devices, including a tablet or smartphone.

If you're the committee chair or project manager, create a separate calendar from your personal calendar, then choose the options to share the calendar and identify the specific people you want to share the calendar with. Decide who will have full access to the calendar, who can make changes to the events (but do nothing more), and who can just see the event details but who can't change them. The latter setting could be used for those members of the society's board who want to see how often a committee or project team meets or what deadlines have been established by the project team. If you want to encourage all of your society's members to see what is going on with a committee or project team (perhaps to entice them to join or to at least attend a meeting), make the calendar public and publicize the link to it using your society's website or e-mail list.

As you and your committee/team members add events to your shared Google Calendar, you can add attachments to the event, such as an agenda, a set of minutes for a meeting, or a draft of a document to be discussed. This may be more productive than the members having to look through their old e-mails to find the documents they need for the meeting.

Notes

The final type of information that a group needs to share among its members is notes: smaller pieces of information that don't necessarily require an entire document. Examples of this are a list of the members and their contact details, the names of upcoming meeting speakers and when they'll present, or the society's account number at a local vendor. Having this information somewhere members can easily access will save a great deal of time and effort for everyone.

In this case, I would recommend that all members create a free Evernote <www.evernote.com> account. Once everyone has created an account, one Evernote user would create a shared notebook (image 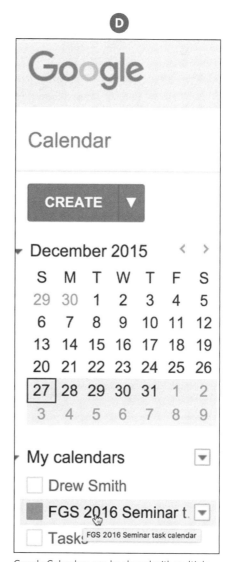); each committee or project team could have its own shared notebook. The person creating the shared notebook can invite others to have access to it, and individuals who have access to the shared notebook can then populate the notebook with whatever notes that need to be shared.

As an alternative to Evernote, the Trello tool described in the previous section

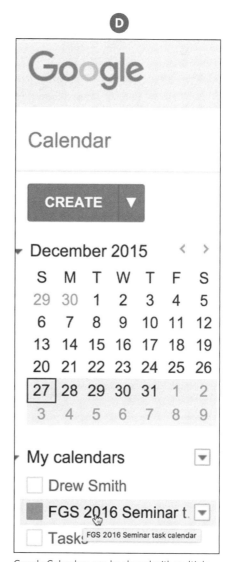

Google Calendars can be shared with multiple users, and you can even create project calendars separate from your personal calendar.

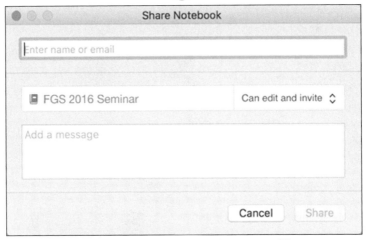

You can share Evernote notebooks with others and even assign different permissions to different individuals (e.g., "Can edit" but not "Can edit and invite").

could also share notes. As with anything else, talk to your group members to see what type of tool they would be most comfortable using, and remember to schedule some time for instruction if some individuals are unfamiliar with the tool.

Keeping Track of Committee Meetings

When you agree to be a volunteer for your local society, you'll usually be placed on a committee and expected to attend meetings. As you might expect, many of the tasks associated with these meetings are relatively straightforward and have been covered in previous chapters: adding meeting dates and times to your calendar, reading and saving relevant e-mails, and placing any assigned to-dos into your task management system. You can use Evernote to archive relevant e-mail and whatever notes you take for yourself at the meeting, and save any related documents into your filing system, probably in a folder set aside for your society and a sub-folder for your committee.

But in this section, I'll cover some more complex tasks you'll need to complete to organize your genealogical volunteering as you take on more responsibilities in genealogical organizations.

Recording Minutes

If you've been asked to take minutes for the committee meetings, you should use a meeting minutes template. If you're using Microsoft Word, you'll find that Microsoft already

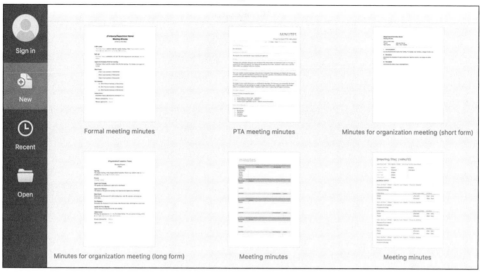

Formal meeting minutes	PTA meeting minutes	Minutes for organization meeting (short form)
Minutes for organization meeting (long form)	Meeting minutes	Meeting minutes

Microsoft Word offers a number of templates for projects, including those for recording minutes from meetings.

provides quite a few minutes templates (just search for *meeting* or *minutes* in the list of templates; see image). Look at each and figure out which is your favorite. Save it as a template in your committee file folder, modify it with any recurring information (such as the name of the society and committee at the top and your own name as the person taking the minutes), resave the template, and open it whenever you are ready to start taking minutes. Always begin by saving it under a new file name, including the name of the society (abbreviating is usually fine unless you're a member of more than one group with the same initials), the name of the committee, the word *minutes*, and finally the date in YYYY-MM-DD format. In that way, all of your minutes will sort together and be listed in chronological order of meeting date.

Your minutes template should include a place for the date, time, and location of the meeting, plus the names of those members who were present/absent and information on any non-member guests. Include a section near the end for the scheduled date, time, and location of the next meeting. If the meeting is conducted in a highly formal way, include items in your template for the call to order, the approval of the agenda, the approval of the previous minutes, and the adjournment; informal meetings are unlikely to need these sections. After you've saved the template into the file for the current meeting, copy into the minutes the meeting agenda so you can easily enter notes with each agenda item during the meeting.

Schedule Meetings with Doodle

Whenever I've chaired a committee, I've used the free Doodle app to find which days and times work best for members. You can use Doodle even without setting up an account, and you can also use it to schedule non-genealogy related events like meals with old friends or family reunions.

The Doodle Wizard takes you step-by-step through the meeting scheduling process. Give the meeting a name and, if you choose, a location and/or description. Provide your name and an e-mail address so you'll have a way to administer the Doodle poll. Next, use the calendar on the screen to mark each possible meeting date that would work. It's probably best not to provide so many choices that your committee members are over-whelmed, but don't provide so few that you'll have some members unable to select any date that would work for them. I would typically aim for a choice of three to five days. Then pick some times on each of those days (Doodle provides you with three slots per day, but you can add more choices than that if you like). Indicate both the proposed start time of the meeting and the proposed end time so your members will know what to expect. To save yourself time, if you're going to offer the same time choices for each date, enter them in the row for the first date then use the link to automatically copy them to all the other dates. (You can always delete any of the time slots you don't want to use for the other dates.)

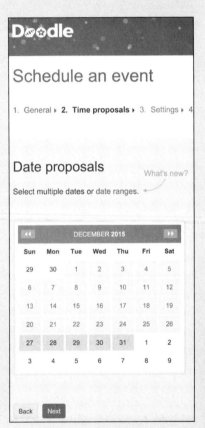

When you're done with these steps, click the Finish button to receive a unique URL to send your committee members. Doodle will also e-mail you with this information, as well as keep you updated each time one of your members takes the poll. I recommend indicating a due date in the subject line of the e-mail to encourage members to complete the poll in a timely manner, making it faster for you to schedule the meeting.

On occasion, you'll find that none of the meeting date/time choices will work for most of your group. But when encountering this problem, I simply create a new Doodle poll using later dates, and try again.

At the conclusion of each agenda item, be sure to record any decisions made by the committee, as well as any to-do items, the dates they're due, and the names of those who will be responsible for them. And when you return home, set aside time to review your minutes for any errors, and add any corrections and e-mail them directly to the committee (or only to the committee chair if that is the agreed-upon practice). You'll want to create a group in your e-mail software's contact list with the e-mail addresses of all the committee members so you can e-mail the entire group at once rather than having to enter each address individually each time.

More technologically savvy committees can approve minutes via e-mail rather than waiting for the next meeting to occur. Once approved, you can add the approval date to the bottom of the minutes, then convert the minutes to a more accessible PDF file format and use whatever method your society has chosen for archiving the minutes. This may involve either a public or a members-only storage area on your society's website.

Chairing a Committee

And what if you're the committee chair? You then have several additional responsibilities, such as: scheduling the date, time, and location of the meeting; communicating that information to the members; soliciting agenda items; finalizing an agenda; reminding the members of any unfinished to-do items that were assigned to them at previous meetings; and chairing the meeting itself. How do you organize each of these important tasks?

While some committees meet on a fixed schedule (for example, the first Saturday of each month), others meet irregularly or as needed. A standing committee may want to set a fixed schedule for its meetings, only adjusting its meeting dates to avoid holidays or other conflicts. Project-based committees, which will likely be disbanded after their projects are complete, may have a different kind of schedule.

Either way, it may be helpful to survey your committee members to find out what date and time will work best for them. I have long depended upon Doodle <**www.doodle.com**>, a great free online tool, for finding the best meeting times; see the Scheduling Your Meeting with Doodle sidebar for more.

Once you have the date and time for your meeting, remember to take whatever steps are necessary to reserve a meeting location. Then you can e-mail your committee with the date, time, and location of the meeting. Remind your committee members to bring their print calendars or calendar devices to the meeting so future meetings can be scheduled at the meeting. If you're unable to find a good meeting date and time for your next meeting at the meeting itself, you can always go back to using Doodle.

In addition to e-mailing your committee about the date, time, and location of the meeting, you may want to invite members to submit topics for the meeting's agenda. Set a deadline of at least a few days prior to the meeting for when you need to have them. Then, when you send a meeting reminder just prior to the meeting, you can include the proposed agenda in the same e-mail. Allow some time on the agenda for brief announcements and include any unresolved issues from previous meetings, as well as status updates on any ongoing committee work. Unless your committee requires a formal agenda approval at the beginning of each meeting, publish your committee's agenda in an appropriate place so other society members can see what your committee is working on. Use the same file-naming scheme that your minutes taker should be using for the minutes. This means that your agendas will have a file name starting with the name of the society, the name of the committee, the word *agenda*, and the date of the meeting in YYYY-MM-DD format.

If you find your meetings are running too long or that important agenda items are getting squeezed out by other items, consider enforcing a time limit for each agenda item and including that on the agenda itself. Ask someone on the committee to serve as a time-keeper, and remind the committee during the meeting when it has run over its time for an item. At that point, you as the committee chair can ask whether the committee wants to extend discussion on the item (with the understanding that it will take away time from other items) or whether members want to table the discussion until a future meeting.

If the committee makes any kind of decision that will require someone to take an action, be sure the item is assigned by name to the individual or individuals responsible. Remind whoever is taking minutes to include these items and names in the minutes. Use your own to-do list system to keep track of these so you can send out reminders as appropriate between meetings.

While you are the committee chair, keep your own copy of the meeting minutes as a reference tool so you can quickly search old minutes to find relevant information. Remember to transfer any to-dos you were personally assigned from the meeting to your own to-do system.

Drew's **To-Dos**

☞ Define projects in such a way that everyone understands what needs to be accomplished and who is responsible for what.

☞ Handle committee meetings by taking notes and maintaining to-do items for reference purposes.

☞ Use shareable software tools such as Evernote and Trello to manage genealogical projects involving more than one person.

GENEALOGICAL SOCIETY COMPARISON WORKSHEET

Getting involved in genealogical and historical societies can help you connect with other researchers, fill in gaps in your family tree, and allow you to give back to the research community. And more importantly, it can also be fun! As you consider seeking membership in societies, keep track of your local societies with this form, downloadable at **<ftu. familytreemagazine.com/organize-your-genealogy>**.

Name			
Website			
Location			
Meeting times			
Major events			
Major databases			
Membership price/dues			

Conclusion

It's All About the Method

Becoming better organized is a journey, not a destination. There will always be some aspect of your genealogy activities that you can be better organized about. Just as you, as a genealogist, can never say, "There, I'm done with my genealogical research," you can never say, "There, I'm as organized as I can be."

Still, you want to avoid spending more time tinkering with your organizational system than you do engaging in actual research. Don't wait until you have the perfectly designed system before you get any real work done. Instead, begin the real work, and make appropriate changes to your methods as you go so your system works more and more smoothly over time.

As someone who enjoys reading books and articles and listening to blogs about productivity and the associated technology tools, I know that some new tool will soon promise to organize my life in an even better way if I just switch to it from whatever I am already using. But if there's one thing I've learned from my own experience and from others who work in these areas, it's that the tools themselves aren't the magic bullets. Just as the next genealogy software program or family tree website won't solve all of your research problems if you're not using the right genealogical research methods, the next productivity tool won't solve all of your organizational problems if you're not using the right productivity methods.

Software tools will come and go, but best practices in methods won't. It's my hope that you've picked up some of those best practices from this book and from the writing and presentations of other genealogy professionals.

If you do decide to take on some new tool in order to become better organized, be aware that you'll need to set aside time to learn it and that the only way to become an accomplished user is to use it as often as you can. You may not want to switch to a new system right in the middle of one of your existing research projects. But if you're thinking of starting a brand-new project, its beginning may be the ideal time to take on a new tool. (As it happens, I did that with the writing of this book.)

Finally, whether you're a genealogy hobbyist or a paid genealogical professional, I hope you'll recognize that the goal here is not to prove to yourself and others how organized you are. Instead, the goal is to accomplish more of the things that bring you joy as you conduct research and other genealogy-related activities. If you're not having fun, why do it?

Oh—and if you got even one useful idea out of this book, would you let me know? I'm especially interested in knowing which chapters and sections were especially useful and worked best for you. Drop me an e-mail at *drew@ahaseminars.com* and share your story with me.

Now, you'll have to excuse me while I go to work on that huge box of unfiled papers sitting in the corner of my home office!

—Drew Smith

appendix

All organized genealogists rely on forms to keep track of their many ancestors and the facts about their lives. You've encountered some forms in individual chapters throughout the book, but this section has some other useful genealogy forms you can use in your research as either forms or as templates for programs like Evernote <www.evernote.com>. As with the other worksheets found throughout the book, you can find downloadable versions of the worksheets that follow online at <ftu.familytreemagazine.com/organize-your-genealogy>.

In this section, you'll find:

- an Ancestral Village Worksheet to record what you know about your ancestors' hometown
- an Ancestor Worksheet to record information about individual ancestors
- a Five-Generation Ancestor Chart to take your family tree back to your great-great-grandparents
- a Family Group Sheet to record basic information about individual family units
- a Genealogy Conference Day Planner to plan your time at multiday educational events like conferences

ANCESTRAL VILLAGE WORKSHEET

Town/village name (in English)	
Names in other applicable languages	
Other historical names (note years of use)	
Geographic coordinates (if known)	
Local government website/contact info	
Date established/your ancestors lived here	
Primary language(s) (note years if applicable)	
Primary religion(s) (note years if applicable)	
Modern county, state, country, etc.	
Historical kingdom, province, state, county, duchy, etc.	
Church parishes the town belonged to	
Governmental seat for the town's region	
Major geological features (river, mountains, etc.)	
Timeline: Note changes in governing authority, boundary changes, major events, etc.	
Gazetteer/other sources used (include page numbers)	

Full Name (maiden name for women): _____

Social Security Number: _____

Nicknames and Alternate Names : _____

Surname Spelling Variations: _____

Birth and Baptism

Birth Date: _____ Birth Place: _____

Baptism Date: _____ Baptism Place: _____

Marriage(s) and Divorce(s)

Name of Spouse(s)	Marriage Date(s)	Marriage Place(s)

Name of Spouse(s)	Divorce Date(s)	Divorce Place(s)

Death

Death Date: _____ Death Place: _____

Burial Date: _____ Burial Church/Place: _____

Obituary Date(s) and Newspaper(s): _____

Military Service

Conflict (if applicable)	Unit	Dates/Years

Migration

From	To	Departure/ Arrival Dates	Companion(s)	Ship (if applicable)

Personal Information

Schools Attended: _____

Religion Church(es) Attended: _____

Hobbies Club Memberships: _____

Children

Child's Name	Birth Date	Birthplace	Other Parent

Friends, Witnesses, and Neighbors to Research

Name	Relationship

APPENDIX

FIVE-GENERATION ANCESTOR CHART

Chart # _____
1 on this chart = _____ on chart # _____

see chart #

16

17

18

19

20

21

22

23

24

25

26

27

28

29

30

31

8
birth date and place
marriage date and place
death date and place

9
birth date and place
death date and place

10
birth date and place
marriage date and place
death date and place

11
birth date and place
death date and place

12
birth date and place
death date and place

13
birth date and place
marriage date and place
death date and place

14
birth date and place
death date and place

15
birth date and place
marriage date and place
death date and place

4
birth date and place
marriage date and place
death date and place

5
birth date and place
death date and place

6
birth date and place
marriage date and place
death date and place

7
birth date and place
death date and place

2
birth date and place
marriage date and place
death date and place

1
birth date and place
marriage date and place
death date and place
spouse

3
birth date and place
death date and place

©2011 FAMILY TREE MAGAZINE

FAMILY GROUP SHEET

of the _____ Family

	Source #		Source #
Full Name of Husband		Birth Date and Place	
His Father		Marriage Date and Place	
His Mother with Maiden Name		Death Date and Place Burial	
Full Name of Wife			
Her Father		Birth Date and Place	
Her Mother with Maiden Name		Death Date and Place Burial	
Other Spouses		Marriage Date and Place	

Children of This Marriage	Birth Date and Place	Death Date, Place and Burial	Marriage Date, Place and Spouse

Day 1

Breakfast Plan	
Morning Sessions	
Lunch Plan	
Afternoon Sessions	
Dinner/Evening Plans	
Booths to Visit	

Day 2

Breakfast Plan	
Morning Sessions	
Lunch Plan	
Afternoon Sessions	
Dinner/Evening Plans	
Booths to Visit	

Day 3

Breakfast Plan	
Morning Sessions	
Lunch Plan	
Afternoon Sessions	
Dinner/Evening Plans	
Booths to Visit	

Day 4

Breakfast Plan	
Morning Sessions	
Lunch Plan	
Afternoon Sessions	
Dinner/Evening Plans	
Booths to Visit	

index

The Accidental Genealogist, 72

adapters (electrical), 173

Alzo, Liz, 72

Amazon.com, 185

Amazon Cloud Drive, 98

Ancestry.com, 122, 144, 145, 147, 151

Ancestry Insider (blog), 189

Ancestry Message Boards, 141

annual reviews, 54–55

Apple iCloud, 20, 98

Apple Mail, 132

apps, 61

    calendar, 20–21

    computer, 61

    health, 22

    mind-mapping, 63–65

    notes, 61–62

    to-do, 46–52

    tracking habits, 15

    travel, 19

    travel preparation, 168

archival repositories, 91

Asana, 47

automatic signatures, 135–136

Backblaze, 100

backups, 125

    online systems, 100–103

    scheduling, 100–102

Belkin Surge Plus, 173–174

binders, 92–93

blog reading

    organizing, 188–189

    tools for, 190

blogs, 110–111, 147

    genealogy, 189–190

bookmarks

    naming, 154–155

    tools for organizing, 155–156

books, 33

    acquiring, 185–186

    organizing, 182–186

brainstorming, 63–67

Brandi, Ralph, 110

breaks

    need for, 21–22, 67

    while traveling, 176

calendaring activities, 18

calendars, 18–21

    plotting tasks on, 52–54

CanoScan scanners, 172

Carbonite, 100

case studies, subdividing projects, 41–44

chargers, 31, 169–170, 173–174

charts, 122–123

checklists, 19

    genealogy workspace, 35

Clooz, 117

cloud-based filing system, 130

cloud-based storage, 18, 61, 69–69, 97–99, 125

Coggle, 63–67

collaboration, 64, 98

    with Evernote, 80–81

    tracking, 45

color-coding, 93

committee meetings

    chairing a committee, 217–218

    scheduling, 216

    taking minutes, 214–215

communication organization

    e-mail, 131–140

    Facebook, 140

    mailing lists, 140–146

    message boards, 140

    paper mail, 129–130

computer apps, 61

computer desks, 27-28

computer displays, 32

conferences, 196-199

converters (electrical),173

copyright issues, 184

corkboards, 33

CrashPlan, 100-102

Cyndi's List, 149-150

d'Aboville System, 89

daily planner, 45

Danko, Stave, 110

data, privatizing, 61

deadlines, 40

Delicious, 156

descendants, identifying, 38

diet, 11

digital copies, 184

digital file name convention tracker, 104

digital voice recorders, 58, 60-62, 174

Diigo, 156

dining rooms, 27

documents, preserving, 91

Doodle, 216

Dragon applications, 62

drawers, 28

Dropbox, 19, 98-99, 102-103, 130

Eastman's Online Genealogy Newsletter (blog), 189

electricity, 30-31

electronic filing systems, 90, 94-97

    backing up files, 100-103

    naming files, 95-96

    selection of devices, 94

e-mail

    automatic signatures, 135-136

    desktop software, 132

    filters for, 19, 138-139

    labels, 136-138

    notifications, 134-135

    selecting an address, 131

    sorting, 139-40

    useful account settings and features, 132-133

emotional needs, 11

Evernote, 19, 58-59

    basics, 68-73

    collaboration, 80-81

    data storage and limits, 69

    for document filing, 130

    dos and don'ts, 77-81

    keeping track of notes with, 64

    Moleskine pages, 59

    notebooks, 73-75, 77-79

use for notes, 213

    organizing articles in, 188

    organizing in, 73-77

    use for packing template, 168

    personal use of, 61

    recording responses in, 146

    as research log, 112-13, 147, 149

    shortcuts, 80

    smart searches, 80

    sorting e-mail with, 139-140

    stacks, 78-79

    table of contents (TOC), 76, 157

    tags, 75, 77, 79

    types of content, 69-71

    Web Clipper, 71-73, 113, 139, 156-157

Evernote organization worksheet, 82

Evidentia, 114-116

    as research log, 147

experts

    hiring, 162

    learning from, 181

external hard drive, 125

Facebook, 64

Facebook groups, 113, 140-143

family charts, as gifts, 38

family events, 38-39

Family History Library, 200

family history publication, 39

Family Tree Books, 186

Family Tree Builder, 116, 118, 121

Family Tree Maker, 118

family trees, 38–39

FamilySearch, 122, 185

FamilySearch.org, 147, 151

FamilySearch Research Wiki, 108, 149–152

feed readers, 190

Feedly, 190, 192–193

file folders, 92–93

file names, 95–96

file organization

    backing up electronic files, 100–103

    cloud-based system, 97–99

    electronic filing systems, 90, 94–97

    organizational schemes, 84–89

    paper-based systems, 28, 89–93

file sharing, 98, 211–212

    scheduling, 212-13

files. *See also* file organization; file sharing

    automatic backup of 18

    synchronization of, 102

filters, for e-mail, 19, 138–139

Findmypast, 148

flash drives, 61, 94, 174

Flip-Pal mobile scanner, 172

foreign languages, 38

furniture, 25, 27-28, 93

GeneaBloggers (blog), 189–190

Geneablogy (blog), 110

Genealogical Institute on Federal Records (Gen-Fed), 199–200

genealogical institutes, 199–200

genealogical projects, and sub-projects, 41–44

Genealogical Research Institute of Pittsburgh (GRIP), 199

Genealogical Society Comparison Worksheet, 219

genealogical society, 39

genealogical sub-project, 41

genealogical subscriptions, auto-renewal for, 18

Genealogy.com, 144–145

Genealogy Gems (blog), 189

Genealogy Guys (blog), 189

Genealogy Guys (podcast), 191

Genealogy Insider (blog), 189

genealogy periodicals, 186–188

genealogy society newsletters, 186–188

genealogy software

    available programs, 116–119

    backing up your research, 125

    identifying new leads and hints, 121–122

    preventing research errors, 120

    recording your findings, 118–120

    visualizing your data, 122–125

genealogy websites, 147–148

generational sub-projects, 41

GenForum, 144–145

GenSmarts, 117

geographical sub-projects, 41

Gmail, 132–134

    labels in, 136–138

goal organization

    creating to-do lists, 45–47

    identifying goals, 37–39

    monitoring progress, 54–55

    subdividing projects, 39–44

    using a calendar, 52–54

goal planning worksheet, 56

goals

    breaking down, 39–41

    identifying, 37–38

    for learning, 180–182

    and to-do lists, 45–47

Google Calendar, 20–21, 212-13

Google Drive, 19, 98

    mind maps in, 63

Google Hangouts, 175, 201

Google's Blogger, 111

GRIP (Genealogical Research Institute of Pittsburgh), 199

habits, 12
    apps for tracking, 15
    chart for tracking, 23
    paper workflow, 14
HDMI connectors, 175
headphones, 174-175
health apps, 22
Henry System, 89
hints, 121-122
How to Archive Family Keepsakes (Levenick), 91
How to Archive Family Photos (Levenick), 91
How to Use Evernote for Genealogy (Scott), 68

iCloud Calendar, 20
idea organization
    with Coggle, 64-67
    with Evernote, 67-81
    mobile and computer apps, 61-62
    paper notebooks, 59-60
    using mind maps, 63-64
    voice recorders, 60-61
ideas, recording, 59
IFTTT, 19
Institute of Genealogy and Historical Research (IGHR), 199-200
internet connection, 31
Internet research. *See also* online research organization
    using bookmarks, 154-157
    conducting your search, 153-154
    identifying record types and collections, 148-150
    scheduling return searches, 158-159
    scouting your sources, 152-153
interviews, 174

journal articles, 186-188
journals, 59. *See also* genealogy periodicals

label printers, 34
labels, 34, 136-137
laptop and travel bag, 169-170
learning organization
    blog reading, 188-193

books, 182-186
conferences, 196-199
genealogical institutes,199-200
goals, 180-182
magazine and journal articles, 186-188
presentations,194-196
webinars, 200-202
Legacy Family Tree, 116, 118
Levenick, Denise May, 91
libraries, 39, 164
LibraryThing, 182-184
lighting, 25, 31-32
lists, 45-47, 122-123

magazine articles, 186-188
mail. *See* e-mail; paper mail
mailing lists, 113, 140-141, 143
meetings, 214-216
    minutes of, 214-215
    notes from, 59
mental wellness, 11
message boards, 113, 140-141, 143-144
Microsoft Office Suite, 18
Microsoft OneDrive, 98
Microsoft OneNote, 67-68
Microsoft Outlook, 18, 10, 132
mind maps, 63-67
    sharing, 64
mobile apps. *See* apps
mobile devices, 31, 48, 61, 94-95, 97-99, 169, 171-172
mobile research office, 169-175
modems, 31
Modified Henry System, 89
Modified Register System (NGSQ System) 88-89
Moleskine notebooks (Evernote), 59
monthly reviews, 55
Morgan, George G., 189
Mozy, 100
MyHeritage, 121, 122, 148

National Archives, 200

Newspapers.com, 155

NGSQ System (Modified Register System), 88–89

note organization

    with Coggle, 64–67

    with Evernote, 67–81

    mobile and computer apps, 61–62

    paper notebooks, 59–60

    using mind maps, 63–64

    voice recorders, 60–61

notebooks, 58–60

notes, 213 –214

    organizing, 58–59

    recording, 59

Office 365 Home, 18

OmniFocus

    completing and recording your task, 51

    defining sub-projects and tasks, 49–51

    downloading, 46–48

    setting up projects and folders, 49

online backup systems, 100–103

online catalogs, 163

online education tracker, 203

online research organization. *See also* Internet research

    challenges, 148

    organizing bookmarks, 154–157

    planning, 148–154

    scheduling return searches, 158–159

online storage, 18. *See also* cloud-based storage

online websites, checklist for, 19

organizational schemes

    Ahnentafel system, 84–87

    alternatives to the number system, 87

    other numbering systems, 87–89

packing, 167–175

packing list, 167–169

    for research trip, 178

    reviewing template for, 176

Packing List (app), 168

Packing Pro, 168–169

paper and pens, 169, 171

paper mail, 129–130

paper workflow habit, 14

paper-based filing systems, 28, 89–93

    archiving materials, 91–92

patience, 12–15

Personal Ancestral File (PAF), 118

photocopies, 184

photos, converting to text, 59

podcasts, 191

power cables, 173–174

power strip, portable, 173–174

presentations, 193–196

print subscriptions, 188

printers, 32–33

progress, monitoring, 54–55

progress review worksheet, 57

projectors, 175

projects, breaking down, 39

questions, online

    asking and recording response, 146

    deciding where to ask, 141–143

    searching for previously answered, 143–145

    subject lines for, 145–146

Register System, 88

relatives, interviewing, 174

Remember The Milk, 47

reports, 122–123

Research Database Worksheet, 160

research

    hiring professionals, 162

    preventing errors in, 120

research habit tracker, 23

research logs, 140, 147

    keeping track of correspondence, 130

    blogs, 110–111, 147

    Evernote, 112–13, 147, 149

    Evidentia, 114–116, 147

research planning worksheet, 126

research process

articulating questions, 106-107

drawing conclusions, 109-110

identifying and investigating sources, 106-108

research process organization

genealogy software, 116-125

maintaining a research log, 110-116

understanding the research process, 106-110

research trip organization. *See also* travel preparation

before your trip, 162-175

during the trip, 175-176

after the trip, 176-177

research trip packing list, 178

ResearchTies, 117

Reunion, 118

RootsMagic, 116, 118, 121-124

Rootsmithing (blog), 110

RootsWeb lists, 141-143

routine, 12-13

safe-deposit boxes, 92

Salt Lake Institute of Genealogy (SLIG), 199-200

Samford University, 199-200

scanning, 175

scanning equipment, 32, 172

scheduling, 211-12

self-organization

automating your workflow, 17-19

avoiding routines, 12-13

using calendars, 19-21

creating habits, 15

mental wellness, 11

simplifying your workspace, 16-17

taking breaks, 21-22

shelf space, 28-29

shredders, 33

Skype, 18, 175

sleep, 11

SLIG (Salt Lake Institute of Genealogy), 199-200

smartphones, 61, 172. *See also* mobile devices

Smith, Drew, 189

Snippets feature (Gmail), 134-135

social networking, 140. *See also* questions, online

software. *See also* genealogy software

for e-mail, 132

for information processing, 67-68 (*see also* Evernote)

for organizing notes, 58

software comparison worksheet, 127

space organization

alternative spaces, 25-27

computer displays, 32

electricity, 30-31

furniture, 27-28

genealogy rooms, 25

internet connection, 31

lighting, 31-32

other equipment, 33-34

scanners and printers, 32-33

spam, 137-138

special collections, 163-164

Steve's Genealogy Blog, 110

storage space, 29-30

subject lines, 145-146

surge protectors, 30

surnames, selection of, 37-38

tablets, 61, 171-172. *See also* mobile devices

taking breaks, 21-22, 67, 176

tasks

plotting on a calendar, 52-54

tracking, 48

time management, 17-18

calendars, 18-21, 52-54

daily planners, 20, 45

to-do lists, 45-47

apps for, 46-47

Todoist, 47

Toodledo, 47

travel apps, 19

travel preparation. *See also* research trip organization
    contacting the resource, 165
    creating an itinerary, 165-167
    packing list, 167-169
    research the repository online, 162
Trello, 207-210, 213-14
triggers, 13-15, 45
TripIt, 166-167
Twitter, 19, 64
typos, 120

uninterruptible power supply (UPS), 30
United States Record Selection Table, 108-109
unpacking, 176-177
USB cables, 173
USB flash drives, 61, 94, 174

VGA connectors, 175
voice recognition technology, 62
voice recorders, digital, 60-62, 174
volunteering organization
    defining and managing projects, 204-207
    organizing shared files and notes, 210-211
    Trello, 207-210

Web Clipper (Evernote), 71-73, 113, 139, 156-157
webinars, 200-202
websites, genealogy, 147-148
weekly reviews, 55
whiteboards, 33
Wi-Fi signal, 31
Willard, Jim, 110
Willard, Terry, 110
workflow
    automating, 17-21
    paper, 14
worksheets
    Evernote organization, 82
    genealogical society comparison, 219
    for goal planning, 56
    for progress review, 57

research database, 160
research planning, 126
software comparison, 127-128
workspace. *See also* mobile research office; space organization
    alternative spaces, 25-26
    checklist for, 35
    genealogy rooms, 25
    perfect, 25-27
    rooms for, 26-27
    simplifying, 16-17
Wunderlist, 47

Zapier, 19

About the Author

Drew Smith is a librarian at the University of South Florida Tampa Library and has an extensive career in education, information technology, and genealogy. He has written numerous articles for national genealogy magazines, especially on the topic of using technology for genealogical research. He is co-host of *The Genealogy Guys Podcast*, which was named one of the best genealogy blogs or websites four times by *Family Tree Magazine*. His previous books include *Advanced Genealogy Research Techniques* (McGraw-Hill Education, 2013) and *Social Networking for Genealogists* (Genealogical Publishing Company, 2009). He lives near Tampa, Florida, with his husband, George, and a number of cats.

dedication

This book is dedicated to one of the most organized people I've ever met: my husband, George G. Morgan.

Acknowledgments

First, my thanks to the many genealogists I've been in contact with during the past twenty-four years. Their questions and problems demonstrated to me that there was a need for this kind of book, and I have learned much from them.

Second, my thanks to many people at F+W Media, including Diane Haddad, who first encouraged me to submit a full book proposal; Allison Dolan, who believed in this book and who shepherded it through the approval process; and editor Andrew Koch, who exhibited amazing patience and who nagged me in all the right ways to complete the manuscript.

Finally, my deepest appreciation goes to my husband, George, whose own writing career inspired me to write this book, and whose support kept me going through those evenings and weekends when it would have been easier to do anything other than create more book content.

ISBN: 978-1-4403-4503-6

Other Family Tree Books are available from your local bookstore and online suppliers. For more genealogy resources, visit **<shopfamilytree.com>**.

20 19 18 17 16   5 4 3 2 1

DISTRIBUTED IN CANADA BY FRASER DIRECT

100 Armstrong Avenue

Georgetown, Ontario, Canada L7G 5S4

Tel: (905) 877-4411

DISTRIBUTED IN THE U.K. AND EUROPE BY

F&W Media International, LTD

Brunel House, Forde Close,

Newton Abbot, TQ12 4PU, UK

Tel: (+44) 1626 323200,

Fax (+44) 1626 323319

E-mail: enquiries@fwmedia.com

fw

a content + ecommerce company

PUBLISHER AND COMMUNITY LEADER: Allison Dolan

EDITOR: Andrew Koch

DESIGNER: Julie Barnett

PRODUCTION COORDINATOR: Debbie Thomas

4 FREE
FAMILY TREE
templates

- decorative family tree posters
- five-generation ancestor chart
- family group sheet
- bonus relationship chart
- type and save, or print and fill out

Download at <ftu.familytreemagazine.com/free-family-tree-templates>

MORE GREAT GENEALOGY RESOURCES

FAMILY TREE MEMORY KEEPER

By Allison Dolan and Diane Haddad

HOW TO USE EVERNOTE FOR GENEALOGY

By Kerry Scott

HOW TO ARCHIVE FAMILY PHOTOS

By Denise Levenick

 Join our community! <facebook.com/familytreemagazine>